PRICING
THE PROFITABLE SALE

The Manager's Guide to Value Pricing

PRICING
THE PROFITABLE SALE

The Manager's Guide to Value Pricing

H. Peter Zell

ARPress
ILLUMINATING IDEAS
EMPOWERING VOICES

ARPress
45 Dan Road Suite 5
Canton MA 02021

Hotline: 1(888) 821-0229
Fax: 1(508) 545-7580

Ordering Information:
Quantity sales. Special discounts are available on quantity purchases by corporations, associations, and others. For details, contact the publisher at the address above.

Printed in the United States of America.

ISBN-13:	Paperback	979-8-89389-290-1
	eBook	979-8-89389-291-8
	Hardback	979-8-89389-292-5

Library of Congress Control Number: 2024908743

The single most important decision in evaluating a business is pricing power. If you've got the power to raise prices without losing business to a competitor you've got a very good business. And if you have to have a prayer session before raising the price by 10 percent, then you've got a terrible business.[1]

Warren E. Buffett

Contents

Preface

Price too high and you lose the sale! Price too low and you can't make money! [2]

Around the clock and around the world thousands upon thousands of sales transactions are being consummated between sellers and buyers. For each of the many diverse products and services offered the seller must first set a price and state the terms of sale to which the buyer must agree before a sales transaction can take place. Determining the price which will be profitable to the seller and acceptable to the buyer is the topic of *Pricing the Profitable Sale*.

(i)

Like its predecessor entitled *Pricing for Profit: The Manager's Guide to Market Oriented Pricing* published by this author seven years ago, *Pricing the Profitable Sale: The Manager's Guide to Value Pricing* was written with two primary audiences in mind. First among these are business and corporate managers with direct pricing responsibilities including general, marketing, product, and brand managers, regional and national sales managers, and individuals specifically charged with pricing of their firms' products and services. The second group includes business school professors and their students in a program leading to the MBA degree. There *Pricing the Profitable Sale* could serve as the primary text in a course on pricing or a supplementary one in an advanced Marketing course.

With so many pricing books on the market already why another one? In perusing a large number of these, the author found most deficient in some major way and began to assign them to three categories. In the first he found popular books written to appeal to people interested in pricing but who have neither the time nor inclination for an in-depth treatment. Pricing advice is generously dispensed much of which is erroneous or misleading. The second category includes standard college texts with some solid information regarding methods and techniques. Because the authors do not want to have their work look like an economics text and possibly discomfort their potential readership, the quantitative side of pricing is treated superficially leaving many open questions. The third group is composed of lengthy scholarly tomes citing an immense body of literature on diverse pricing hypotheses and theories accompanied by often complex mathematics. The result is a smorgasbord of diverse pricing advice that can leave the average practitioner overwhelmed and bewildered.

(ii)

Based on this assessment, the author suspected that there may exist a niche market for a book that fitted in-between the last two categories and appeal to marketers who prefer a quantitative treatment of the topic yet that is easy to follow and, most importantly, useful. In *Pricing the Profitable Sale* the need for higher mathematics is avoided by use of incremental difference equations to yield formulas and graphs that are more transparent and useful than those given in the pricing literature of the third group. But these simple formulas, whose derivation goes not much beyond Algebra 101, are not meant as an end in themselves but a means to an end. In fact, the reader may ignore their development and still obtain a good foundation in market oriented pricing practice and techniques.

The rewards of this quantitative approach are a much deeper understanding of pricing in general and price-setting in particular. Above all, the book is meant to be practical and assist pricers in making sound pricing decisions. Thus, *Pricing the Profitable Sale* presents twenty pricing propositions and two general pricing rules of thumb which the pricer can use over and over as a guide in solving his or her pricing problems. The book also provides definitive answers to such important questions as, Is the pursuit of sales and market share growth compatible with profit growth?, Can one price be used to maximize both sales and profit for a given product or service?, What are the optimal prices that maximize sales revenue and profit for a specific product or service?, and Why does a company's sales revenue often go up while profits decline and vice versa?

Throughout *Pricing the Profitable Sale* the reader will find numerous pricing problems and their solutions worked out in detail both mathematically and graphically. In addition, two hypothetical case studies on sales revenue maximization in the transportation industry and profit maximization in the fast foods business, respectively, appear in the Appendix. To reduce the marketer's dependence on the given formulas and minimize the necessary calculations, several tables are included listing the computed values.

(iii)

Pricing the Profitable Sale consists of fifteen chapters each of which stands on its own to be read or passed over without loss of continuity. The first three cover fundamental concepts including a discussion of pricing of products and services in general, an evaluation of "cost plus' pricing methods, and the types of costs and their relevance in pricing. Standard break-even analysis and contribution analysis and their different uses are introduced next. The demand curve and the law of demand are taken up in Chapter 6. Iso-Profit Analysis, which follows, allows the marketer to determine whether, in a contemplated price adjustment, she or he should lower or raise the price to leave profits unimpaired. The various pricing strategies used by firms to reach their goals are reviewed in Chapter 8 while the important topic of value pricing is introduced next.

With the following five chapters a number of concepts and ideas are introduced that are mostly new to the pricing literature. Chapters 10 and 11 introduce the manager to methods and techniques to improve profits and the challenges posed by price and market share competition. In the next three chapters the pricer is given the formulas and charts needed to arrive at the optimal prices to either maximize sales revenue or contribution (profits) on the short run for any of her or his products or services. The book concludes with an overview of the legal issues governing pricing that should be taken into account by all employees, from top management down, so as to be in compliance with relevant federal antitrust laws.

Pricing the Profitable Sale is not intended to replace any of the leading pricing texts of the day but rather to complement these. Thus, in this book only passing attention is paid to pricing policy and its implementation, the organizational structure required to effectively implement pricing strategies and policies, foreign and multinational sales, promotional and communication issues, or the all-important relationships between sellers and the different levels in their distribution chains. Many of these topics are beyond the scope of this work and adequately covered elsewhere.

This revised version of the original *Pricing for Profit* includes some major changes. Parts of the book have been completely rewritten and updated. To make the work more user-friendly, important points are more fully explained and several graphs and tables have either been eliminated or replaced by more useful ones. All the original formulas found in *Pricing for Profit* have been retained while the pricing propositions and rules of thumb found there have been rewritten for added clarity and usefulness.

Since marketers are generally not much interested in how certain formulas were derived and only need to know that they work, the lengthy section of proofs appearing in Appendix I of *Pricing for Profit*, with the exception of two items, has been deleted. Interested readers will find this information in the former title which will continue to appear in print.

(iv)

Some marketers will undoubtedly reject the approach taken in this book claiming that pricing cannot be done by formula. They are, of course, correct because finding the right price is a very complex issue that goes beyond simply computing a price and implementing it. Yet, interestingly, these same people are likely to themselves use the most popular pricing method, known as "cost-plus," which is, of course, precisely what they are objecting to. As will be demonstrated in this book, that method ignores existing market conditions and yields suboptimal results. Would it not be preferable to instead use a formula method that addresses these conditions and bring about more optimal results if implemented?

Others will say that companies like Alphabet (Google), Apple, Meta (Facebook), and Microsoft earn billions in profits every fiscal quarter without using the pricing rules and guidelines proposed in this book. They too are partially correct. These firms are immensely profitable through their unique and highly desirable products and services, their monopoly positions, and other competitive factors. Consequently, they can leave millions of dollars "on the table" by using unsound, suboptimal pricing methods without adverse affects. But this book was not written for them but for managers of ordinary business firms and corporations that are either struggling to survive or else moderately or highly successful and profitable and looking for ways to do even better.

Some readers will object to the emphasis on company profits in this book. Yet profit is certainly a legitimate and worthy goal for every company manager. Most importantly, profits ensure company survival in a very competitive world. The focus should not be on how or how much profit these companies and their owners and shareholders make but on how the money is used. Is it conscionable for top executives of some publicly traded companies to earn multimillion dollar salaries and keep most of their paychecks in a country where one in ten families must rely on government food stamps to survive?

Some Americans have advocated that these behemoths and their wealthy owners and executives pay a surtax to help eliminate poverty especially among children. "Let them make all the money they want," they say, "just don't let them keep it." Why not use the extra funds from hefty surcharges on yearly incomes of the wealthiest citizens to guarantee every American family a minimum income? Others have proposed such funds be pooled to eliminate world hunger. Why not build desalination plants and pipelines in parts of Africa where water is desperately needed to grow crops and at the same time alleviate the migration crisis which, together with the Covid-19 pandemic, climate change, and the war in Ukraine, is one of the biggest challenges of the day? These are important social issues and obviously much beyond the scope of this book.

(v)

On a personal note, I came to appreciate the importance of proactive, market oriented pricing after a disastrous experience in my first marketing position after obtaining my MBA degree. When I joined a Pittsburgh-based conglomerate for work at their Chicago facilities, this division had seen a continuous erosion of sales, market share, and profits for a number of years. While the company had a stellar reputation for its quality products that were much in demand by electric utility companies nationwide, upper management adhered to a very rigid pricing scheme based on production and overhead costs. With declining sales and mounting losses, the Chicago division had to be shuttered resulting in job terminations for hundreds of many talented and devoted employees who had been with the company for decades.

The debacle sparked my interest in pricing and, after my transfer to another division of the company, I started to devote many off-hours to find an alternative to so-called "cost-plus" pricing as it was practiced at the Chicago division. After reading the relevant pricing literature and finding little in the way of practical rules and guidelines but many unproved and questionable assertions instead, I decided to use my mathematical expertise to solve some price optimization problems. The outcome was two unpublished papers which I mailed to well-known experts in the field of pricing for their comments.[3] When I left this company to work for a small, start-up in their marketing and sales department, I was fortunate in that the owners were not professional managers and very open to new management and marketing ideas.

To assist with their company's pricing problems, the owners brought in Daniel A. Nimer, a well-known pioneer in value-based pricing, for a two-day seminar.[4] Mr. Nimer told participants, among other things, that "Price determines cost and not vice versa," "A product that is unique requires a unique price," and "What is really important in pricing is perceived value." His concept was revolutionary at a time when "cost-plus" was the model of choice at most firms. Subsequently, I decided to write a book based on my previous work effort but because of my corporate assignments, which included several extended stays overseas, it had to await my retirement for its writing and publication.

Product and services pricing is a complex but extremely important exercise that draws on many academic disciplines including accounting, economics, finance, jurisprudence, marketing, mathematics, psychology, and sociology. Clearly, it is an interdisciplinary and exciting field of study to which many people have made important contributions. Yet despite the importance and seriousness of the topic, one also speaks of the "pricing game." This would suggest that there is some measure of fun and enjoyment attached to pricing. This I can confirm from my corporate marketing experiences and reconfirm now. It was certainly a pleasure working on this book and I hope that my readers will enjoy reading and using it at least as much as I enjoyed writing it.

Notes

1. Warren E. Buffett is the CEO of Berkshire Hathaway Inc. and one of the world's most successful and wealthiest investors. He made the quoted remark before the Financial Crisis Inquiry Commission (FCIC) during a 2010 hearing. The comment was reported by Bloomberg News at www.bloomberg.com/news/articles on February 17, 2011 under the heading "Buffett Says Pricing Power More Important Than Good Management."

2. Benson P. Shapiro, "Precision Pricing for Profit in the New World Order," *Harvard Business School Note 9-999-003*, 7 Dec. 1998. (www.hbsp.harvard.edu/product/999003-PDF-ENG?).

3. The author's early work on price optimization was summarized in two manuscripts, namely, *Price Optimization for Industrial Products* dated March 6, 1979 and *Pricing for Maximum Profits* of October 25, 1982. Among the professors he contacted for an evaluation of his work during 1979-1983 were: Philip Kotler of the Graduate School of Management, Northwestern University; Thomas T. Nagle of the Graduate School of Business, University of Chicago; Alfred R. Oxenfeldt of the Graduate School of Business, Columbia University; and Benson P. Shapiro of the Graduate School of Business Management, Harvard University.

All four professors responded and the author is indebted to each for his helpful comments that ranged from a cautiously supportive "While I have not been able to give it more than a skim, clearly you are developing interesting theory" from Professor Kotler to a decidedly negative opinion from Professor Shapiro who wrote: "It is a well put together piece which shows a good understanding of cost structure and price impact. But, it is really not new knowledge. Rather it is a clever and able manipulation using existing knowledge and generally known techniques. You certainly did a complete job of working out the equations and the graphs."

Professor Nagle thought my work to be "standard textbook material for a graduate economics class" and informed me of his forthcoming book to be entitled *The Strategy and Tactics of Pricing* due in mid-1984. Professor Oxenfeldt wrote that he did not view price-setting "as a mathematical problem, one of profit maximization ..." but rather as "a complex series of judgments about rivals, resellers, suppliers as well as ultimate customers." Nevertheless, he found the *Iso-Profit Chart* I sent him "very useful." (See Chapter 7 for a description of this chart).

4. The Nimer seminar on pricing strategy, tactics, and policy entitled *Pricing for Profit: Using Price as a Strategic Weapon* was sponsored by Emily Jonas Hill and Roger Gettys Hill and their firm Gettys Manufacturing Company, makers of servomotors and drives for the machine tool industry. It was held at the Racine Motor Inn in Racine, Wisconsin on April 29 and 30, 1980.

CHAPTER

1

The Art and Science of Pricing

Pricing is at once a science and an art.... Scientific, artful pricing can provide the firm with the maximum profits obtainable during any specific state of economic weather.[1]

This chapter presents a brief introduction to price and the pricing of goods and services. Topics covered include the role of price at the micro- and macro-economic levels, the relationship between price and the other marketing mix strategy variables, the uniqueness of the price variable, pricing objectives, and the two major approaches to pricing in use today.

1.1 The Role of Price in the Economy

How a business firm's products and services are priced is crucial to its success and viability. Prices set too high may throttle demand and require the product's eventual withdrawal from the market. If prices are set too low, the firm may experience large but unprofitable sales. Thus, price can determine what can be sold and in what quantities and, perhaps more importantly, whether or not a business will be profitable. A business enterprise cannot consistently sustain losses without being in jeopardy of becoming extinct.

At the macroeconomic level, the price system in a free-market economy, as our own, ensures the proper allocation of scarce resources both human and non-human. Such resources include labor, raw materials, machinery, buildings, and land. Where such a system is inoperative, as was the case in the former socialist (Marxist) economies of Eastern Europe (the Soviet Union, the German Democratic Republic, Poland, Czechoslovakia etc.), scarce resources are employed for the production of goods and services for which there may be no or little demand while products and services needed and wanted by consumers are regularly in short supply or often not available at all.

In such economies, instead of letting the market determine price and production levels, state central planners typically mandated production levels for all goods together with the prices to be charged. These state-controlled economies collapsed around the year 1990 and mutated into free-market economies. Once freed from the shackles of Marxist economic dogma, these countries began to flourish resulting in strong and politically engaged middle classes. The pricing of goods and services was an integral part of this process as prices based on supply and demand replaced state-mandated ones.

According to two prominent economists and authors, "Present-day economies are a mixture of socialism and private enterprise."[2] Some of an economy's output is produced in the private sector which is predominantly profit-oriented. A second part is in the public sector, often termed socialist, which is generally not profit-oriented, such as public transportation, while a third is in the not-for-profit sector that includes schools, hospitals, and charitable organizations. In *Pricing the Profitable Sale* we are almost exclusively concerned with private sector pricing.

1.2 Price as a Marketing Strategy Variable

The major marketing strategy variables have been identified as Product, Price, Advertising and Promotion, and Distribution and are often referred to as the *four Ps* (Product, Price, Promotion, and

Place).[3] More recently one has come to refer to these four variables as *Product, Price, Communication,* and *Distribution.* Price is seen to be just one element available to the marketer for reaching the firm's marketing objectives. All four variables should be viewed as co-equal in importance to the marketing effort and therefore never be treated in isolation but rather be made part of a comprehensive marketing strategy.

The four marketing strategy variable are closely interrelated. The greatest product or service ever dreamed up will not sell at any price if there is no demand for it. Likewise, the most desirable product will not sell well if it is priced wrong for the intended product-market. Furthermore, potential customers must know about the existence of the product or service which may not be the case if it has not been properly advertised and promoted. Finally, if there is no convenient place for potential customers to acquire the product or service, sales are likely to suffer or may not materialize at all.

Clearly then, all marketing activities, including pricing, must be coordinated and goal oriented for optimum results. Specifically, the individual strategy variable goals, including those for pricing the product or service, must be consistent with each other and support the overall objectives for the intended target market or markets.

1.3 The Uniqueness of Price

Among the mix of four marketing strategy variables, price has some very unique properties. One of these, and perhaps the most important, is its direct and strong impact on profits. In fact, two consultants with McKinsey and Company, the world's oldest and most prestigious global consulting firm, found that a small percentage improvement in the sell price has a far greater impact on profitability than do similar improvements in variable cost, fixed cost, and sales volume. "The fastest and most effective way for a company to realize its maximum profit is to get its pricing right," they noted.[4] This notion was echoed by pricing authors Dolan and Simon who wrote that "Price drives profit like no other factor."[5]

Another unique feature of the price variable is that it is the only one of the four that does not generate significant costs. All the others—product development and manufacture, advertising and sales promotion, and distribution—involve money outlays. Price changes can be implemented with virtually zero cost. That is not to say that a price is never without costs. If it is the wrong price for the product or service, it can be very costly. Price is also the easiest and quickest among the variables the marketer can change. This is valuable in case of a sudden change in the market that could impact sales and profits. Finally, price is the only strategy variable which generates revenue by which the company's investments and costs can be recouped and a profit earned.

Despite its uniqueness and importance to a company's fortunes and viability, the pricing function ranks low in priority for writers of standard marketing texts. In the leading marketing text for over half a century, *Marketing Management* by Kotler and Keller, the topic does not appear until the latter half of their voluminous book. Also, it is estimated that less than 10% of business schools offer a stand-alone pricing course. This means that the only pricing exposure MBA students are likely to obtain is in a first or advanced marketing course.

Pricing is also the least understood among the marketing strategy variables. According to Kotler and Keller, "Executives complain that pricing is a big headache—and one that is getting worse by the day."[6] Not surprisingly, this topic has spawned a profusion of pricing consultancies beginning with the late Dan Nimer's one-man operation to huge international firms such as Simon-Kucher & Partners with over 1,200 employees in twenty-five countries.[7]

1.4 Pricing as Art and Science

Pricing is both an art and a science. A sell price is a number and pricing involves the manipulation of numbers by means of simple or more complex mathematical formulas. Furthermore, the results of price changes are measurable in terms of sales revenue, market shares, and profits or losses. Quantifiable parameters and measurable results are the hallmark of scientific inquiry. Pricing, therefore, may properly be classified as a science much like biology, economics, mathematics, physics, and the social sciences are. The analytical tools developed and used in *Pricing the Profitable Sale* are meant as another step in that direction.

At the same time, pricing is an art because not every pricer is equally proficient in applying pricing principles and techniques to actual pricing situations. Pricing is, after all, much more than using computed values to establish the price of a new product or adjust the price of an established one. That is why some marketers and pricers are eminently successful while others are not. Considering that the information available to the pricer is always imperfect and incomplete and the behavior of customers and competitors is never entirely predictable, much skill and intuition is still required for successful pricing moves, both in size and timing. Clearly, the quality of management's pricing decisions has a profound impact on a company's fortunes.

1.5 Pricing Objectives

Depending on the industry they are in and the markets they serve, firms usually establish marketing objectives to be achieved. Pricing goals typically differ among the firm's product-markets and may be for either the short or long term. Also, a company may have multiple goals for the same product-market because the goals are not necessarily exclusive. Among the most common pricing objectives are these:

* Profits

* Sales revenue

* Market share

* Price leadership

* Image

* Meeting competition

Empirical studies have shown profit maximization to be the most common goal found in practice.[8] In fact, among publicly held companies, profit-oriented pricing goals predominate. Within these mostly equity-financed firms there is a strong incentive and expectation for quarterly increases in earnings, dividend payouts, share prices, and market capitalization. Furthermore, a good and uninterrupted earnings stream is desirable to pay down debt, fund research and new product development, and finance future expansion.

The second most common objective is sales revenue. The need for growth is a strong motivating factor for many top managers. This objective is closely related to that of market share, i. e., the percentage of industry sales of a particular product or product class the company accounts for. In the automobile and aeronautics industries among others, market share is measured by sales volume (number of units sold) rather than sales revenue. Either way, market share is a measure of the company's relative standing within an industry, its market power, and its viability. It is often made the pricing goal as it has been shown that firms with a dominant position in the industry tend also be the most profitable.

Among the other pricing goals, price leadership goals are especially prevalent in industries and markets with few competitors. The price leader gets to set the prices which will ensure that it is and remains the most profitable in its industry. Image as a pricing goal is especially important in the luxury goods industries. Products are usually premium-priced and purchased on account of the aura of exclusivity they convey. Some companies have goals that simply seek to match the prices of competitors. This is not a pro-active but safe approach to the market.

More altruistic pricing goals include those in furtherance of some worthwhile cause such as preserving a clean and healthy environment, combating hunger and diseases, or ensuring employment for disadvantaged people. However, even with these socially engaged firms, profits can never be far from consideration. As noted British pricing author André Gabor has written: "It is undeniable that profit maximization is seldom, if ever, the sole aim of a firm, but it seems that most, if not all the other legitimate aims of businessmen are either means towards furthering profitability or can be pursued in the long run only if the firm is working profitably."[9]

While these objectives are useful for giving the marketing and pricing effort the needed direction, they are insufficient to make a plan actionable. Management must, in addition, develop more detailed goals to include specific performance levels and deadlines that are measurable. Examples of such specific product pricing goals are:

* Achieve break-even sales by (date)

* Improve profits by 5% by (date)

* Increase sales revenue by 10% by (date)

* Maintain market share at 20% through at least (date)

These goals must obviously be realistic and in line with the other marketing strategy variables for the particular product-market.

1.6 Pricing Methods

One can distinguish between two major approaches to pricing. Both are in common use world-wide but differ radically in their focus and the results achieved. The late Peter Drucker, a well-known management guru and educator, described the two methods as "cost-led pricing" and "price-led costing."[10] The cost-based approach to pricing focuses on the company's costs and is generally known as *cost-plus pricing* the "plus" referring to the markup that is added to product costs to arrive at a sell price. It is by far the older and more widely used of the two pricing methods. Cost-plus pricing may be described by this simplified flow diagram:

$$\textit{Product} \longrightarrow \textit{Cost} \longrightarrow \textit{Price} \longrightarrow \textit{Customer}$$

In this method, the product is developed after which its costs are determined. A total unit cost for manufacturing and marketing the product is then computed to which a suitable profit margin is added to obtain the sell price. This package of product, price, and terms of sale is offered to the customer who is then free to choose between it and other competing product offerings on the market.

The more modern approach to pricing is customer and market rather than seller oriented and is variously referred to as *market oriented, value oriented, perceived value,* or simply as *value pricing.* In this approach, the focus has shifted away from the seller to the customer and prices are based on the product's perceived value to the customer and the product-market segment being served. The approach is the reverse of the above as illustrated by this new event sequence:

$$\textit{Customer} \longrightarrow \textit{Price} \longrightarrow \textit{Cost} \longrightarrow \textit{Product}$$

The marketing process begins with customers and their wants and needs in a product or service and the value it represents to this product-market segment of potential customers, i. e., its *perceived value.* The price is the one these potential customers are able and willing to pay for the product or service offered. This information tells the company what the costs must be to cover its manufacturing, marketing, and overhead costs and make an acceptable profit. Product development to meet the product and price specifications is the final link in the chain.

Pricing the Profitable Sale is devoted to the customer oriented approach to pricing. However, because of the continuing popularity of cost-plus pricing, the following chapter will review this pricing method in more detail and point out some of its advantages but also its severe limitations for pricing profitably.

Notes

1. Spencer Tucker, *Pricing for Higher Profit*, 5.

2. Ross Eckert and Richard Leftwich, *The Price System and Resource Allocation*, 18.

3. The four Ps were popularized by Professor E. Jerome McCarthy of Michigan State University in his *Basic Marketing: A Managerial Approach* first published in 1960.

4. Michael Marn and Robert Rosiello, "Managing Price, Gaining Profit," *Harvard Business Review on Pricing*, 46-49.

5. Robert Dolan and Hermann Simon, *Power Pricing*, 24.

6. Philip Kotler and Kevin Keller, *Marketing Management*, 377.

7. Hermann Simon and Martin Fassnacht, *Price Management*, 17.

8. Robert Dolan and Hermann Simon, supra at 32.

9. André Gabor, *Pricing*, 32.

10. Peter F. Drucker, "The Information Executives Truly Need," *Harvard Business Review*, January-February 1995, 58. (www.hbsp.harvard.edu/product/95104-PDF-ENG).

CHAPTER

2

Cost-Plus Pricing

Cost-plus pricing is, historically, the most common pricing procedure because it carries an aura of financial prudence.[1]

Products and services have traditionally been priced by a cost-based method which carries the generic term of *cost-plus* and is also known as full-cost, absorption cost, or markup pricing. According to pricing consultants and authors Simon and Fassnacht, around 75% of companies practice cost-oriented pricing.[2] While many marketing texts no longer discuss cost-plus or do so in passing only, every marketer should have at least some familiarity with it even though its use cannot be recommended. In fact, this chapter could be subtitled "How *not* to price your products or services."

In this chapter the basics of cost-plus pricing are discussed together with a list of the benefits the method promises. Overhead allocation, which is a requirement of the method, is covered next and an example of pricing by overhead allocation presented. The chapter concludes with a summary of both the promised benefits and actual shortcomings of cost-plus as a pricing method.

2.1 The Method

While it is generally true that a firm must eventually recover all of its costs before it can generate a profit regardless of which pricing method is used, be it cost-plus or value pricing, in cost-plus pricing the firm seeks to recover the product's full cost, including a portion of company overhead, on each and every sale. In other words, each unit sold must bear its share of company overhead costs with the assumption being that if these costs are covered by the sell prices, a full recovery of all overhead costs will be achieved and the firm will always be profitable.

Overhead may be defined as that portion of a company's costs that cannot be objectively traced to the manufacture and marketing of any of its products such as the direct labor and material costs expended. From a practical standpoint this means that the company's total overhead costs, i.e., costs that it incurs regardless of the level of output, must be distributed among its products in a process known as *overhead allocation*.

For a one-product firm, the product's sell price could be computed using this simple formula:

$$P = (VC + F / Q) \times (1 + m) \quad \text{Eq. (2.1)}$$

where,

P = Sell price ($)
VC = Unit variable cost ($)
F = Total fixed (overhead) cost ($)
Q = Sales volume (units)
m = Profit markup (%)

In the above expression, VC, the unit variable cost, is the cost directly associated with the production and marketing of this particular product. The total fixed cost, F, is the company's overhead cost. This cost must be divided by the product's sales volume to arrive at an overhead cost per unit. The profit factor, m, is a percentage profit markup expressed as a decimal.

Example

Alpha Company's Product X, its only product, costs $20 to produce and market and the firm's yearly overhead cost is $100,000.

If total forecasted sales for the year are 10,000 units, the unit overhead cost charged to Product X is $10 ($100,000 / 10,000). Suppose that a profit of 20% is to be made on each sale. By Equation (2.1), the product's sell price would be:

$$P = (\$20 + \$10) \times 1.2 = \$36$$

Depending on the competitive situation, the markup percentage and thus the price could be raised or lowered. This is, in fact, the only manner in which some flexibility could be applied to this pricing scheme. Also noteworthy is that the sales volume Q must be known in advance even though there is no guarantee that this number of units will actually be sold at the computed price.

2.2 Overhead Allocation

Since a company typically produces and markets more than one product, its total overhead cost must be *allocated* among these different products. There are any number of allocation formulas a firm may choose from but, to make the method work, it must consistently apply the same formula to all its products. We shall illustrate use of three typical allocation formulas and compute sell prices in a three-product company. These formulas for the overhead rate are:

$$\text{Rate} = \frac{\text{Overhead}}{\text{Direct labor cost}} \qquad (I)$$

$$\text{Rate} = \frac{\text{Overhead}}{\text{Direct material cost}} \qquad (II)$$

$$\text{Rate} = \frac{\text{Overhead}}{\text{Direct labor + material costs}} \qquad (III)$$

These and many other allocation formulas and their application may be found in the pricing and cost accounting literature.[3]

2.3 Application

The following example will illustrate the method in the case of a manufacturing company with three products.

Illustrative Example: Sun Valley Products Co.

Sun Valley Products manufactures and markets three products with these manufacturing costs:

	Product A	Product B	Product C
Direct labor ($)	10.00	20.00	20.00
Direct material ($)	20.00	10.00	20.00

The company's annual projected overhead is $200,000 while labor and material costs are projected to be $100,000 and $400,000, respectively. The overhead rates to be applied are therefore:

Formula I) $200,000 / $100,000 = 2.0 \times$ Labor
Formula II) $200,000 / $400,000 = 0.50 \times$ Material
Formula III) $200,000 / $500,000 = 0.40 \times$ (Material + Labor)

The total cost charged to each product and the product's sell price including a 10% markup is therefore:

	Product A	Product B	Product C
Direct labor	10.00	20.00	20.00
Direct material	20.00	10.00	20.00
Formula I			
Overhead	20.00	40.00	40.00
Total cost	50.00	70.00	80.00
Sell price	*55.00*	*77.00*	*88.00*
Formula II			
Overhead	10.00	5.00	10.00
Total cost	40.00	35.00	50.00
Sell price	*44.00*	*38.50*	*55.00*
Formula III			
Overhead	12.00	12.00	16.00
Total cost	42.00	42.00	56.00
Sell price	*46.20*	*46.20*	*61.60*

As this tabulation shows, each product covers a considerable range in sell prices depending on the allocation formula used and the product's relative labor and material content. Nevertheless, if the sales and accounting departments have projected total quantity sales and material and labor costs accurately, the firm should see a profit at year's end regardless of which formula is used, provided, of course, that customers are willing to buy the products at the prices offered.

2.4. The Case Against Cost-Plus Pricing

From a modern marketing point of view, cost-plus pricing makes little sense for a number of reasons. As we have seen in the previous section, overhead cost allocation is arbitrary resulting in distorted full costs and prices. But there is a deficiency that is even more fundamental and egregious. Thus, cost-plus pricing completely ignores all-important price-volume relationships, i. e., the fact that companies and individuals will buy fewer products from a specific supplier when prices are high and vice versa assuming, of course, that there are substitute products on the market. Also ignored are customers' value perceptions of products and services and their willingness to pay for these. The concept of value pricing is treated in Chapter 9.

Another shortcoming is that sales volumes must be forecast even before the sell prices have been determined. That is obviously not realistic because the number of units of a products sold is heavily dependant on the prices charged. Furthermore, the method seeks to impose sell prices on the market based on the company's cost structure. That is possible only if the firm has acquired a monopoly position in the market it serves, i.e., it must be able to dictate to the market what customers buy and in what quantities and at what prices. That is generally not possible in a free-market economy.

Among the more specific deficiencies of cost-plus pricing are these:

* The method, if judiciously applied, rejects all sales below the full-cost price thereby foregoing any contribution to overhead costs and profits on such sales.

* Premium pricing and profit opportunities from such factors as product uniqueness, customer value perceptions, and brand loyalty are not taken advantage of so that the firm is essentially "leaving money on the table" on many sales.

* Because of their cost-based nature, prices are in an inverse relationship with business activity in that they are too high during periods of low demand, i.e., weak markets, when downward pressure on prices is highest and too low in strong markets when sales are brisk and price sensitivity is low.

* The most serious problem is what pricing experts and authors Nagle and Müller have called a *death spiral* in which the firm prices itself out of the market because a price increase leads to lower sales which causes average unit costs to rise requiring a further price increase and so on.[4] Many financially healthy companies with sought-after products and services have come to ruin by being caught up in this destructive phenomenon.

In summary, cost-plus pricing has some value in establishing a price level where no other benchmarks are available but it should never serve as the primary pricing tool inasmuch as it yields suboptimal results which can, in extreme cases, lead to dire consequences for the firm.

2.5 Why "Cost-Plus" Remains Popular

As noted at the beginning of this chapter, cost-plus pricing despite its many shortcomings is still much in use, either by itself or in combination with other methods, and for some fairly good reasons. Among the benefits often cited are these:

* The method yields a definitive price which is not the case for value-oriented pricing where subjective estimates of customers' perceived values of products and services are required.

* Where the profit markups are reasonable, sell prices tend to be fair and equitable to both buyers and sellers.

* Computation and administration of sell prices is a simple routine requiring a minimum of time, effort, and expertise.

* Insofar as there are no major variances between actual and projected overhead costs and sales volumes, the firm will never incur a loss but always operate profitably.

* The firm can count on a steady stream of income as costs are fully and continuously recovered by ongoing sales.

* Prices are readily explained and, where necessary, justified to corporate buyers and government agencies especially in cases of alleged antitrust violations.

* Provided costs remain relatively stable, cost-plus pricing fosters long-term price stability in the industry.

* Cost-plus pricing can always be made responsive to market conditions by adjusting profit markups to make product offerings more competitive.

In the next chapter we shall look at cost and contribution dollars to company overhead and profit which are both fundamental to understanding the pricing function.

Notes

1. Thomas Nagle and Georg Müller, *The Strategy and Tactics of Pricing*, 4.

2. Hermann Simon and Martin Fassnacht, *Price Management*, 175.

3. For a more thorough discussion of overhead allocation, see Spencer Tucker, *Pricing for Higher Profit*, 43-49; Kent Monroe, *Pricing*, 2nd ed., 228-239; and André Gabor, *Pricing*, 58-66. This topic is also treated in standard texts on cost accounting such as *Horngren's Cost Accounting: A Managerial Emphasis*.

4. Thomas Nagle and Georg Müller, supra at 5.

CHAPTER

3

Cost and Contribution

A fundamental principle in market-based pricing is to recognize that price is a statement of value, not a statement of costs.[1]

At this point the reader should be convinced that pricing a product or service based on its costs is not the way to achieve profitability goals. Is cost, then, relevant at all in pricing and, if so, how relevant? This is one question we hope to answer in this chapter. But first, we need to examine the nature of costs and how they arise. Next we examine the contribution margin and total contribution dollars and how these allow marketers to recoup their companies' direct and overhead costs and earn a profit. At the conclusion of the chapter, a first set of pricing guidelines is presented.

3.1 The Nature and Origin of Costs

A firm incurs costs in a number of ways and these may be divided into two broad categories—direct and indirect costs. Direct costs are, in turn, classified as variable or fixed. Marketers and pricers are mostly interested in the direct costs while top management will be more focused on the indirect costs. All executives and managers though will share the common goal of keeping all costs down to maintain and improve profitability.

3.1.1 Direct Costs

As their name implies, *direct costs* are costs that are directly attributable, traceable, and assignable to a profit entity whose profitability one wishes to examine such as a single product, a product line, a sales territory, a target market, a customer account, or an individual salesperson. These direct costs, which have also been called the *out-of-pocket costs* or *incremental costs*, are the *costs of doing business* and exist only because a specific product or other profit entity exists. If it did not exist or if it were to be discontinued, all associated direct costs would vanish.

Direct Variable Costs: For a product, *direct variable costs* increase in direct proportion to the number of units produced and sold and would include, but not be limited to, hourly labor and raw materials that went into the product, sales commissions, and royalties. Figure 3.1 (a) illustrates the relationship between direct variable cost and volume. As may be noted, at zero volume direct variable cost is zero and increases in direct proportion to sales volume.

Figure 3-1
Direct Variable and Fixed Costs

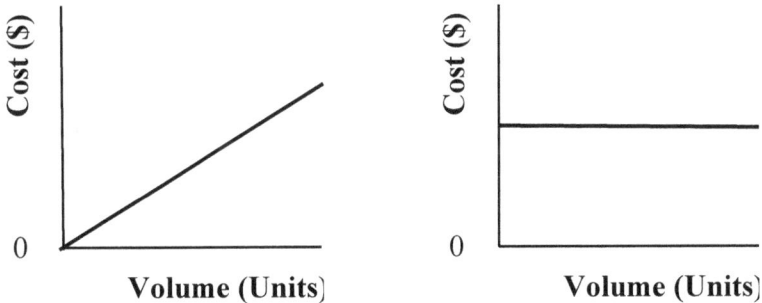

(a) Variable cost   (b) Fixed cost

Direct Fixed Costs: Unlike the variable costs, *direct fixed costs* do not increase with the number of units produced and sold but remain constant with volume. In other words, these costs are independent of the activity level and are not zero if production were to cease. These costs would look like Figure 3-1(b). Direct fixed costs, sometimes called *specific programmed costs*, would include costs incurred for a specific product or service such as modification or improvement, advertising and sales promotion, and warehousing.

For example, suppose a promotional campaign was planned together with a price change for a specific product, then the costs incurred must be charged to that particular product thereby reducing its profit after the price change. Or suppose the price of a product was reduced and the increased demand was expected to require an expansion in production capacity. Then the added costs, such as for additional machinery or fixtures, would be chargeable to this product. Similarly, suppose a hotel's management decided to combine several rooms to make a suite, then the conversion costs would have to be taken into account in the new profit calculations.

3.1.2 Indirect Fixed (Common) Costs

Costs that are not directly attributable, traceable, and assignable to a specific product or other profit entity are known as *indirect fixed costs* or common costs. Sometimes they are referred to as *overhead costs or* simply as *overhead*. These costs are shared by all the products and are therefore common costs or the *costs of being in business*. They cannot be changed in the short term for a number of reasons including legal and contractual, moral, and ethical. Common costs include employee salaries, general and administrative, sales and sales support, depreciation, mortgages, leases, rentals, loan interest, insurance, advertising and promotion, research and development, professional services, employee travel, and utilities.

The above is the most important information on costs a marketer and pricer needs to know. Typically, developing accurate cost data for pricing purposes, including a product's average unit variable cost, is the responsibility of the firm's cost accountants. For a more thorough and nuanced discussion of the topic, the interested reader may wish to consult the relevant literature including a text on cost accounting.[2]

3.2 The Basic Formulas

Profit is the difference between sales revenue and total cost and expressed symbolically:

$$I = R - C \qquad \text{Eq. (3.1)}$$

where,　　　I = Profit (before taxes)
　　　　　　R = Sales revenue
　　　　　　C = Total cost

Let it be assumed that the total cost C consists of only direct variable costs and indirect fixed (overhead) costs but no direct fixed (programmed) costs. If the latter are present, these can be dealt with separately by accounting means.

With this restriction, Equation (3.1) becomes:

$$I = R - V - F \qquad \text{Eq. (3.2)}$$

where,　　　V = Total variable cost
　　　　　　F = Indirect fixed (overhead) cost

Sales revenue, in turn, is the product of the sell price and the number of units sold (sales volume):

$$R = P \times Q \qquad \text{Eq. (3.3)}$$

where,　　　P = Sell price
　　　　　　Q = Sales volume (units)

while the total variable cost is:

$$V = VC \times Q \qquad \text{Eq. (3.4)}$$

where,　　　VC = Unit variable cost

Combining Equations (3.2) through (3.4), the general expression for profit is:

$$I = (P - VC)\,Q - F \qquad \text{Eq. (3.5)}$$

In words, the profit earned from a firm's product or service is the difference between the sell price and its unit variable cost multiplied by the number of units sold minus the indirect fixed (overhead) cost associated with the production of that item.

3.3 How Important is Cost in Pricing?

While there is a consensus that costs must never be allowed to drive sell prices, one cannot ignore the fact that costs have a profound impact on profits. Equation (3.1) indicates that, as a first approximation, there are only two ways by which profits may be raised and that is by either raising sales revenue or reducing total cost. Now, as will be shown below, the relationship between profit and sales revenue is not a linear one, i.e., an increase in sales revenue does not guarantee an increase in profit.

That leaves *cost reduction* as the only undisputable option for improving profitability. Clearly then, low total costs are of fundamental importance to profitable operations. How relevant then are costs in incremental price adjustments meant to improve profitability? The answer is that it depends on which of the costs described above we mean.

For *incremental* price changes, neither the unit variable cost of a product nor the fixed (overhead) cost associated with production of that product can be expected to change. Therefore, these costs do not significantly impact profits. This can easily be demonstrated as follows:

If we take Equation (3.5) for profit and designate "0" as the parameters before an incremental price change and "1" after the change, the profit before and after the change can be written as:

$$I_0 = P_0 \, Q_0 - VC_0 \, Q_0 - F_0$$
$$I_1 = P_1 \, Q_1 - VC_1 \, Q_1 - F_1$$

If one lets $VC_1 = VC_0$ and $F_1 = F_0$, as previously stipulated, and lets Δ stand for an incremental change, then the incremental profit change as a result of an incremental price change is given by:

$$\Delta I = I_1 - I_0 = \Delta R - VC_0 \, \Delta Q \qquad \text{Eq. (3.6)}$$

In words, the incremental profit change following an incremental price change of an item equals the sales revenue change less the product of the item's unit variable cost and the change in sales volume. Since the overhead cost F does not appear in Eq. (3.6), indirect fixed (overhead) costs are *not relevant* in incremental price change computations.

Regarding the common notion that a revenue increase leads to improved profits, Equation (3.6) indicates that this is not necessarily the case.[3] This outcome can only hold if the second term on the right ($VC_0 \times \Delta Q$) is negative which means that, since VC_0 is always positive, ΔQ must be negative. This, in turn, implies (by the law of demand) an incremental price increase ΔP. As will be shown later, incremental price increases can lead to profit increases as well as to profit losses. Clearly, the sales revenue versus profit relationship is more complex.

3.4 Contribution

By the term *contribution* is meant the amount of revenue remaining from the sale of a product or service after the direct variable costs have been deducted. This remainder will *contribute* to pay down indirect fixed (overhead) costs plus earn a profit. A company can begin earning such a profit only after sufficient contribution dollars have been generated to cover its overhead costs. Total contribution to overhead and profit is the difference between sales revenue and total variable cost:

$$\mathbf{K = R - V} \qquad \text{Eq. (3.7)}$$

where,   K = Total contribution

Inserting Equations (3.3) and (3.4) into Equation (3.7), total contribution may also be expressed as:

$$\mathbf{K = (P - VC) \, Q} \qquad \text{Eq. (3.8)}$$

The expression in parentheses in Equations (3.5) and (3.8) is a key profitability metric known as the *unit contribution margin* which is defined as the difference between a product's sell price and its unit variable cost. Thus, the unit contribution margin expressed in dollars is given by:

$$\text{CM (\$)} = P - VC \qquad \text{Eq. (3.9)}$$

The dollar contribution margin may also be expressed as a percentage of the sell price:

$$\text{CM (\%)} = \frac{P - VC}{P} \qquad \text{Eq. (3.10)}$$

The actual percentage is obtained, as usual, by multiplying the right-hand side of Equation (3.10) by 100%. While the contribution margin can be expressed either as a dollar amount or as a percentage and distinguished by the two notations given above, we shall generally use CM to stand for either. Which one is meant becomes immediately clear from the context since any formula must be dimensionally correct.

The total contribution K earned by a firm with n products is simply the sum of the individual contributions:

$$K = (P_1 - VC_1) \, Q_1 + (P_2 - VC_2) \, Q_2 + \, ... \, (P_n - VC_n) \, Q_n$$

Example

Suppose Alpha Company has three products each with a different direct variable cost—$8 for product A, $5 for product B, and $2 for product C—but, for competitive reasons, each product is being sold at the same price of $10. The respective contribution margins are by Equations (3.9) and (3.10):

Product A: CM ($) = $10 – $8 = $2   CM (%) = $2 / $10 = 20%
Product B: CM ($) = $10 – $5 = $5   CM (%) = $5 / $10 = 50%
Product C: CM ($) = $10 – $2 = $8   CM (%) = $8 / $10 = 80%

Clearly, Product C is the most profitable as every sale brings in $8 of contribution or 80% of the sell price. Product A is the least profitable with only 20% of the sell price available for contribution.

An easy way to understand contribution is to look on the unit contribution margin (P – VC) as the basic *building block* by which the firm can recover its overhead costs and earn a profit. Suppose we were required to build a wall of a certain dimension in a month's time. In our analogy, suppose that wall represented the firm's overhead costs. Assume further that we used these (P – VC) building blocks to build the wall. If we could complete the wall before the end of the month, any additional blocks could be used to build something else.

In the business context, additional blocks would generate profits. If an insufficient number of blocks arrived in time, the wall would be left unfinished. For the business, the result would be a dollar loss for the month instead of profits. Clearly, success depends on the size of the building blocks (P – VC), their number (Q) and their rate of arrival. Ideally, the unit contribution margin and quantity would both be as large as possible and sales would be brisk.

3.5 Contribution or Profit?

Marketers talk more about contribution dollars than profits because calculating a profit requires one to know the indirect fixed (overhead) cost F which, as we have seen in Chapter 2, involves cost allocation when considering individual products. Contribution K, on the other hand, can be calculated without knowledge of overhead costs. The relationship between profit I and contribution K is found by inserting Equation (3.7) into Equation (3.2):

$$\mathbf{I = K - F} \qquad\qquad \text{Eq. (3.11)}$$

Thus, profit is simply total contribution less overhead costs meaning that total contribution must exceed overhead costs before a profit is made.

Since, as was shown above, the overhead costs do not enter into incremental price change calculations provided these costs are the same before and after the change, one can easily show the equivalency of profit and contribution changes. Thus, using "0" for a value before an incremental price change and "1" after a change and letting $F_1 = F_0$, one has from Eq. (3.11):

$$I_1 - I_0 = K_1 - K_0 - F_0 + F_0$$
$$\Delta I = \Delta K \qquad\qquad \text{Eq. (3.12)}$$

This means that we can use the terms incremental contribution change and incremental profit change interchangeably since a dollar change in one results in an equal dollar change in the other.

3.6 Pricing Guidelines (I)

The above mathematical relationships lead us to our first pricing observation or proposition.

Pricing Proposition 1

Where indirect fixed (overhead) costs are the same before and after an incremental price change:

a) Only direct variable costs are relevant in profit computations.

b) Changes in total contribution are equivalent to changes in profit.

In general, it is more practical to work with total contribution and total contribution changes rather than profit and profit changes since this avoids the overhead allocation problem discussed before.

Notes

1. Michael Morris & Gene Morris, *Market Oriented Pricing*, 2.

2. More information on costs and their role in pricing decisions may be found in Kent Monroe, *Pricing*, Chapter 10, and Thomas Nagle and Georg Müller, *The Strategy and Tactics of Pricing*, Chapter 9.

3. Sometimes even well-known pricing texts leave the strong impression that profits may be improved by simply selling more product. For example, in André Gabor, *Pricing*, 30, one reads: "Even though exceptions are possible, increased sales generally mean improved profitability, that is to say, growth is not so much a rival aim as rather a means by which higher returns can be obtained."

CHAPTER

4

Break-Even Analysis

Used appropriately and with an understanding of its limitations, break-even analysis can be useful for a number of important business decisions.[1]

Break-even analysis and, more specifically, the *break-even chart*, was a product of the Great Depression of the early 1930s at which time the very survival of many small businesses was at stake. The federal government encouraged business owners and managers to familiarize themselves with this simple yet powerful tool by which they could easily determine the necessary combination of costs, sell prices, and sales revenues that would ensure profitable operations.

Before we construct a break-even chart, it will be useful to first review its mathematical foundation. Following this, a practical example will illustrate drawing and using the chart and applying the break-even formulas to answer the questions posed in a feasibility study for a potential new product.

4.1 The Concept

The continuing popularity enjoyed by the break-even chart is mainly due to the fact that it is not only practical but easy to construct requiring the drawing of only two lines on a grid after which the break-even point can be read off directly. Furthermore, changes in the price and costs can be easily accommodated and their impact on the break-even point graphically demonstrated.

While traditional break-even analysis ignores market-oriented factors such as product demand and competition and is therefore of limited usefulness in setting or adjusting prices of existing products, it is ideally suited for use in product feasibility studies where, during the product conceptual stage, management needs to determine whether a proposed new product should be developed or dropped from further consideration.

Break-even analysis is based on the concept of contribution introduced in the previous chapter in which total product cost is separated into its two primary components, namely, a total variable cost which increases in direct proportion to the number of units produced and an indirect fixed cost which is independent of volume output and commonly known as overhead. The break-even point is reached when the sales revenue for the product just equals the product's total cost, i.e., the price-volume operating point at which profits are exactly zero.

4.2 The Break-Even Formulas

The basic equation relating a product's total cost, sales revenue and profits is from Equation (3.1) in the previous chapter:

$$I = R - C \qquad \text{Eq. (4.1)}$$

where, I = Profit ($)
          R = Sales revenue ($)
          C = Total product cost ($)

From Equation (3.5), the expanded form of this equation is:

$$I = (P - VC)\,Q - F \qquad \text{Eq. (4.2)}$$

where, P = Sell price ($)
          VC = Unit variable cost ($)
          Q = Sales volume (units)
          F = Indirect fixed (overhead) cost ($)

Rewriting Equation (4.2) for the sales volume, one obtains:

$$Q = \frac{I + F}{P - VC} \qquad \text{Eq. (4.3)}$$

At the break-even point I = 0 giving us a break-even quantity of:

$$\mathbf{Q_{BE}} = \frac{\mathbf{F}}{\mathbf{P - VC}} \qquad \text{Eq. (4.4)}$$

Since, by definition, the product's unit contribution margin is:

$$CM\ (\$) = P - VC \qquad \text{Eq. (3.9)}$$

the break-even quantity becomes:

$$\mathbf{Q_{BE}} = \frac{\mathbf{F}}{\mathbf{CM\ (\$)}} \qquad \text{Eq. (4.5)}$$

In words, the break-even quantity at which neither a profit is made nor a loss incurred for a given product is the product's fixed cost divided by its unit dollar contribution margin.

The break-even sales revenue is then:

$$R_{BE} = Q_{BE} \times P \qquad \text{Eq. (4.6)}$$

Sometimes it is desirable to know what the profit or loss is above or below the break-even point, respectively. If one lets:

$$I_{AB} = \text{Profit above or below the BEP}$$
$$I_{BE} = \text{Profit at the BEP}$$

one obtains, from Equations (4.3) and (4.5):

$$I = CM\ (\$) \times Q - F$$

$$I_{AB} - I_{BE} = CM(\$) \times Q_{AB} - F - CM(\$) \times Q_{BE} + F$$

But since at the BEP, the profit I_{BE} is zero, one has:

$$I_{AB} = (Q_{AB} - Q_{BE}) \times CM\ (\$) \qquad \text{Eq. (4.7)}$$

In words, the profit (or loss) outside the BEP is the product of the difference between the actual and break-even quantities and the product's unit dollar contribution margin.

The above formulas let a manager know how much product the company needs to sell and at what average price level during a given time period to ensure that the firm's overhead is fully covered. The same formulas may also be used for the product feasibility study mentioned above by simply letting F, the indirect overhead cost, become the direct fixed (programmed) cost incurred in developing and marketing the planned new product. The outcome will let the manager know what quantity sales are needed at what price level in a given period of time to break even and thus whether the planned project is feasible or not.

4.3 Application

An example will demonstrate the use of break-even analysis in a hypothetical feasibility study for a new product concept.

Illustrative Example: EMD Industries

EMD Industries is a medium-sized manufacturer of electro-mechanical devices such as automatic gate openers as used in exclusive residential areas and garage door openers for residential and commercial use. Recently, Yvonne, a long-time employee in the company's marketing department, came up with an exciting new product idea.

The product would be an electronic sensor system that gave off a buzzer sound inside the home to alert people in rural and certain urban areas with curbside mailboxes that they had received mail. She brought the idea to Brian, the marketing manager, who immediately recognized the product's market and profit potential. Brian subsequently asked for a meeting of the new products committee composed of the president and managers of the accounting, engineering, finance, marketing, and production departments.

At the first meeting, some members objected to adding the product to the line since they considered it a bad fit. However,

Brian was able to convince them that Product X could draw on the company's expertise in sensor technology, was relatively simple to develop and manufacture, and, furthermore, could be sold through one of their major distribution channels.

At a later meeting, it was learned that Mail-A-Lert, the name Brian had chosen for Product X, would cost about $40,000 to develop and bring to market. This would include purchasing some additional machinery and shop fixtures, building a prototype, plus costs associated with an initial promotional campaign. Furthermore, there was a consensus that, once full-scale production was under way, Mail-A-Lert could be produced for as little as $20 per unit.

Since the product was unique, i.e., there was no substitute available on the market and demand was expected to be high, Brian felt that he could market Mail-A-Lert to home improvement retailers such as The Home Depot and Lowe's at the premium price of $100. But before giving the green light, the new products committee needed to know what the chances were of the proposed new product becoming profitable within a year of market introduction. Brian responded by making a break-even analysis.

4.3.1 Break-Even Chart Solution

The Mail-A-Lert parameters were:

$$P = \$100$$
$$VC = \$20$$
$$F = \$40,000$$

On the break-even chart shown in Figure 4.1, the horizontal (x) axis represents the number of units sold. The vertical (y) axis is simply labeled dollars. The sales revenue line begins at the origin where quantity and sales revenue are zero. For the second point, Brian picked a quantity of 600; it yielded a sales revenue of $60,000 ($100 × 600 units). Connecting the origin with this second point gave him the sales revenue line.

For the cost line, he noted that the total cost is the sum of the fixed cost ($40,000) and the total variable cost. His first point was therefore at $40,000 on the y-axis. At a quantity of 600, the total variable cost was $12,000 ($20 × 600 units). Adding the two costs, he obtained $52,000 which was the second point on this line. Connecting the two points gave him the total cost line.

The break-even point (BEP) occurs where the sales revenue and total cost lines intersect. We note from the chart that the break-even quantity Q_{BE} and beak-even sales revenue R_{BE} are 500 units and $50,000, respectively. In the region where the sales revenue line lies

Figure 4-1
Break-Even Chart for Mail-A-Lert

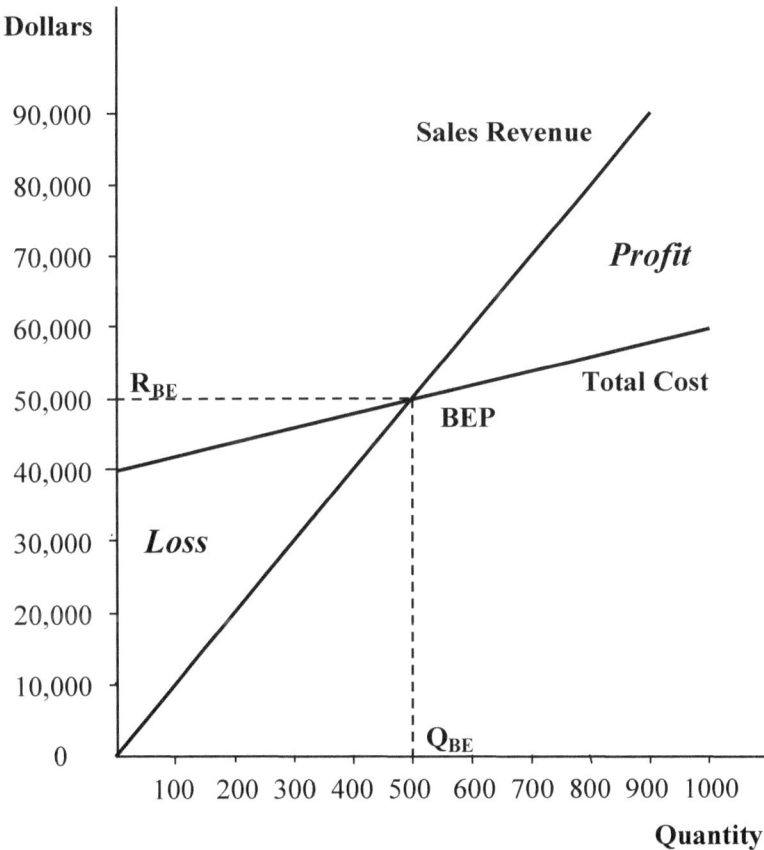

below the total cost line, Mail-A-Lert will be unprofitable. To the right of the BEP, where sales revenue exceeds total cost, it will result in a profit. The amount of profit or loss is the vertical distance between the two lines. For example, if 600 units were sold, profits earned would be $8,000 ($60,000 – $52,000).

Besides the standard break-even chart shown, many variations have come into existence. Tucker, a prominent pricing consultant and strong proponent of break-even analysis, has shown how to construct composite break-even charts that allow the determination of a single break-even point for several products with different variable costs.[2]

4.3.2 Formula Solution

By Equation (3.9) of Chapter 3 the unit contribution margin is:

$$CM\ (\$) = \$100 - \$20 = \$80$$

By Equations (4.5) and (4.6), the break-even quantity and break-even sales revenue for the first year are therefore, respectively,

$$Q_{BE} = \frac{\$40,000}{\$80} = 500 \text{ units}$$

$$R_{BE} = \$100 \times 500 \text{ units} = \$50,000$$

This agrees with the chart solution.

Suppose the profit at a quantity of 600 units was desired. By Equation (4.7) one finds:

$$I_{AB} = (600 - 500) \times \$80 = \$8,000$$

If management decided that just breaking even did not suffice but that an additional profit of $10,000 during the year was required, by Equation (4.3), the quantity to be produced and sold during this time period would rise to:

$$Q_{I} = \frac{\$40,000 + \$10,000}{\$80} = 625 \text{ units}$$

4.4 Break-Even vs. the Unit Contribution Margin

Combining Equation 3.10 of Chapter 3 and Equation 4.4 above one obtains another useful expression that relates the break-even quantity and the percentage unit contribution margin.

$$Q_{BE} = \frac{F}{P \times CM\,(\%)} \qquad \text{Eq. (4-8)}$$

To further assist the new products committee, Brian used the above formula to illustrate the various pricing options available in case

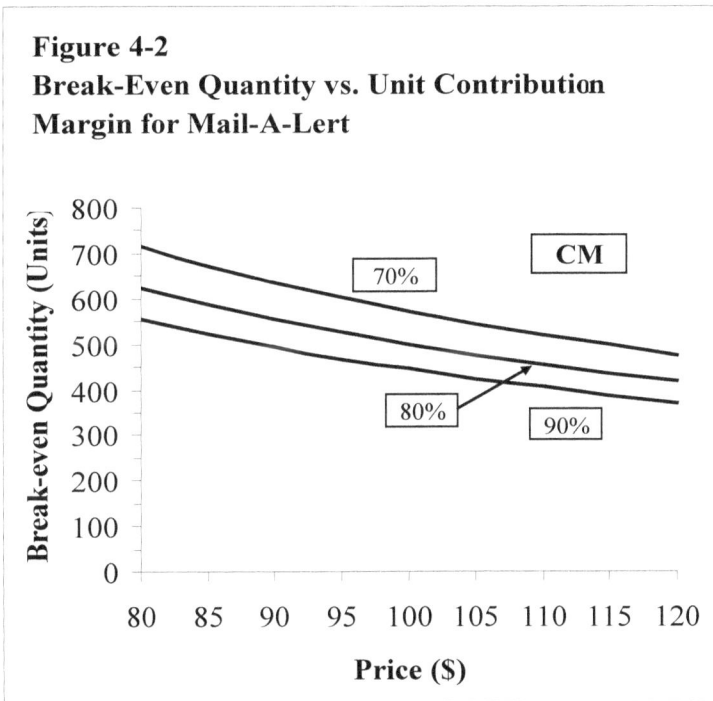

Figure 4-2
Break-Even Quantity vs. Unit Contribution Margin for Mail-A-Lert

EMD Industries decided to offer the product at a price different from $100 or if the estimate of the product's unit variable cost turned out to be faulty. In Figure 4-2 the three curves show the new break-even quantities for unit contribution margins of 70%, 80%, and 90% and for sell prices from $80 to $120. (The estimated unit contribution margin was 80%).

Clearly evident from Figure 4-2 is that i) a higher price leads to a corresponding decrease in the required sales volume to break even at all percentage unit contribution margins, and ii) a decline in the product's unit contribution margin, caused by an increase in the unit variable cost, raises the required sales volume at all price levels. Changes in direct fixed cost F could, of course, also be computed and tabulated or graphed if desired.

The next chapter deals with contribution analysis and how it can be used to estimate the comparative profitability among different company products as well as the relative profitability of price change alternatives.

Notes

1. Kent Monroe, *Pricing*, 278.

2. See Spencer A. Tucker, *Pricing for Higher Profit*, 101-117, for a discussion of his Break-even System. Standard break-even analysis is also covered in André Gabor, *Pricing*, 58-60; in Michael Morris & Gene Morris, *Market Oriented Pricing*, 93-99; in Kent Monroe, *Pricing*, 269-278; and in Hermann Simon & Martin Fassnacht, *Price Management*, 178-180.

CHAPTER

5
Contribution Analysis

*The underlying logic of contribution analysis is that
a product or service should be held accountable
only for those costs directly traceable to its
production, sales, and distribution.*[1]

It is not uncommon for management to be faced with the
seeming paradox of increasing sales revenue but declining profits and
vice versa. In this regard not much has changed since the mid-1930s
when a company's president asked his controller for an explanation
after sales had increased but profits declined by substantial amounts.
The controller, Jonathan Harris by name, provided the answer by
separating costs into volume-dependant variable costs and volume-
independent fixed costs. This was the beginning of an accounting
system known as *direct costing.*[2] It allowed management to study
the profitability of individual products at different price and sales
levels.

The concept of contribution was introduced in Section 3.4
of Chapter 3. The reader will recall from Equation (3.8) that total
contribution is the difference between a product's sales revenue and
its total variable cost:

$$K = R - V = (P - VC)\, Q \qquad \text{Eq. (5.1)}$$

where, K = Total contribution ($)

$$R = \text{Sales revenue (\$)}$$
$$V = \text{Total variable cost (\$)}$$
$$P = \text{Sell price (\$)}$$
$$Q = \text{Sales volume (units)}$$
$$VC = \text{Unit variable cost (\$)}$$
$$P - VC = \text{Unit contribution margin (\$)}$$

The contribution income statement on which contribution analysis is based differs markedly from the typical income statement used for financial analysis. We begin by showing and comparing the two. Using an illustrative example, we next apply the contribution analysis in two situations where it is ideally suited. One is in determining the relative profitability of a firm's line of products. The other is in evaluating the profit impacts of price change options for each product.

5.1 The Contribution Income Statement

The traditional quarterly or annual income statement is not suitable to a product profitability analysis because it lumps all costs, both direct and overhead, together under various aggregate cost categories. In somewhat simplified form such a *traditional income statement* would look like this:

	Sales revenue
Less:	Cost of goods sold
Less:	General sales & administrative expenses
Less:	Depreciation
	Operating profit
Less:	Other expenses
	Pretax profit

Such an income statement can also be very misleading because it strongly suggests that to improve the bottom line, a manager's best option, aside from reducing costs, is to increase sales revenue. We know, of course, from Chapter 3 that there is no direct unqualified relationship between sales revenue and total contribution and profit.

The *contribution income statement* does away with these problems and takes the following form:

Sales revenue

Less: Total variable cost

Total contribution

Less: Direct fixed cost

Net contribution

Less: Indirect fixed (overhead) cost

Pretax profit

This income statement gives us the framework for a profitability analysis.

5.2 Profitability Analysis

Profitability analyses are not limited to individual products or product lines. Any profit entity such as a product-market segment, sales territory, customer group, customer account or even individual salesperson may be evaluated and compared with others in terms of contribution dollars generated. We illustrate the method by examining the profitability of three models of a typical company's product offering.

Illustrative Example: Maricopa Enterprises Ltd. (I)

Maricopa Enterprises was founded three years ago by some entrepreneurial individuals who, while still in college, decided to design, manufacture, and market a line of innovative products for the healthcare industry. While more products are still in the development stage, Maricopa Enterprise's only product on the market at this time is a portable medication organizer and dispenser called TimerX which holds a patient's daily supply of prescription and over-the counter drugs and vitamins.

This pocket dispenser, which includes a microprocessor, comes in three models for sale to three distinct market segments. The three models differ in several respects including the number of medication chambers and event alerts, the manner in which the medication events may be set (time interval or specific time of day), the manner in which the patient is alerted to an event (visual, vibrating, or beep alarm), the construction details, and the warranty period (from one to three years).

The standard model TimerX-S includes all the features most in demand and sells for $100. Its unit variable cost is estimated to be $60. To attract the very price-sensitive segment of the market and compete with a bargain brand known as Pop-a-Pill, the economy model TimerX-E was introduced and is available for just $60. Its unit variable cost is $45. For patients who want a product with all the bells and whistles and do not mind paying $200, the premier TimerX-P can be had. Its variable cost per unit is $80. Maricopa Enterprise sells its products nationwide through a number of drugstore chains.

During the previous month, the company sold 3,000 units of the standard, 1,000 of the low-cost, and 500 of the premium-priced models yielding monthly sales revenue of just under one-half million dollars. In line with modern pricing philosophy, the sell prices bear no direct relationship to the products' cost of manufacture, i. e., its direct variable cost, but are based on what management believes reflect their customers' value perceptions and willingness to pay. In fact, the unit variable cost differences among the three models are much less than their price differences.

The monthly contribution statement for the TimerX brand is shown in Table 5.1 at the end of this chapter. The computations are straightforward and follow the contribution income statement given in Section 5.1 above. To show how direct fixed (programmed) costs are accounted for, let it be assumed that during the month the company expended $10,000 promoting the premium model TimerX-P including a targeted advertising campaign and showcasing the product at a trade show. Since this expenditure was specifically for the benefit of this model, it is a programmed cost and included as a direct fixed cost under the TimerX-P model reducing the total contribution by that amount.

As Table 5-1 indicates, the premium model TimerX-P was the most profitable on a per unit basis with $120 or 60% of the sell price going to contribution. However, in terms of net contribution dollars the standard model was the most profitable bringing in $120,000 in net contribution dollars, or 65% of the $185,000 total, followed by the premium model at $50,000 or 27% of the total. The company overhead, i. e., outlays which could not be directly assigned to any of the three models and were common to the firm and its products, was $100,000 leaving a pre-tax profit of $85,000 or 18.5% of sales revenue.

Summarizing the results of Table 5.1 one has:

	TimerX-E	TimerX-S	TimerX-P
% of Sales Revenue	13.0	65.2	21.8
% of Total Contribution	7.7	61.5	30.8

This information may also be presented in graphical form as in Figure 5-1 where sales revenue for the three models is shown together with the respective *net* contribution dollars earned after the total variable costs for the three models and the direct fixed cost for TimerX-P are deducted. This type of chart is quite useful and recommended for general marketing and pricing analyses. Thus, where contribution dollars earned are much out of proportion with sales revenue for the model in comparison to the other models, the chart can point to possible pricing issues and necessary corrective measures.

Clearly, for the standard model, net contribution closely tracks sales revenue and both account for nearly two thirds of their totals. For the economy model both sales revenue and net contribution generated are relatively small. Why then would Maricopa Enterprises not simply drop TimerX-E from the line? The reasons are strategic. This model draws sales, however small, from the Pop-a-Pill brand and there is a good chance that, given a choice, customers will opt for the standard model which they see as a better value.

Figure 5-1
Sales Revenue and Net Contribution for TimerX Brand

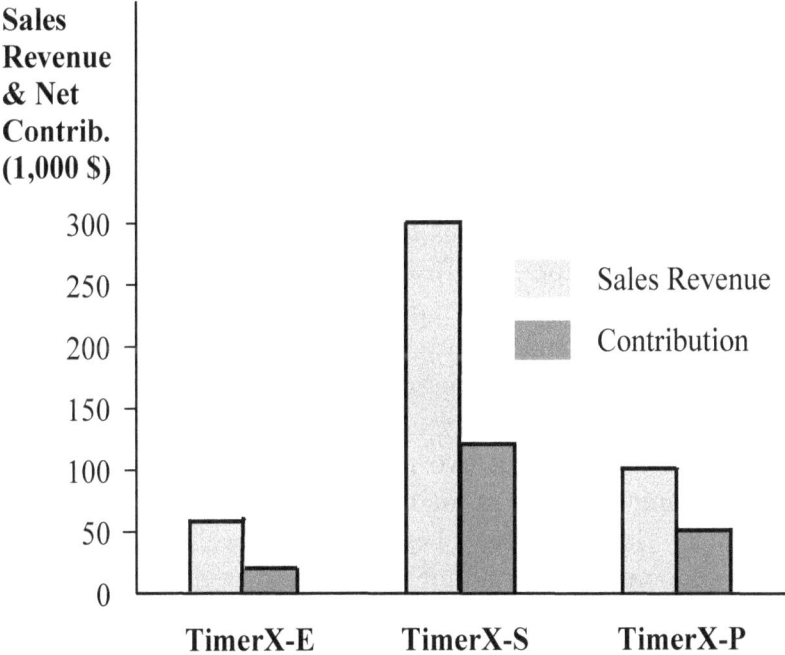

5.3 **Contribution Pricing**

Contribution analysis may also be employed to evaluate different price change options in terms of profitability. However, to make such an analysis the pricer needs to make some assumptions regarding the price-volume relationship and, specifically, he or she must estimate the percentage change in the quantity sold as a result of a percentage price change. In the following chapter (Chapter 6) we shall refer to this important price-volume relationship as the price elasticity of demand (P.E.D.). This metric is defined by:

$$\text{P.E.D.} = - \frac{\text{Percentage change in quantity demanded}}{\text{Percentage change in price}}$$

Thus, for example, if a price reduction of 10% results in a quantity increase of 5%, the P.E.D. would be 0.5 (5% / 10%). If a price increase of 5% results in quantity decline of 10%, the P.E.D. would be 2.0 (10% / 5%).

An example, a continuation of the one introduced in the previous section, will illustrate the method.

Illustrative Example: Maricopa Enterprises Ltd. (II)

After reviewing the latest profitability statements for the TimerX brand, Maricopa Enterprises' management has decided to initiate some price changes to increase sales revenue but, more importantly, the bottom line. To achieve this goal, an informal pricing committee consisting of the president and the vice presidents for Marketing & Sales, and Finance, needs to know the total contribution impacts to these proposed price changes: A price reduction of either 5% or 10% for the economy model and price increases of either 5% or 10% for the other two models. The options selected must lead to an improvement in total contribution of at least 10% to be acceptable. The committee's best estimates for the P.E.D.s are: 2.0 for the economy model, 1.0 for the standard model, and 0.5 for the premium model.

As part of this analysis, the accounting department prepared Table 5-2 appearing at the end of this chapter. It should be noted that in actual practice, more and smaller price increments in either direction would be chosen to identify the most profitable price. Also noteworthy in this tabulation is that the proposed price increases are expected to lead to sales volume declines and the price reductions to sales volume increases. This is in line with the law of demand covered in the following chapter.

Reviewing Table 5-2, the following can be concluded. The price of the economy model should not be changed as any change would substantially reduce total contribution. For the standard model, a price increase from $100 to $110 would be advantageous since it would increase total contribution by over 10%. Likewise, the premium model's price should be raised from $200 to $220. These price changes would add $21,500 in total contribution which is an increase of 11.0%. This all assumes, of course, that the estimated price-volume relationships at the present operating point (POP) prior to any price changes are reasonably correct.

5.4 Establishing Price Limits

What should the lowest price be at which a product is offered for sale? In other words, what should be its *price floor*? According to Tucker and other pricing experts it should be the direct variable cost also known as the product's *out-of-pocket (oop)* cost.[3] Oop costs are specifically incurred in the manufacture and sale of the product or service and consist of direct labor, direct materials, and direct overhead cost at any level. We have previously labeled this cost as the product's unit variable cost VC. Thus, in *Pricing the Profitable Sale* we shall define the price floor as:

$$P_F = VC \qquad \text{Eq. (5.2)}$$

In periods of business downturns selling at oop prices would allow a manufacturer to keep the doors open and retain a skeleton force of highly skilled labor until business improved. However, a business cannot survive if it does not find a way to eventually cover its overhead costs. Therefore, Equation (5.2) may be called the product's *short-term* price floor whereas the *long-term* price floor is the product's total unit cost (incremental plus fixed). This cost, we know, is neither easy to determine nor useful for pricing purposes.

The view that the price floor should be a product's average unit variable cost is not shared by everyone. Thus, Nagle and Müller, while conceding that theoretically the price floor is the product's variable cost, argue that: "The feasible price floor for a product that is positively differentiated is the price of the next-best competitive alternative."[4] In other words, if there is a comparable product or service on the market it should serve as the price floor. The reason given is that it tends to mitigate a price war. In this author's view such a price has no quantitative foundation and is too shaky and unstable to be of practical value.

With the lower limit of a product's price thus established, what should be the upper limit? Should it simply be whatever the market will bear as some pricing experts have proposed? A better answer would be the price that either maximizes sales revenue or total contribution and profits depending on the marketing goal for the product. Any price points other than these optimal ones would lead to suboptimal results, i. e., sales revenues and total contributions that are not at their maximum levels achievable under the prevailing price-volume conditions for the product.

For the TimerX brand previously discussed, for example, one can distinguish among four price points—the price at the present operating point (POP), the price floor and the optimal prices for either sales revenue or profit maximization. These are:

	TimerX-E	TimerX-S	TimerX-P
P_0	$60.00	$100.00	$200.00
P_F	45.00	60.00	80.00
[P]	45.00	100.00	300.00
P*	67.50	130.00	340.00

where, P_0 = Sell price before a price change
P_F = Price floor
[P] = Sell price for maximum sales revenue
P* = Sell price for maximum total contribution

How these optimal prices were determined can be found in Chapters 13 and 14 of *Pricing the Profitable Sale* where price optimization for sales revenue and contribution maximization, respectively, are covered. These sell prices are valid only if the estimates for the price elasticity of demand and unit contribution margin are correct, namely, P.E.D.s of 2.0, 1.0, and 0.5 and unit contribution margins of 25%, 40%, and 60% for the economy, standard, and premium models, respectively.

We note that for sales revenue maximization the standard model is already at the optimum price of $100 but $30 below the optimum price for contribution maximization. Interestingly, for the economy model the optimum price for revenue maximization is $45 which also happens to be the price floor. This is a good illustration for what marketers often experience, namely, that striving for maximum revenue and market share can be, and often is, fatal to the bottom line.

5.5 Pricing Guidelines (II)

We conclude this chapter with another pricing proposition:

Pricing Proposition 2

Under normal circumstances, no product should be sold below its average unit variable cost because no contribution to overhead and profit can be earned below this cost and price.

The following chapter on market demand is especially important to pricers because without a good understanding of the relationship between customer demand for goods and services and the prices charged, it is difficult, if not impossible, to set and adjust prices to yield optimal results.

Notes

1. Michael Morris & Gene Morris, *Market Oriented Pricing*, 93.

2. Kent Monroe, *Pricing*, 2nd ed., 160.

3. Spencer Tucker, *Pricing for Higher Profit*, 90-91.

4. Thomas Nagle and Georg Müller, *The Strategy and Tactics of Pricing*, 135-136.

Table 5-1
Contribution Statement for TimerX Brand by Product Model

Item	Product Model			Totals
	TimerX-E	TimerX-S	TimerX-P	
Sell price ($)	60.00	100.00	200.00	—
Unit variable cost ($)	45.00	60.00	80.00	—
Unit contribution margin ($)	15.00	40.00	120.00	—
Unit contribution margin (%)	25.0	40.0	60.0	—
Sales volume (units)	1,000	3,000	500	4,500
Sales revenue ($)	60,000	300,000	100,000	460,000
Total variable cost ($)	45,000	180,000	40,000	265,000
Total contribution ($)	15,000	120,000	60,000	195,000
Total contribution (%)	25.0	40.0	60.0	42.4
Direct fixed cost ($)	0	0	10,000	10,000
Net contribution ($)	15,000	120,000	50,000	185,000
Net contribution (%)	25.0	40.0	50.0	40.2
Common fixed cost ($)	—	—	—	100,000
Pretax profit ($)	—	—	—	85,000

Table 5-2
Price Change Analysis for TimerX Brand

Model	TimerX-E		TimerX-S		TimerX-P	
Present sell price ($)	60.00	60.00	100.00	100.00	200.00	200.00
Price change (%)	-5.0	-10.0	5.0	10.0	5.0	10.0
New sell price ($)	57.00	54.00	105.00	110.00	210.00	220.00
Unit variable cost ($)	45.00	45.00	60.00	60.00	80.00	80.00
Unit contribution margin ($)	12.00	9.00	45.00	50.00	130.00	140.00
Present sales volume (units)	1,000	1,000	3,000	3,000	500	500
Change in sales volume (%)	10.0	20.0	(5.0)	(10.0)	(2.5)	(5.0)
New sales volume (units)	1,100	1,200	2,850	2,700	488	475
Sales revenue ($)	62,700	64,800	299,250	297,000	102,375	104,500
Total variable cost ($)	49,500	54,000	171,000	162,000	39,000	38,000
Total contribution ($)	13,200	10,800	128,250	135,000	63,375	66,500
Present total contribution ($)	15,000	15,000	120,000	120,000	60,000	60,000
Change in contribution ($)	(1,800)	(4,200)	8,250	15,000	3,375	6,500
Change in contribution (%)	(12.0)	(28.0)	6.9	12.5	5.6	10.8

CHAPTER

6

Market Demand

*Market demand for a product is the total volume that
would be bought by a defined customer group in a
defined geographical area in a defined time period
in a defined marketing environment under a defined
marketing program.[1]*

The focus of modern market oriented pricing is on the
buyer and specifically on his or her value perceptions of certain
products and services and relative ability and willingness to pay for
these. The present chapter formally introduces two very important
concepts that are invaluable to the study of pricing, namely, the law
of demand and the price elasticity of demand both of which have
already been mentioned in the previous chapter. These originated
with British economist Alfred Marshall, one of the founders of
neoclassical economics, whose groundbreaking work *Principles of
Economics* was first published in 1890 and remains relevant to this
day.

The major part of this chapter will be devoted to the second
of these concepts, namely, the price elasticity of demand (P.E.D.)
since it is the real key to profitable pricing. In fact, it is doubtful that
a marketing professional can effectively price a product or service
without both a good understanding of its meaning and use and
knowing something about the specific price sensitivities of her firm's

products and services. This is not to say that the P.E.D. has found universal favor with marketers. Some pricing authors (who will remain anonymous) have either ignored or downplayed the critical importance of this metric.[2] The chapter also includes information on how a product's P.E.D. may be estimated either through formal research or from information within the firm. It concludes with the price cross-elasticity of demand, another important pricing metric.

6.1 Marketing Terms

To ensure author and reader are on the same page, it will be useful to review some common marketing concepts and terms.[3] An aggregate of buyers for a given product or service is described as a *market* for that product or service as opposed to an *industry* which is an aggregate of suppliers of such products or services. Thus one speaks of the market for automobiles, laptops, or movie pictures and the automobile, computer, or entertainment industry. By *market demand* one means the number of units of a specific product sold or expected to be sold in a given time period.

Demand may be primary or selective. *Primary demand* is for a *product class* like automobiles while *selective demand* would be for a specific make or model of automobile. Primary demand must exist before selective demand can occur. For example, when a new product class like the cell phone first came on the market, the innovator's first task was to generate primary demand for it before shifting to selective demand for its particular brand of cell phones once competing models were being offered. In *Pricing the Profitable Sale*, we are mainly concerned with selective demand.

Market segmentation has become a cornerstone of modern marketing. It means partitioning an overall market for specific products and services into smaller submarkets or market segments. A *market segment* consists of a group of buyers who share similar characteristics, product wants and needs, and the means and willingness to pay for these. Once identified, firms may then choose one or more of these market segments to serve. These become *target markets* for their marketing efforts with customized product, price, advertising and promotion, and distribution strategies.

The focus in this book is, of course, on just one of these strategy variables, namely, the price charged for a specific product or service. Price can have many meanings—it could be the list price, the price charged by a distributor, a fully discounted price paid by the end-user, or some other price in the distribution chain. Paying attention to how the price is stated is important because it determines the product's dollar unit contribution margin which is the difference between its price and direct unit variable cost. If this price is either over- or understated so will be the product's computed profitability.

Figure 6-1
Hypothetical and Linear Demand Curves

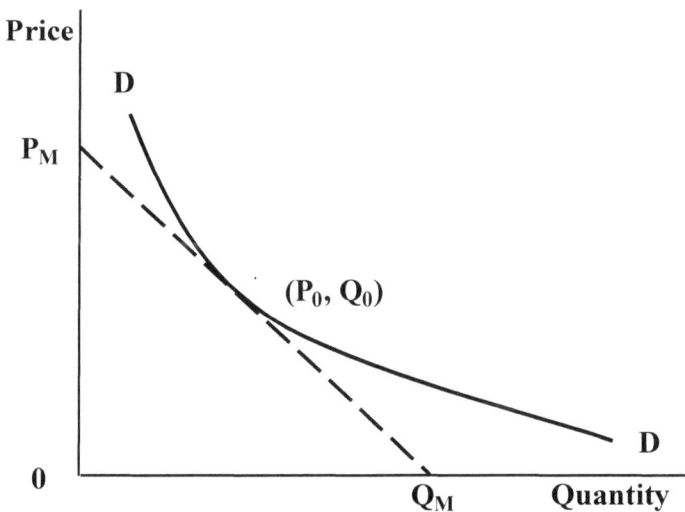

6.2 The Law of Demand

The *law of demand* states that, other things being equal (ceteris paribus), quantity demanded varies inversely with price or, stated differently, customers will buy more product at a lower than at a higher price. Clearly, this economic principle only expresses what common sense and experience would dictate but it does have major practical and theoretical implications. A tabulation of sell price versus the number of units purchased at each price over a given time period is known as a *demand schedule*. A graphical representation of the law of demand is the *demand curve* which is illustrated in Figure 6-1. Curve DD represents the typical downward-sloping demand curve for some fictional product.

As may be noted, quantity appears on the horizontal and price on the vertical axis. This is the traditional Marshallian representation of the demand curve and is the reverse of a conventional curve which places the independent variable (price) on the horizontal x-axis and the dependent variable (quantity) on the vertical y-axis. Using a conventional representation with the x-axis being the price axis, this curve is known as a *price response curve* (PRC). The curve's shape is the same in either case. In *Pricing the Profitable Sale* we shall make use of both types of curves.

While the demand curve is useful as a visual representation of the law of demand, it is of little practical use in pricing for at least two reasons. First, a marketer is not likely to know what the demand curves for his or her firm's diverse products look like. All that is really known is the present price-volume operating point (POP) indicated by (P_0, Q_0) on Figure 6.1. All other points on the demand curve are unknown. If they were known, the marketer would be only a step or two away of being able to compute the optimal prices that would maximize sales revenue or profits.

The second fundamental difficulty with the demand curve is that its location and shape is subject to frequent change due to factors both within and outside the firm. A point on the demand curve simply means that these are the number of units being sold during a given time period (month, quarter etc.) at this particular price. Movement along the present demand curve can occur only under ceteris paribus conditions, i.e., in the absence of any other major changes in another marketing strategy variable besides the product's price.

Changes that would significantly alter the shape of a product's demand curve include major product modifications, quality improvements or issues, deletions or additions to the line, raising or lowering the advertising budget, and any availability or delivery improvements or issues. Also impacting the product's demand curve would be major changes in a directly competing product including its market introduction, its purchase price, or any other marketing strategy variable or product lineup of a competitor. For these reasons, the demand curve would be an unreliable guide for pricing purposes.

Below the demand curve in Figure 6-1 appears a straight-line approximation to this curve, known as a *linear demand curve*, which is drawn tangent (having the same slope) to the demand curve at the present price-volume operating point (P_0, Q_0). This curve, unlike the hypothetical demand curve, is very useful for both pricing purposes and establishing rules and guidelines of a general nature. The linear demand curve intersects the price axis at P_M, the maximum price a customer is willing to pay for the product. This parameter is sometimes known as the *reservation price*. The curve intersects the horizontal axis at Q_M, the maximum number of units of the product customers are willing to purchase during a given time period.

Is the law of demand always valid? The answer is "not always but nearly always." People buy more of a product if they can get it for less except in the case of certain luxury goods for which the high prices themselves are the source of their attraction. For some well-heeled buyers these satisfy a need to possess something so exclusive that only they and a few others can afford it. Thus, there have been instances where the prices of high-end goods such as certain alcoholic beverages, perfumes, and clothing labels were reduced to stimulate demand when the opposite occurred, i.e., the quantities sold actually declined as their prices were lowered. Where quantity demanded varies directly with price, economists speak of *Giffen's Paradox*.

6.3 The Price Elasticity of Demand (P.E.D.)

In the absence of a reliable demand curve, a product's price sensitivity at the present price-volume operating point (P_0, Q_0) can serve as a useful substitute for pricing purposes. Knowing the price elasticity of demand (P.E.D.) can tell the marketer what sales volume changes to expect from a contemplated price change and predict its impact on sales revenue and profits.

6.3.1 The P.E.D. Formulas

A product's price elasticity of demand is defined as the relative responsiveness of quantity demanded to a change in price. If one lets the coefficient of price elasticity be denoted by the lowercase Greek epsilon (ϵ), the P.E.D. can be expressed as:

$$\epsilon = \frac{\text{Percentage change in quantity demanded}}{\text{Percentage change in price}} \qquad \text{Eq. (6.1)}$$

For incremental movements in price and volume, the *point price elasticity of demand*, simply also called the *price elasticity of demand*, is defined as:[4]

$$\epsilon = - \frac{Q_1 - Q_0}{Q} \div \frac{P_1 - P_0}{P} \qquad \text{Eq. (6.2)}$$

where, P_0, P_1 = Price before and after a change, respectively
Q_0, Q_1 = Quantity before and after a price change, respectively

As may be noted, ϵ is dimensionless. Letting the uppercase Greek delta (Δ) denote "the change in," this equation may be rewritten as:

$$\epsilon = - \frac{\Delta Q}{\Delta P} \times \frac{P}{Q} \qquad \text{Eq. (6.3)}$$

For incremental changes only, P and Q may be the original (P_0, Q_0) or changed (P_1, Q_1) prices and quantities, respectively, as the price elasticity of demand will be very closely the same.

The reader may wonder why the above two formulas are preceded by a negative sign. This is a convention introduced by Alfred Marshall. Since, by the law of demand, price and quantity are in an inverse relationship, the negative sign will ensure that the coefficient of price elasticity is always a *positive* number. We shall follow this convention throughout this book since it is much easier to relate to and manipulate positive numbers than negative ones. All one needs to remember is that a price *reduction* will *increase* the number of units sold and a price *increase* will *reduce* the quantity sold. In *Pricing the Profitable Sale*, the P.E.D. will always be considered to be a *positive* number.

While the above formulas are useful for computing the P.E.D. given a hypothetical or linear demand curve, they are cumbersome to work with and present no clear way to translate the marketer's knowledge of the price sensitivity of a product into an estimate of its P.E.D.. To correct this deficiency, throughout *Pricing the Profitable Sale* the following simplified notation for the P.E.D., based on Equation (6.1), will be employed:

$$ \boldsymbol{\epsilon} = - \frac{\blacktriangle Q}{\blacktriangle P} \qquad \text{Eq. (6.4)} $$

where, $\blacktriangle Q$ = Percentage incremental quantity change
                 $\blacktriangle P$ = Percentage incremental price change

Using Equation (6.4), a marketer can easily estimate a product's price elasticity coefficient ϵ at the present price-volume operating point (P_0, Q_0) provided he or she has a good feel for the product's price sensitivity at that point. One way this coefficient can be determined by the marketer, or other knowledgeable individuals within the firm, is by answering a simple question, for example, "What percentage sales volume change could one expect with a 10% price change?"

If, for example, a 10% price reduction is expected to increase sales volume by 25%, the product's P.E.D. would be 25% ÷ 10%

or 2.5. Similarly, if a 10% price increase is expected to result in a volume decline by 5%, the product's P.E.D. would be 5% ÷ 10% or 0.5. As may be noted, any negative signs may be ignored since we have defined the P.E.D. to be a positive number regardless of the direction of the price change.

6.3.2 Sales Revenue and the P.E.D.

The size of the elasticity coefficient establishes whether demand is elastic or inelastic at the (P_0, Q_0) point. This lets the marketer know where on the product's linear demand curve this price-volume point is located. This, in turn, gives him or her a good indication whether the sell price should be raised or lowered to improve sales revenue. The demand classification rule is:

If ϵ is	Demand is
> 1.0	*Elastic*
= 1.0	*Unitary elastic*
< 1.0	*Inelastic*

In addition to these three demand conditions, one can identify two special cases. Thus, when $\epsilon = 0$, demand is said to be *perfectly inelastic* and when $\epsilon = \infty$, demand is described as *perfectly elastic*.

If demand for the product is *inelastic* at the present price-volume operating point (P_0, Q_0), a small price change will produce a proportionally smaller change in sales volume whereas if it is *elastic*, the proportional sales volume change will be larger than the price change. At *unitary elasticity*, the change in sales volume will be in direct proportion to the price change.

More importantly, in which direction sales revenue changes with an incremental price change depends directly on the P.E.D. at the present price-volume operating point (P_0, Q_0). The relationship between a price change, the resulting revenue change and the P.E.D. is as follows:[5]

	$\epsilon_0 < 1.0$		$\epsilon_0 > 1.0$	
Price	Up	Down	Up	Down
Revenue	Up	Down	Down	Up

Hence, in the case of inelastic demand ($\epsilon_0 < 1.0$), when a product's price is raised, its sales revenue too rises and when the price is lowered, its sales revenue likewise declines. In other words, price and revenue are in synch. The opposite is true in the case of elastic demand ($\epsilon_0 > 1.0$). In that case, a price rise leads to a sales revenue decline and a price reduction to a revenue increase. Here price and revenue are out of synch. We shall later use the above relationships between price and sales revenue to state an important pricing rule of thumb for the case of sales revenue maximization.

Figure 6-2
Price Elasticities Along Linear Demand Curve

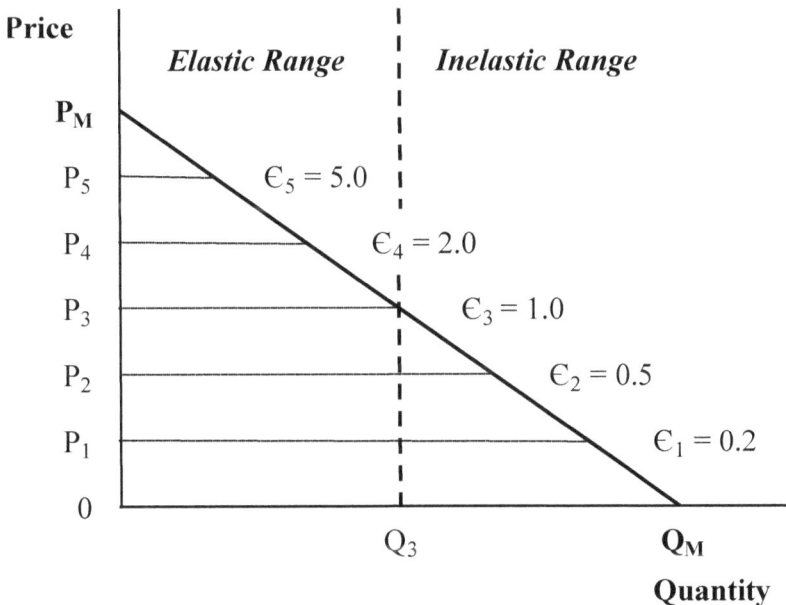

6.3.3 The Demand Curve and the P.E.D.

At least two common misconceptions about the linear demand curve exist and require clarification. The first is that the P.E.D., i.e., the coefficient of price elasticity, may be obtained by computing the slope of the linear demand curve. That is not the case because the coefficient $\mathcal{E}$ is the *dimensionless* ratio of two *percentages* (quantity and price) and not simply the ratio of quantity and price. The latter ratio would not make $\mathcal{E}$ dimensionless.

The second misconception is that the demand curve for a specific product or service, and specifically the linear demand curve, is either elastic or inelastic. That is not correct either. It is, however, correct to speak of a demand curve as being more elastic or inelastic than another similar curve. For example, if a linear demand curve tends toward the horizontal one may correctly term demand for the product it represents to be elastic and, if this curve appears more vertical, one may speak of demand for this product to be inelastic.

The typical demand curve is neither elastic nor inelastic. In fact, it is both. In the upper region of a linear demand curve, where the price is high and demand is low, demand is elastic. At the lower end, in the region of low prices and high demand, demand for the product is inelastic.

To illustrate this point, Figure 6-2 shows a typical linear demand curve on which five values of price elasticity of demand P.E.D., from 0.2 to 5.0, have been posted. Incidentally, these values may easily be determined by inspection.[6] As may be noted, the coefficient of price elasticity varies all along the demand curve with price elasticities increasing as one moves toward the left and higher price points and lower sales volumes. The dividing point is found at unitary price elasticity ($\mathcal{E} = 1.0$) where demand changes from inelastic to elastic. In other words, demand is elastic to the left and inelastic to the right of the price at which the P.E.D. equals one.

The maximum sales revenue for a particular product is achieved at the price at which the P.E.D. is exactly 1.0. Figure 6.2 clearly shows why this is the case. Thus, if one selects any price on the y-axis and draws a line horizontally to the demand curve and from there draws a vertical line to the x-axis and multiplies the quantity found there by the selected price one obtains the sales revenue for that price and quantity.

As may be noted, this product represents a rectangle within the triangle of the demand curve and the two axes. The largest possible rectangle and thus the maximum sales revenue is obtained where the P.E.D. is 1.0. In the diagram this maximum sales revenue is represented by the rectangle $P_3 \times Q_3$. All other rectangles that may be drawn within this space are smaller yielding smaller sales revenues.

An interesting point is that the triangular area under the linear demand curve is the sales revenue potential for this product, i.e., $R_P = \frac{1}{2}(P_M \times Q_M)$. The rectangle $P_3 \times Q_3$ mentioned above represents exactly one half of this potential sales revenue. The small triangles above and to the right of this rectangle represent the other half of R_P.

6.4 Pricing Guidelines (III)

With the above analysis and observations, the following additional pricing proposition can be offered. It follows directly from the relationship between a price change, the resulting revenue change, and the P.E.D. given in Section 6.3.2 above.

Pricing Proposition 3

Price change for sales revenue maximization,

a. No incremental price change for sales revenue improvement is required where a product's price elasticity of demand at the present price-volume operating point (P_0, Q_0) is equal to 1.0 ($\epsilon_0 = 1.0$).

b. Where a product's price elasticity of demand at the present price-volume operating point (P_0, Q_0) is larger than 1.0 ($\epsilon_0 > 1.0$), lowering the price will raise sales revenue; if it is less than 1.0 ($\epsilon_0 < 1.0$), raising the price will also raise sales revenue.

The simple pricing rule of thumb given in Pricing Proposition 3.b.

above allows the pricer to immediately know the required direction, up or down, of a contemplated price change.

6.5 Price Sensitivity Estimation

Considering its importance to pricing, both in segmenting markets and adjusting prices, it is perhaps not surprising that firms are much interested in the price sensitivities of their various products and services and consequently spend considerable amounts of money and time obtaining estimates. The marketing literature dealing with this topic is extensive and pricing texts sometimes devote an entire chapter to price sensitivity analysis.[7] Extensive consumer research has been done to get a solid handle on this elusive pricing metric but, because marketing research is beyond the scope of *Pricing the Profitable Sale*, the present section is confined to an overview only of the diverse techniques and tests that have been devised, their advantages and disadvantages, and their relative costs. It ends with some suggestions on estimating price sensitivities using information available within the firm

6.5.1 Research Techniques

Several techniques have been devised for gauging the price sensitivities of potential buyers in terms of either actual purchases or intentions to purchase certain products and services. Pertinent information may be collected from the analysis of sales data, customer surveys, and sensitivity experiments.

An economical way of obtaining price sensitivity information is found in the analysis of historical sales data. Where a firm is linked to its retailers as part of an inventory management system, scanner data will allow tracking of sales volume changes in response to price changes that is especially timely and useful. Care must be taken that sales changes are truly reflective of the price changes and not some other variable. For this, the data are usually subjected to some statistical analysis.

Where a product is still in the planning stage, the measurement of product preferences and purchase intentions has proved useful. In the so-called *price response survey*, respondents in the target market are asked price-related questions designed to elicit information on the willingness or probability of a purchase at various price points. From this data, a downward sloping curve may be constructed showing purchase probability on the vertical and price on the horizontal axis. The disadvantage of this technique is that with its focus on the purchase price, respondents may become unrealistically price conscious which could lead to distorted results.

In a controlled pricing experiment, the sell price (independent variable) is changed and its effect on the sales volume (dependent variable) is measured while all other variables that might influence the dependant variable are held constant. In a retail environment, such experiments may be conducted in stores or in a laboratory facility that closely duplicates the actual buying experience. In-store experiments are conducted without the buyers' knowledge and usually include a control store where prices are not changed so that possible extraneous non-price influences can be taken into account. A laboratory purchase experiment, on the other hand, has the advantage that the researcher can select the participants and control all variables that could impinge on the purchase decision.

Conjoint analysis, also known as *trade-off analysis* or *conjoint measurement*, is a relatively new and powerful experimental technique for new product development and pricing.[8] The heart of the technique is a sequential paired comparison in which respondents are asked to state their preferences between two product profiles with different attributes and attribute levels. The technique allows the marketer to assign a monetary value to any of a number of specific attributes and levels and after manipulation of the data predict what buyers would be willing to pay for various combinations of attributes. Special conjoint software is required and expert guidance recommended in conducting the experiment and evaluating the data. The method is necessarily expensive and an option for only large and profitable companies.

6.5.2 Internet Data

Firms and individuals that sell on the Internet can count on a veritable bonanza of quality price sensitivity information to guide their pricing decisions. The essence of P.E.D. determination for a product or service is, of course, finding the ratio of the percentage change in sales volume in response to a percentage change in price. The Internet seems tailor-made for the collection of this type of marketing data because prices can be changed almost continuously and the effects on sales volume found in real time which is something not possible any other way.[9] The Internet is also very cost-effective considering the huge outlays often involved in traditional price-sensitivity research. In addition, some firms have successfully used the Internet to price-segment their larger market in order to serve these smaller segments more efficiently and profitably.

6.5.3 Internal Company Data

Other than the Internet, there is perhaps no better place for obtaining information on a product's P.E.D. than within the firm and specifically from the sales force, distributors and other distribution channel members, and loyal customers. Purchasing agents are known for telling salespeople something like this: "We like your product but you are simply not competitive. If you could drop your price by 5%, we would be willing to buy another x units per month from you." Sometimes a salesperson may tell his or her sales manager: "The people at Alpha Company really like our product and the best part is that we have no competition." Both scenarios reveal much about the relative price sensitivities for a company product at these two firms and offer clues about whether prices should be maintained at present levels or need to be adjusted to improve sales revenue or profits.

To obtain relevant P.E.D. information the pricer should question knowledgeable people within the firm and then apply some elementary statistics to this raw data to obtain a number that represents the best estimate available. Sales personnel will rarely be able to answer a direct question about the size of the P.E.D. which means that the pricer must frame the question so that this ratio may be computed from the responses. Two typical questions might be:

i) "If we were to lower our price for Product X by 10% today, how many more units could we expect to sell next month over this month? or,

ii) "If we were to raise our price for Product X by 10% today, how many fewer units could we expect to sell next month from this month?

To evaluate these responses, two simple statistical techniques, the *weighted average* and the *expected value*, may be used. If one were to tally the sales force, for example, it is likely that the sales manager and more experienced salespersons would be more knowledgeable than the others. Consequently, their assessment should carry more weight. Thus, if one lets ε_a, ε_b,......ε_n be the price elasticity coefficients computed from the responses of the individual sales persons and w_a, w_b,......w_n be the respective weights assigned to each, the *weighted average* would be:

$$\varepsilon = \frac{\varepsilon_a \times w_a + \varepsilon_b \times w_b + ... \varepsilon_n \times w_n}{w_a + w_b + ... w_n} \qquad \text{Eq. (6.5)}$$

An alternative way would be to select the most knowledgeable individual, presumable the sales manager, and let him or her assign probabilities P to estimates of the product's P.E.D.. The *expected value* would then be:

$$\varepsilon = \varepsilon_1 \times P_1 + \varepsilon_2 \times P_2 + ... \varepsilon_N \times P_N \qquad \text{Eq. (6.6)}$$

where, $P_1 + P_2 + ...P_N = 1.0$.

Example

Suppose Alpha Company's sales manger and four members of his sales force—two experienced salespeople and two trainees—were asked to estimate the P.E.D. of Product X at the present price-volume operating point (P_0, Q_0). The sales manager estimates the P.E.D to be 1.6, the two salespeople 1.3 and 1.6, and the two trainees 2.0 and 0.9, respectively. Furthermore, suppose their respective P.E.D. estimates have been assigned weights of 3.0 (sales manager), 2.0 (salespeople), and 1.0 (trainees). Then, by Equation (6.5), one obtains:

$$\epsilon = \frac{1.6 \times 3.0 + 1.3 \times 2.0 + 1.6 \times 2.0 + 2.0 \times 1.0 + 0.9 \times 1.0}{3.0 \times 1 + 2.0 \times 2 + 1.0 \times 2}$$

$$\epsilon = 13.5 / 9.0 = 1.50$$

Using the sales manager's estimates only and the corresponding probabilities P he or she assigned to each, one obtains by Equation (6.6):

ϵ	P	$\epsilon \times P$
1.4	0.2	0.28
1.5	0.5	0.75
1.6	0.2	0.32
1.7	0.1	0.17
	1.0	1.52

Thus, according to the company's sales force, Product X's present P.E.D. is 1.50. A 5% price reduction, for example, would increase sales volume by 5% × 1.5 or 7.5% and, by our pricing rule of thumb, also sales revenue since the P.E.D. is larger than 1.0. By the sales manager's assessment, the product's P.E.D. is slightly more elastic than that estimated by his sales force.

6.6 The Price Cross-Elasticity of Demand

Another pricing metric of interest to marketers is the so-called *price cross-elasticity of demand*. While the P.E.D. is a measure of the percentage sales volume change as a result of a percentage price change in the same product, the price cross-elasticity of demand (C.E.D.) relates the percentage price change in one product to the percentage sales volume change in another.

Thus, if a price reduction in one product causes a sales volume increase in another, the two products are considered *complements*. If a price reduction in one results in a sales volume decline in another, the two products are *substitutes*. The two products can belong to the same firm or one to a competitor. Typical complementary products are razors and razor blades while pork and beef on a shopper's grocery list may be substitutes.

Analogous to Equation (6.3) for the P.E.D., the C.E.D. is defined as:[10]

$$\epsilon_X = \frac{\Delta Q_A}{\Delta P_B} \times \frac{P_B}{Q_A} \qquad \text{Eq. (6.7)}$$

where P_B is the price of product B and Q_A the demand for product A while Δ stands for the "change in."

One can determine whether two products complement each other or are substitutes by this classification rule:

If ϵ_X is	The products are
Positive	*Substitutes*
Negative	*Complements*

This is important for the marketer to know because if a product's price is lowered to increase demand, for example, it is not desirable to have it take away sales from another product unless, of course, the product is a competitor's.

Example

Armatec Company is a manufacturer of "smart guns" that allow safe storage of handguns at home by incorporating a locking mechanism that may only be released by entering a PIN code on a radio controlled device worn on the owner's wrist. Until recently, Pistol Model AP-1 sold for $100 while the wrist unit cost another $25. Weekly sales for the combination were 1,000 units.

Because Model AP-1 and wrist unit AC-7 must be purchased together they are complementary products and a price change in the AP-1 would be followed by a sales volume change in both the AP-1 and AC-7, namely, upward in the case of a price reduction and downward for a price increase. We therefore do not need to use Equation (6.7) to establish that the two models are complements.

The Armatec line also includes the more expensive Model AP-2 with additional features and functions. When its price was recently cut from $150 to $130, weekly sales of the Model AP-1 soon dropped to 800 units. How are the two models related, i.e., are they complements or substitutes? Letting "A" represent the Model AP-1 and "B" the Model AP-2 in Equation (6.7) one obtains:

$$\epsilon_X = \frac{1,000 - 800}{\$150 - \$130} \times \frac{\$150}{1,000} = 1.50$$

Since $\epsilon_X > 0$, the two models are considered substitutes. Clearly, as a result of the price reduction in the Model AP-2, some customers were willing to switch from Model AP-1 to the Model AP-2. This could mean that with the price reduction in the AP-2, the two models were no longer sufficiently differentiated in terms of features, functions, and price so that some Armatec customers now considered the premium-priced model a better value.

Notes

1. Philip Kotler and Kevin L. Keller, *Marketing Management*, 111.

2. One pricing author writes near the beginning of his book: "Because the phrase price elasticity is so often misused and confused,   I rarely use it in conversations and will not use it again in this text." Another writer advises his readers: "Chances are that you have heard the term elasticity used in pricing. And for that reason, it's an important term to understand even though it isn't an integral component of setting the most profitable price. Elasticity answers the question, 'If price is changed, what will happen to revenue?'"

3. Most of these concepts and terms are more thoroughly covered in standard marketing texts. See, for example, Philip Kotler and Kevin L. Keller, *Marketing Management*.

4. J. P. Gould and C. E Ferguson, *Microeconomic Theory*, 94-95.

5. Gould and Ferguson, supra at 111

6. On Figure 6-2, the coefficient of price elasticity at a particular price P_X on the linear demand curve is the ratio of the distance on the y (price)-axis between 0 and P_X to the distance between P_X and the reservation price P_M. For example, the P.E.D. at price P_2 is $\varepsilon_2 = P_0P_2 \div P_2P_M = 2 \div 4 = 0.50$. See Gould and Ferguson, supra at 97-99.

7. For P.E.D. measurement techniques, see, for example, Chapter 8 (Measurement of Price Sensitivity) in Thomas Nagle and Georg Müller, *The Strategy and Tactics of Pricing*; Chapter 9 (Research Methods for Pricing Decisions) in Kent Monroe,

Pricing; Chapter 3 (Price Response Estimation) in Robert Dolan and Hermann Simon, *Power Pricing*; and Chapter 3 (Analysis: The Economics of Price) in Hermann Simon and Martin Fassnacht, *Price Management*.

8. For a good introductory treatment of conjoint analysis, see Kent Monroe, *Pricing*, 244-248; Thomas Nagle and Georg Müller, *The Strategy and Tactics of Pricing*, 192-197; and Hermann Simon and Martin Fassnacht, *Price Management*, 116-127.

9. Walter Baker, Michael Marn, and Craig Zawada, "Price Smarter on the Net," *Harvard Business Review on Pricing*, 155-170.

10. Gould and Ferguson, supra at 67-68.

CHAPTER

7

Isoprofit Analysis

Far too often, price changes get made with little or no analysis of their likely financial impact on profitability.[1]

Most products on the market have been there for enough time for sales revenues, market shares, operating profits, and competition to have stabilized. However, while sell prices too have become settled, this does not mean that price has lost its significance as a marketing strategy variable. On the contrary, managers of mature products are constantly trying to improve results by price adjustments.

Before changing an established price, be it up or down, a marketer needs to know whether such a move will be profitable or not. As is well known, a pricing error can potentially lead to huge losses even though the price adjustment may have been relatively minor. This chapter introduces what has until now served as the primary analytical tool by which a marketer can evaluate the relative profitability of contemplated price change options. The relevant formulas are developed and two sets of tables presented by which this determination can be made without much time or effort. The chapter ends with an example to demonstrate use of the technique.

The presumptive originator of the technique called it *equal profit analysis* while in the later pricing literature it has also become known as *breakeven sales analysis* or simply *breakeven analysis*.[2] In *Pricing the Profitable Sale* the term *isoprofit analysis* is used instead because when this author first came across it in the cited monograph and developed the required formulas and tables to make practical use of it, he did not want to employ the phrase *break-even analysis* and have it confused with the much older technique by that name. The name is not important as long we have the same thing in mind.

7.1 Background

While the technique is now widely known and used, its origin is obscure but presumably lies with a 1960 monograph written by a University of Michigan economist named Wilford J. Eiteman who sought to reconcile economic theory with business practice in regard to profit maximization. Eiteman researched the price setting procedures at various manufacturing firms in different industries by conducting personal interviews and found that business managers had little knowledge of economic theory and used their own technique to maximize yearly profits.

He summarized his findings in these words: "Managers were found to determine the *profit-maximizing* combination of price and volume for their firms by a technique that did not make use of the concepts of marginal revenue and marginal costs. They decided upon the profit-maximizing combination by use of a curve which, for lack of a better term, the author has called an 'equal profit curve.'"[3]

What Eiteman did find was that in their attempt to maximize profits, managers envisioned a *hypothetical demand curve* for their product from which they could infer the volume change necessary as a result of a price change that would leave profits the same as before the price change. He gave no formula for the calculation of an equal profit curve but from his tabulations one can infer this relationship:

$$\frac{\text{Profit} + \text{Overhead}}{\text{Volume of Output (in units)}} + \text{Average Variable Cost} = \text{Price}$$

When profit plus overhead is held constant, the volume of output made a variable, and a fixed average variable cost used, a required price can be computed. A plot of Price (on the y-axis) versus Volume (on the x-axis) yields an equal profit curve. Using such curves, Eiteman could infer whether particular price changes would increase or reduce profits. His graphical technique has not proved useful for evaluating price change options but a formula now in common use appears in Section 7.3 below together with a simple derivation.

Figure 7-1
Typical Isoprofit Curve

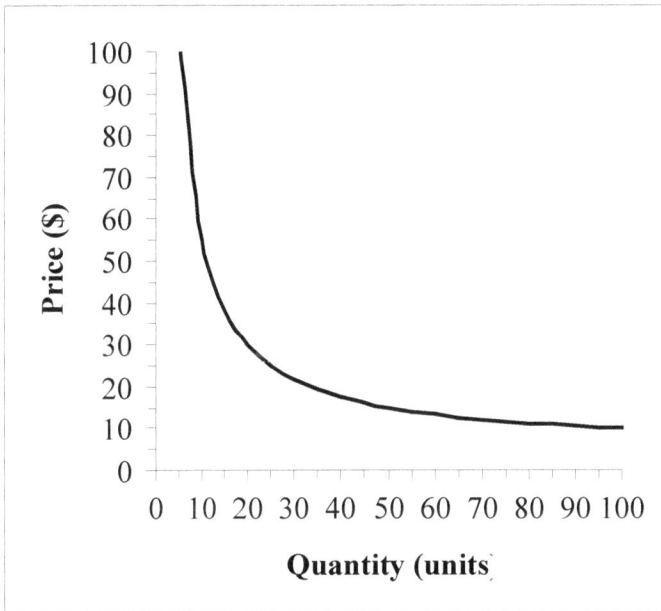

Example

Suppose Alpha Company's management wanted to see an isoprofit curve for one of their products with these parameters: Price $P_0 = \$10$, direct unit variable cost $VC_0 = \$5$, and sales volume $Q_0 = 100$ units. Using Equation (7.7) below, the formula for this curve is:

$$Q_1 = 500 / (P_1 - 5)$$

The desired isoprofit curve for this product is shown in Figure 7-1. It tells management the number of units to be sold in the event of a price change if profits are to be maintained. As may easily be verified, all price-quantity points on this curve yield the same total contribution, namely, $500. Interestingly, the shape of this curve is very similar to the hypothetical demand curve shown in Figure 6-1 of the previous chapter.

7.2 The Rationale Behind the Technique

The concept of the demand curve and the law of demand was taken up in the previous chapter. Briefly, the law of demand simply says that more units of a product will be sold at a lower price than at a higher one. When a price is reduced, the number of units sold typically increases while an increase in the sell price will cause a drop in demand. Either a cut in the sell price or a price rise will thus change the sales volume in the opposite direction leading to a change in the total contribution level and profit as well. Isoprofit analysis (or break-even sales analysis) is designed to answer two questions:

i) In the case of a contemplated *price reduction*:
 What is the *minimum required sales volume increase* that will leave total contribution and profit unchanged?

ii) In the case of a contemplated *price increase*:
 What is the *maximum allowable sales volume reduction* that will leave total contribution and profit unchanged?

This begs the question why a marketer would be interested to know what price change would leave total contribution and profit the same as before the change. The answer is that isoprofit analysis sets the boundaries on profitable sales volume changes. Thus, in the case of a price reduction, the marketer can expect total contribution and profits to rise as long as the sales volume increase is larger than the minimum required. In the case of a price increase, the marketer can expect a total contribution and profit increase if the sales volume reduction is less than the maximum allowable. While the technique does not tell him or her by how much the sell price should be changed or what the contribution gain will be, it does tell the pricer the range of price changes which will be profitable and which not.

In most cases, isoprofit analysis is better suited to evaluating price change options than contribution analysis (Chapter 5) because instead of taking the proposed price change and *running it up the flagpole* to arrive at an answer on profitability, the marketer is presented with the facts on which he or she can make an informed judgment whether the allowable or required sales volume changes can be expected to materialize. If not, the price change should not be implemented. The technique has another significant advantage in that the values on allowable and required sales volume changes as a function of price changes can be tabulated so that the pricer can simply look up the numbers and save computation time and effort.

7.3 The Isoprofit Formulas

In developing the isoprofit formulas we proceed in the usual manner. In Equation (3.8) of Chapter 3 we defined the total contribution K as the product of the unit contribution margin $(P - VC)$ and the sales volume Q:

$$K = (P - VC)\,Q \qquad\qquad \text{Eq. (7.1)}$$

If one lets the subscripts 0 and 1 stand for a parameter before and after a price change, respectively, one obtains:

$$K_0 = (P_0 - VC_0)\,Q_0 \qquad\qquad \text{Eq. (7.2)}$$
$$K_1 = (P_1 - VC_1)\,Q_1 \qquad\qquad \text{Eq. (7.3)}$$

The change in total contribution as a result of a price change is:

$$\Delta K = K_1 - K_0 \qquad\qquad \text{Eq. (7.4)}$$

But since, for isoprofit, the total contribution change $\Delta K = 0$:

$$K_1 = K_0 \qquad\qquad \text{Eq. (7.5)}$$

Combining Eq. (7.2), Eq. (7.3), and Eq. (7.5) and solving for the new sales volume, one obtains the basic isoprofit formula:

$$Q_1 = Q_0 \times \frac{P_0 - VC_0}{P_1 - VC_1} \qquad \text{Eq. (7.6)}$$

But since for incremental price changes we can assume that $VC_1 = VC_0$, this expression becomes:

$$\frac{Q_1}{Q_0} = \frac{P_0 - VC_0}{P_1 - VC_0} \qquad \text{(Eq. (7.7)}$$

In order to put Equation (7.7) into a form suitable for tabulation, we need the sales volume change expressed as a percentage. The percentage change in sales volume resulting from a price change is:

$$\blacktriangle Q = \frac{Q_1}{Q_0} - 1 = \frac{P_0 - P_1}{P_1 - VC_0} \qquad \text{Eq. (7.8)}$$

Since $P_1 = P_0 + \Delta P$, Equation (7.8) can be rewritten as:

$$\blacktriangle Q = \frac{-\Delta P}{\Delta P + CM_0 \, (\$)} \qquad \text{Eq. (7.9)}$$

This is the isoprofit formula expressed in terms of dollars. By dividing numerator and denominator on the right side by P_0 one obtains the percentage formula suitable for tabulation:

$$\blacktriangle Q = \frac{-\blacktriangle P}{\blacktriangle P + CM_0 \, (\%)} \qquad \text{Eq. (7.10)}$$

where, $\blacktriangle Q$ = Incremental sales volume change (%)
$\blacktriangle P$ = Incremental price change (%)
$CM_0 \, (\%)$ = Unit contribution margin prior to the price change

Equation (7.10) allows the marketer to compute the percentage of *required* sales volume increase in the case of a price reduction and the *allowable* sales volume reduction in the case of a price increase.

Example

Suppose Alpha Company's Product X has a percentage unit contribution margin of 45%. What would be the isoprofit volume changes for price changes of 5%? From Equation (7.10):

i) For a 5% price reduction:

$$\blacktriangle Q = -(-0.05)/(-0.05+0.45) = 0.125$$

Hence, a 5% price reduction would require a minimum sales volume change of $+0.125 \times 100\%$ or $+12.5\%$ to keep profits as before.

ii) For a 5% price increase:

$$\blacktriangle Q = -(0.05)/(0.05+0.45) = -0.100$$

This means that for a 5% price increase the maximum allowable sales volume change would be $-0.100 \times 100\%$ or -10.0%.

7.4 Reference Tables

Doing the above exercise for every contemplated price change could become tedious and it is more convenient to rely on tabulations of isoprofit values.

7.4.1 Required and Allowable Volume Changes

Table 7-1 at the end of this chapter lists the isoprofit sales volume changes in percent for unit contribution margins from 5% to 100% and contemplated price changes ranging from 1% to 30% as computed using Equation (7.10).[4] Specifically, the *minimum required* percentage sales volume increase in the case of a price reduction is shown in Table 7-1(a) while Table 7-1(b) lists the *maximum allowable* percentage sales volume reduction for a price increase. For non-incremental (high) price reductions at low margins, this formula can yield required sales volume increases above 100%. Since a doubling of the required sales volume in the absence of any cost changes (which these formulas presuppose) is not realistic, these isoprofit points are excluded.

7.4.2 Required and Allowable P.E.D.s

The reader may have observed that when one computes the required or allowable percentage sales volume change for a given percentage price change one implicitly also determines the required or allowable price elasticity of demand since the percentage price and volume changes are directly related via the P.E.D.. Hence, in the example in Section 7.3 above, the minimum required P.E.D. for a 5% price reduction is 12.5% / 5% or 2.5. The maximum allowable P.E.D. for a 5% price increase is 10.0% / 5% or 2.0. This begs the question, Why not compute and tabulate the required or allowable P.E.D. as a result of a price change directly? Then the two questions of Section 7.2 could be rephrased thus:

i) In the case of a contemplated price *reduction*:
What is the *minimum required P.E.D.* that will leave total contribution and profit unchanged?

ii) In the case of a contemplated *price increase*:
What is the *maximum allowable P.E.D.* that will leave total contribution and profit unchanged?

The required formula is easily derived. In the previous chapter, Equation 6.4, the P.E.D. is defined as:

$$\varepsilon = - \blacktriangle Q / \blacktriangle P$$

so that Equation (7.10) becomes.:

$$\varepsilon = \frac{1}{\blacktriangle P + CM_0 (\%)} \qquad \text{Eq. (7.11)}$$

Equation (7.11) gives the *minimum required P.E.D.* for a price reduction and the *maximum allowable P.E.D.* for a price increase to leave total contribution and profits unchanged.

Based on Equation (7.11), Table 7-2 at the end of this chapter lists the isoprofit price elasticities of demand for unit contribution margins from 5% to 100% and contemplated price changes from 1% to 30%. Specifically, the *minimum required P.E.D.* for a price reduction appears in Table 7-2(a) while Table 7-2(b) lists the *maximum allowable P.E.D.* for a price increase.

Example

Returning to Alpha Company's Product X of Section 7.3 above and using Equation (7.11), one obtains:

i) For a 5% price reduction:

The minimum required P.E.D. is $1 / (- 0.05 + 0.45) = 2.5$

ii) For a 5% price increase:

The maximum allowable P.E.D. is $1 / (0.05 + 0.45) = 2.0$

These are the results obtained previously.

Figure 7-2(a)
Isoprofit Curves: Price Change vs. Sales Volume Change

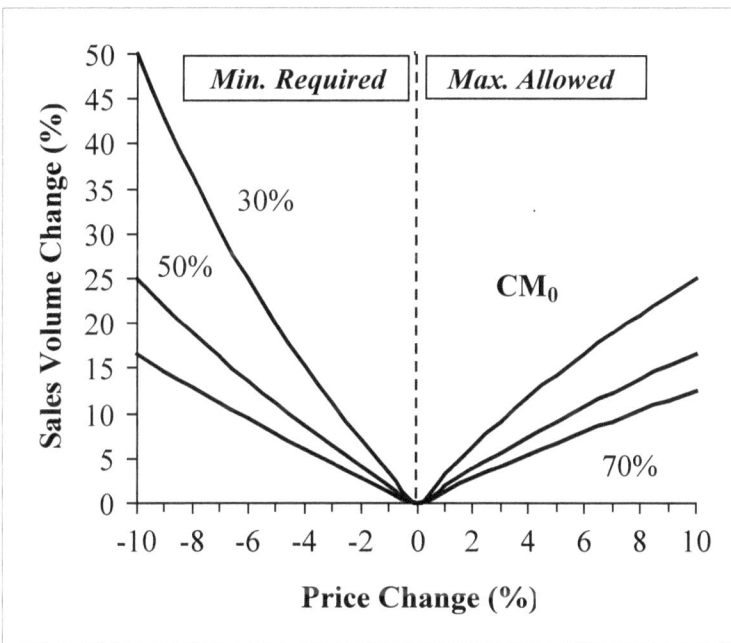

7.5 Graphical Analysis

For viewing trends and allowing for generalizations, a graphical representation of the data is often more useful than a mere tabulation of numbers. Figure 7-2(a) shows a graph of the isoprofit sales volume changes for price changes between –10% and +10% and unit contribution margins of 30%, 50%, and 70%. The region to the left of the vertical line at a zero price change, shows the minimum *required* sales volume increases and to the right the maximum *allowable sales volume* reduction. The graph in Figure 7-2(b) shows the price elasticity of demand required or allowed for a price reduction and increase, respectively, for three values of percentage unit contribution margin. Again, the region to the left of the vertical line at a zero price change shows the minimum *required* P.E.D. for a price reduction and to the right of this line the maximum *allowable* P.E.D. for a price increase.

Figure 7-2 (b)
Isoprofit Curves: Price Change vs. P.E.D.

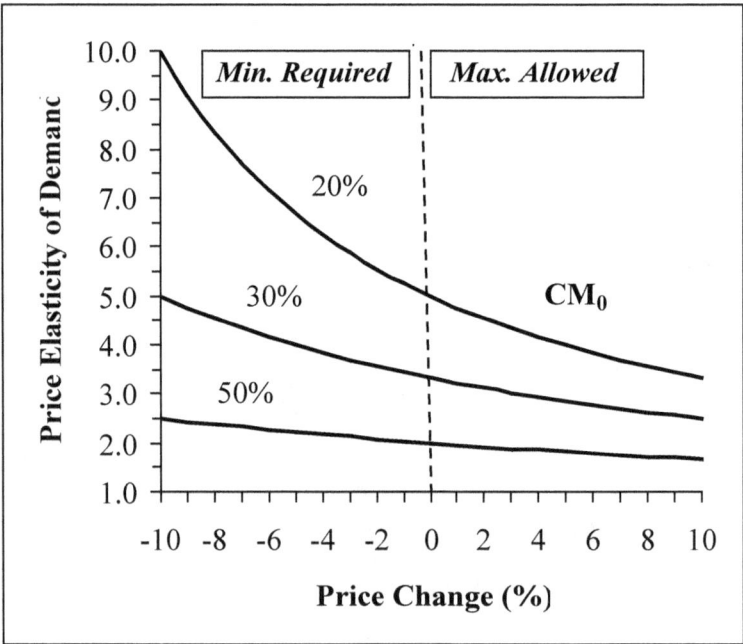

Of particular interest is the P.E.D. at which the percentage price change is zero. Letting $\blacktriangle P = 0$ in Equation (7.11) one obtains the optimal price elasticity of demand:

$$\epsilon^* = \frac{1}{CM_0\ (\%)} \qquad\qquad \text{Eq. (7.12)}$$

Referring to Figure 7-2(b), for each percentage contribution margin CM_0 (%), the isoprofit P.E.D. lies at the crossover point between negative and positive price changes. At that price point, no price change is needed and the present price should be held.

7.6 Pricing Guidelines (IV)

On hand of the isoprofit formulas of Equations (7.10), (7.11), and (7.12), and Figures 7-2(a) and 7-2(b), the following additional pricing propositions can be stated:

Pricing Proposition 4

The lower a product's unit contribution margin, the higher,

a) must be the percentage sales volume increase and price elasticity of demand to make an incremental price reduction profitable.

b) are the allowable percentage sales volume reduction and price elasticity of demand to make an incremental price increase profitable.

Pricing Proposition 5

Price change for total contribution (profit) maximization:

a. No incremental price change for profit improvement is required where a product's price elasticity of demand at the present price-volume operating point (P_0, Q_0) is equal to the reciprocal of its unit contribution margin CM_0 (%).

b. Where a product's price elasticity of demand at the present price-volume operating point (P_0, Q_0) is higher than the reciprocal of CM_0 (%), lowering the price will raise profits; if it is less than the reciprocal of CM_0 (%), raising the price will also raise profits.

Pricing Proposition 5 gives a simple pricing rule of thumb by which the pricer can quickly determine whether the contemplated price change should be up or down. All that is required is to compare the reciprocal of the product's unit contribution margin with its estimated P.E.D. at the present price-volume operating point.

7.7 Application

The following example will demonstrate use of the technique.

Illustrative Example: Maricopa Enterprises Ltd. (III)

As may be recalled from Section 5.2 of Chapter 5 (Contribution Analysis), Maricopa Enterprises manufactures and markets a medication dispensing device known as TimerX which is sold in three versions—economy, standard, and premium. In Section 5.3 of that chapter we noted that the company's pricing committee had decided on a price reduction for the economy model and price increases for the other two models. The price elasticities were estimated to be 2.0, 1.0, and 0.5, respectively. The parameters for the three product models are therefore:

	TimerX-E	TimerX-S	TimerX-P
Sell price, P_0 ($)	60.00	100.00	200.00
Contribution margin, CM_0 (%)	0.25	0.40	0.60
Price elasticity, P.E.D.	2.0	1.0	0.5
Optimal P.E.D, $1 / CM_0$ (%)	4.0	2.5	1.7

Referring to the pricing rule of thumb above and Table 7-2, the range of profitable price changes are:

TimerX-E
Since the P.E.D. of 2.0 is less than the optimal P.E.D. (ε*) of 4.0, the price should be raised. With a CM_0 (%) of 25% and a P.E.D. of 2.0, by Table 7-2(b), the maximum allowable price increase is 25%. Optimal price range: $60 - $75.

TimerX-S
Since the P.E.D. of 1.0 is less than the optimal P.E.D. (ε*) of 2.5, the price should be raised. With a CM_0 (%) of 40% and a P.E.D. of

1.0, by Table 7-2(b), the maximum allowable price increase is at least 30 %.
Optimal price range: $100 - $130 (minimum).

TimerX-P
Since the P.E.D. of 0.5 is less than the optimal P.E.D. (ε^*) of 1.7, the price should be raised. With a CM_0 (%) of 60% and a P.E.D of 0.5, by Table 7-2(b), the price may be increased by at least 30%.
Optimal price range: $200 - $260 (minimum).

7.8 Implementing Price Changes

Once the profitability of a certain price change has been determined, such as by isoprofit analysis or another means, the next issue should be whether it should be implemented. The reason is that the firm with its products and services is just one player in the field—the other two are its customers and its competitors. Customers generally resist paying higher prices and may switch to a competitor while competitors may view a price cut, especially a substantial one, as a hostile act to seize additional market share. As pricing authors Nagle and Müller have pointed out, "Done poorly, a pricing move can have disastrous consequences."[5]

The first task for the pricer should be to establish the validity of the underlying assumptions leading to a price change option and, specifically, the sell price, the unit contribution margin, and the price elasticity of demand prior to the planned price change. The product's net sell price and contribution margin are data normally generated internally by the firm and should, in theory at least, present no major hurdle to being determined with a fair degree of accuracy. Price elasticity data, on the other hand, is a judgmental factor based on experience and, consequently, there is always a danger of significantly under- or overestimating the market's price sensitivity for a product. This is another reason for proceeding with caution.

Caution is also recommended in the use of the published tables for isoprofit or breakeven analyses, including the ones given in this chapter, because these are based on a linear demand curve and meant for incremental price changes only. Some of the tables appearing in other texts list price changes of over 30% in either direction (a price range of 60%) which is not very realistic.

A comparison of the hypothetical and linear demand curves (Figure 6-1 of Chapter 6) shows how these two would normally diverge before and after the POP meaning that price changes too far removed from that point on the hypothetical demand curve no longer adequately predict the quantity changes. Furthermore, the sales volume change for price increase may substantially differ from that for a price reduction. It is therefore highly recommended that the tables not be used for incremental price changes exceeding about 15% - 20% in either direction. The tabular listings for larger price changes should be used for trend analyses only.

The second question to be asked is, Are other options available besides a price change? Chances are that there are many. We shall discuss some of these later in the book. A major factor to be considered by the marketer is the stage the particular product or service is in its life cycle. Product life cycle pricing is discussed in the following chapter.

Notes

1. Thomas Nagle and Georg Müller, *The Strategy and Tactics of Pricing*, 213.

2. For breakeven sales analysis with breakeven formula and chart see, for example, Thomas Nagle and Georg Müller, supra at 145, 214-219. Incidentally, in their Appendix 9B, these authors use an interesting graphical method to derive Equation (7-9) given above. Break-even formulas and associated tables of computed values are also found in Robert Dolan and Hermann Simon, *Pricing Power*, 22-23; André Gabor, *Pricing*, 71-74; and Kent Monroe, *Pricing*, 287-290.

3. Wilford J. Eiteman, *Price Determination in Oligopolistic and Monopolistic Situations*, 6.

4. Table 7-1 is an adaptation of the author's 2-page flyer: H. P. Zell & Associates, *Iso-Profit Chart*. (U.S. copyright registration no. TX 1-158-252 dated July 25, 1983).

5. Thomas Nagle and Georg Müller, supra at 270.

Table 7-1 (a)
Isoprofit Price Reduction: Minimum Required Sales Volume Increase (%)

CM₀ (%)	Price Change (%)													
	-1.0	-2.0	-3.0	-4.0	-5.0	-6.0	-7.0	-8.0	-9.0	-10.0	-15.0	-20.0	-25.0	-30.0
5	25.0	66.7	—	—	—	—	—	—	—	—	—	—	—	—
10	11.1	25.0	42.9	66.7	100.0	—	—	—	—	—	—	—	—	—
15	7.1	15.4	25.0	36.4	50.0	66.7	87.5	—	—	—	—	—	—	—
20	5.3	11.1	17.6	25.0	33.3	42.9	53.8	66.7	81.8	100.0	—	—	—	—
25	4.2	8.7	13.6	19.0	25.0	31.6	38.9	47.1	56.3	66.7	100.0	—	—	—
30	3.4	7.1	11.1	15.4	20.0	25.0	30.4	36.4	42.9	50.0	100.0	—	—	—
35	2.9	6.1	9.4	12.9	16.7	20.7	25.0	29.6	34.6	40.0	75.0	—	—	—
40	2.6	5.3	8.1	11.1	14.3	17.6	21.2	25.0	29.0	33.3	60.0	100.0	—	—
45	2.3	4.6	7.1	9.8	12.5	15.4	18.4	21.6	25.0	28.6	50.0	80.0	—	—
50	2.0	4.2	6.4	8.7	11.1	13.6	16.3	19.0	21.9	25.0	42.9	66.7	100.0	—
55	1.8	3.8	5.8	7.8	10.0	12.2	14.6	17.0	19.6	22.2	37.5	57.1	83.3	—
60	1.7	3.4	5.3	7.1	9.1	11.1	13.2	15.4	17.6	20.0	33.3	50.0	71.4	100.0
65	1.6	3.2	4.8	6.6	8.3	10.2	12.1	14.0	16.1	18.2	30.0	44.4	62.5	85.7
70	1.4	2.9	4.5	6.1	7.7	9.4	11.1	12.9	14.7	16.7	27.3	40.0	55.6	75.0
75	1.4	2.7	4.2	5.6	7.1	8.7	10.3	11.9	13.6	15.4	25.0	36.4	50.0	66.7
80	1.3	2.6	3.9	5.3	6.7	8.1	9.6	11.1	12.7	14.3	23.1	33.3	45.5	60.0
85	1.2	2.4	3.7	4.9	6.3	7.6	9.0	10.4	11.8	13.3	21.4	30.8	41.7	54.5
90	1.1	2.3	3.4	4.7	5.9	7.1	8.4	9.8	11.1	12.5	20.0	28.6	38.5	50.0
95	1.1	2.2	3.3	4.4	5.6	6.7	8.0	9.2	10.5	11.8	18.8	26.7	35.7	46.2
100	1.0	2.0	3.1	4.2	5.3	6.4	7.5	8.7	9.9	11.1	17.6	25.0	33.3	42.9

Table 7-1 (b)
Isoprofit Price Increase: Maximum Allowable Sales Volume Decrease (%)

CM_0 (%)	Price Change (%)													
	1.0	2.0	3.0	4.0	5.0	6.0	7.0	8.0	9.0	10.0	15.0	20.0	25.0	30.0
5	16.7	28.6	37.5	44.4	50.0	54.5	58.3	61.5	64.3	66.7	75.0	80.0	83.3	85.7
10	9.1	16.7	23.1	28.6	33.3	37.5	41.2	44.4	47.4	50.0	60.0	66.7	71.4	75.0
15	6.2	11.8	16.7	21.0	25.0	28.6	31.8	34.8	37.5	40.0	50.0	57.1	62.5	66.7
20	4.8	9.1	13.0	16.7	20.0	23.1	25.9	28.6	31.0	33.3	42.9	50.0	55.6	60.0
25	3.8	7.4	10.7	13.8	16.7	19.3	21.9	24.2	26.5	28.6	37.5	44.4	50.0	54.5
30	3.2	6.2	9.1	11.8	14.3	16.7	18.9	21.0	23.1	25.0	33.3	40.0	45.4	50.0
35	2.8	5.4	7.9	10.3	12.5	14.6	16.7	18.6	20.4	22.2	30.0	36.4	41.7	46.1
40	2.4	4.8	7.0	9.1	11.1	13.0	14.9	16.7	18.4	20.0	27.3	33.3	38.5	42.9
45	2.2	4.3	6.2	8.2	10.0	11.8	13.5	15.1	16.7	18.2	25.0	30.8	35.7	40.0
50	2.0	3.8	5.7	7.4	9.1	10.7	12.3	13.8	15.2	16.7	23.1	28.6	33.3	37.5
55	1.8	3.5	5.2	6.8	8.3	9.8	11.3	12.7	14.1	15.4	21.4	26.7	31.2	35.3
60	1.6	3.2	4.8	6.2	7.7	9.1	10.4	11.8	13.0	14.3	20.0	25.0	29.4	33.3
65	1.5	3.0	4.4	5.8	7.1	8.4	9.7	11.0	12.2	13.3	18.7	23.5	27.8	31.6
70	1.4	2.8	4.1	5.4	6.7	7.9	9.1	10.3	11.4	12.5	17.6	22.2	26.3	30.0
75	1.3	2.6	3.8	5.1	6.2	7.4	8.5	9.6	10.7	11.8	16.7	21.0	25.0	28.6
80	1.2	2.4	3.6	4.8	5.9	7.0	8.0	9.1	10.1	11.1	15.8	20.0	23.8	27.3
85	1.2	2.3	3.4	4.5	5.6	6.6	7.6	8.6	9.6	10.5	15.0	19.0	22.7	26.1
90	1.1	2.2	3.2	4.3	5.3	6.3	7.2	8.2	9.1	10.0	14.3	18.2	21.7	25.0
95	1.0	2.1	3.1	4.0	5.0	5.9	6.9	7.8	8.7	9.5	13.6	17.4	20.8	24.0
100	1.0	2.0	2.9	3.8	4.8	5.7	6.5	7.4	8.3	9.1	13.0	16.7	20.0	23.1

Table 7-2 (a)
Isoprofit Price Reduction: Minimum Required Price Elasticity of Demand (P.E.D.)

CM_0 (%)	Price Change (%)													
	-1.0	-2.0	-3.0	-4.0	-5.0	-6.0	-7.0	-8.0	-9.0	-10.0	-15.0	-20.0	-25.0	-30.0
5	25.0	33.3	50.0	100.0	—	—	—	—	—	—	—	—	—	—
10	11.1	12.5	14.3	16.7	20.0	25.0	33.3	50.0	100.0	—	—	—	—	—
15	7.1	7.7	8.3	9.1	10.0	11.1	12.5	14.3	16.7	20.0	—	—	—	—
20	5.3	5.6	5.9	6.3	6.7	7.1	7.7	8.3	9.1	10.0	20.0	—	—	—
25	4.2	4.3	4.5	4.8	5.0	5.3	5.6	5.9	6.3	6.7	10.0	20.0	—	—
30	3.4	3.6	3.7	3.8	4.0	4.2	4.3	4.5	4.8	5.0	6.7	10.0	20.0	—
35	2.9	3.0	3.1	3.2	3.3	3.4	3.6	3.7	3.8	4.0	5.0	6.7	10.0	20.0
40	2.6	2.6	2.7	2.8	2.9	2.9	3.0	3.1	3.2	3.3	4.0	5.0	6.7	10.0
45	2.3	2.3	2.4	2.4	2.5	2.6	2.6	2.7	2.8	2.9	3.3	4.0	5.0	6.7
50	2.0	2.1	2.1	2.2	2.2	2.3	2.3	2.4	2.4	2.5	2.9	3.3	4.0	5.0
55	1.9	1.9	1.9	2.0	2.0	2.0	2.1	2.1	2.2	2.2	2.5	2.9	3.3	4.0
60	1.7	1.7	1.8	1.8	1.8	1.9	1.9	1.9	2.0	2.0	2.2	2.5	2.9	3.3
65	1.6	1.6	1.6	1.6	1.7	1.7	1.7	1.8	1.8	1.8	2.0	2.2	2.5	2.9
70	1.4	1.5	1.5	1.5	1.5	1.6	1.6	1.6	1.6	1.7	1.8	2.0	2.2	2.5
75	1.4	1.4	1.4	1.4	1.4	1.4	1.5	1.5	1.5	1.5	1.7	1.8	2.0	2.2
80	1.3	1.3	1.3	1.3	1.3	1.4	1.4	1.4	1.4	1.4	1.5	1.7	1.8	2.0
85	1.2	1.2	1.2	1.2	1.3	1.3	1.3	1.3	1.3	1.3	1.4	1.5	1.7	1.8
90	1.1	1.1	1.1	1.2	1.2	1.2	1.2	1.2	1.2	1.3	1.3	1.4	1.5	1.7
95	1.1	1.1	1.1	1.1	1.1	1.1	1.1	1.1	1.2	1.2	1.3	1.3	1.4	1.5
100	1.0	1.0	1.0	1.0	1.1	1.1	1.1	1.1	1.1	1.1	1.2	1.3	1.3	1.4

Table 7-2(b)
Isoprofit Price Increase: Maximum Allowable Price Elasticity of Demand (P.E.D.)

CM_0 (%)	1.0	2.0	3.0	4.0	5.0	6.0	7.0	8.0	9.0	10.0	15.0	20.0	25.0	30.0
5	16.7	14.3	12.5	11.1	10.0	9.1	8.3	7.7	7.1	6.7	5.0	4.0	3.3	2.9
10	9.1	8.3	7.7	7.1	6.7	6.3	5.9	5.6	5.3	5.0	4.0	3.3	2.9	2.5
15	6.3	5.9	5.6	5.3	5.0	4.8	4.5	4.3	4.2	4.0	3.3	2.9	2.5	2.2
20	4.8	4.5	4.3	4.2	4.0	3.8	3.7	3.6	3.4	3.3	2.9	2.5	2.2	2.0
25	3.8	3.7	3.6	3.4	3.3	3.2	3.1	3.0	2.9	2.9	2.5	2.2	2.0	1.8
30	3.2	3.1	3.0	2.9	2.9	2.8	2.7	2.6	2.6	2.5	2.2	2.0	1.8	1.7
35	2.8	2.7	2.6	2.6	2.5	2.4	2.4	2.3	2.3	2.2	2.0	1.8	1.7	1.5
40	2.4	2.4	2.3	2.3	2.2	2.2	2.1	2.1	2.0	2.0	1.8	1.7	1.5	1.4
45	2.2	2.1	2.1	2.0	2.0	2.0	1.9	1.9	1.9	1.8	1.7	1.5	1.4	1.3
50	2.0	1.9	1.9	1.9	1.8	1.8	1.8	1.7	1.7	1.7	1.5	1.3	1.3	1.3
55	1.8	1.8	1.7	1.7	1.7	1.6	1.6	1.6	1.6	1.5	1.4	1.3	1.3	1.2
60	1.6	1.6	1.6	1.6	1.5	1.5	1.5	1.5	1.4	1.4	1.3	1.3	1.2	1.1
65	1.5	1.5	1.5	1.4	1.4	1.4	1.4	1.4	1.4	1.3	1.3	1.2	1.1	1.1
70	1.4	1.4	1.4	1.4	1.3	1.3	1.3	1.3	1.3	1.3	1.2	1.1	1.1	1.1
75	1.3	1.3	1.3	1.3	1.3	1.2	1.2	1.2	1.2	1.2	1.1	1.1	1.0	1.0
80	1.2	1.2	1.2	1.2	1.2	1.2	1.1	1.1	1.1	1.1	1.1	1.0	1.0	0.9
85	1.2	1.1	1.1	1.1	1.1	1.1	1.1	1.1	1.1	1.1	1.0	1.0	0.9	0.9
90	1.1	1.1	1.1	1.1	1.1	1.0	1.0	1.0	1.0	1.0	1.0	0.9	0.9	0.8
95	1.0	1.0	1.0	1.0	1.0	0.9	1.0	1.0	1.0	1.0	0.9	0.9	0.8	0.8
100	1.0	1.0	1.0	1.0	1.0	0.9	0.9	0.9	0.9	0.9	0.9	0.8	0.8	0.8

CHAPTER

8

Pricing Strategies

*Although different strategies can achieve profitable
results even within the same industry, nearly all
successful pricing strategies embody three principles.
They are value-based, proactive, and profit-driven.*[1]

A strategy is a comprehensive plan for attaining a given objective which, in a marketing and pricing context, is usually the maximization of total contribution (profit), sales revenue, or market share. To be most effective, such a pricing strategy must be subordinate to the overall marketing strategy for each product-market or market segment the company has chosen to serve. Therefore, one may define a pricing strategy as a plan for directing and coordinating price-related activities in support of the chosen product-market strategy. In this chapter various pricing strategies are discussed including general, life cycle, and industry-specific ones.

8.1 General Pricing Strategies

Most business enterprises define themselves in terms of the markets and, specifically, the product-market segments they serve. In the case of manufacturing, some firms focus on highly unique and differentiated products for select market segments while others find opportunities in commodity type goods that differ little from those of competitors but appeal to a broader customer base. Some companies have positioned themselves as suppliers of high-quality state-of-the-art products while still others choose to serve the more price sensitive portion of the market. Some retailers are considered upscale in terms of their merchandise offerings while others operate as general merchandisers or as discounters. How companies *position* themselves in the marketplace also defines their primary pricing strategies.

Marketing theorists have identified three basic pricing strategies being employed by firms, namely, skim, penetration, and neutral pricing. The first two were proposed by Columbia University Professor Joel Dean in late 1950 as a guide to new product pricing.[2] They are still useful for that purpose but are of more general applicability as well because companies typically do not decide on a product-by-product basis on whether to skim or penetrate the market but use the same pricing strategy for all of their products or services.

8.1.1 Skim Pricing

In skim pricing a firm skims the cream of demand for its products or services by pricing these relatively high resulting in large unit contribution margins but usually at the expense of sales volume and market share. It is the strategy of choice for firms whose products or services are highly unique and differentiated. Demand for such products and services tends to be relatively price inelastic, i.e., buyers are less concerned with the price they pay than the satisfaction they gain from ownership and use. Many manufacturers and retailers of such goods, which typically carry well recognized brand names, use skim pricing to great advantage.

8.1.2 Penetration Pricing

Penetration pricing, also called *volume pricing*, represents the other pricing extreme. It is a strategy that is most suitable for firms that have positioned themselves to serve the more price-sensitive segments of a larger market. Prices are kept relatively low to penetrate markets and generate volume at the expense of unit contribution margins. This strategy works best for companies that enjoy a cost advantage over competitors by the efficient management of their resources. Its big advantage is that it keeps out competitors with less efficient operations. A penetration price is not necessarily the lowest price for the product in the specific product-market served but rather it is a low price in relation to a customer's value perception of the product. In the retail industry, discounters such as Walmart and Costco are typical penetration pricers.

8.1.3 Neutral Pricing

Neutral or *parity pricing* is the strategy of choice for firms for which neither of the two extremes, skim or penetration pricing, seems appropriate   in the product-markets they serve. A neutral price is a middle price designed to generate good volume sales and, at the same time, respectable unit contribution margins. Neutral pricers prefer not to use price as a major marketing tool but rather rely more on non-price strategy variables such as product innovation and advertising and sales promotion to gain sales and market share.

8.2 Life Cycle Strategies

One of the best known and most useful marketing concepts is that of the product life cycle (PLC) which maintains that every product on the market has a finite life much like humans and animals. It is furthermore postulated that every product passes through a number of distinct stages each of which represents challenges and opportunities that marketers must address to meet long-term marketing and profitability goals. The concept had been around for some years when in a 1965 *Harvard Business Review* article by a well-known business consultant and writer, Theodore Levitt, popularized it for use as a guide to strategic marketing decision making.[3]

Four distinct stages for the PLC have been identified, namely, introduction, growth, maturity, and decline. A hypothetical product life cycle and its four stages appears in Figure 8-1. The horizontal

(x) axis is labeled time and, depending on the particular product, could be measured in weeks, months, or years. Some new products and services are stillborn while others, often classified as fads, may have lives of only weeks or months while still others may be around for decades. In accordance with Levitt's description of the PLC, the vertical (y) axis has been labeled sales volume meaning the number of units of the product actually sold.

In the marketing literature the vertical axis is often labeled sales or sales revenue in dollars. This is done to allow the addition of a hypothetical profit curve for the four stages. In the view of this author, that is not a sound practice for data analysis because prices change over time and certain discounts may be offered to diverse customer groups at various times. This will distort the shape of the PLC and obscure where each of the four stages begins and ends. Nor should one be plotting shipments leaving the factory floor but product actually purchased by the end user. Shipped goods may be stored and never purchased and, in addition, there will be random time lags between shipments and between shipments and purchases.

The four PLC stages have been more fully described as follows.

8.2.1 The Introduction Stage

In most industries and markets new products and product innovations are an important factor for driving company growth and profits. More than that, product innovation is a necessity for survival especially for firms offering industrial or consumers products for which technology is changing rapidly. During the introductory PLC stage, sales start at zero and may languish there for some time before they begin to take off if they do so at all. For some products, such as a new version of an Apple iPhone, a Samsung Android phone, or another make of smart phone, the introductory stage is fairly short as many users of the previous model simply switch to the newer one as the old one is phased out. Pricing a new model presents no major problem since there is sufficient history to serve as a guide.

Figure 8-1
Hypothetical Product Life Cycle (PLC)

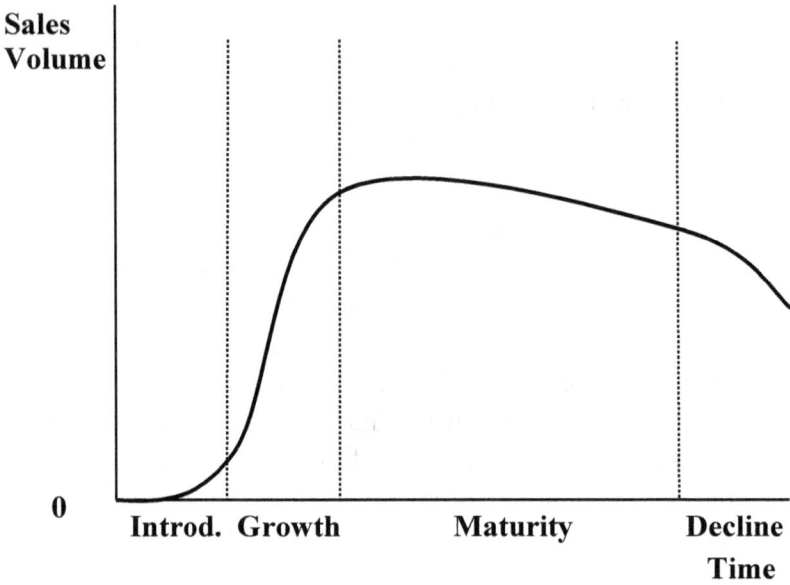

The situation is quite different in two other situations. One is the case for a true innovation, i.e., a product or service so new and different that the general public cannot yet relate to it. Examples of past innovations include the automobile replacing the horse and buggy, the refrigerator replacing the ice box, the airplane replacing the steamship for overseas travel, the compact disc replacing the gramophone record, and the cell phone replacing or supplementing the land line phone.

For such products, the innovator's first task is to generate *primary demand* for the new product class by focusing the marketing effort on a customer group known as *early adopters*. For consumer goods, these are usually affluent young people receptive to new product ideas. Advertising and sales promotion must be geared to build product awareness and educate potential customers on product usage and benefits. The other situation is where the firm is entering a new product-market segment of a larger market in which it has no or little prior experience.

For an innovation during this introductory stage competition is minimal or small especially if it is protected by patents, trade secrets, and trademarks. Potential competitors with similar product concepts may watch from the sidelines to see whether the innovation catches on or fizzles before committing their own resources to product research and development. Due to relatively few sales and heavy advertising and promotional costs, this stage can be expected to show losses or minimal profits at best. Pricing a true innovation can be difficult since there are no comparable products on the market to use as a guide. In the second case, where the company is entering a new product-market, the task of setting an appropriate introductory price is equally challenging. In both cases the two pricing options are skim and penetration pricing introduced in Section 8.1 above.

Skim Pricing

Skim pricing can be recommended where these conditions hold:

* Competitor entry will be difficult because of one or more entry barriers such as patent protection, required financial resources, manufacturing capabilities, and channel requirements.

* Demand can be expected to be relatively inelastic, i.e., potential buyers will not be overly sensitive to the purchase price.

* A high reference price is to be set to allow *sequential skimming* that will attract more price sensitive buyers with lower-priced versions of the basic product.

* Initial production capacity is limited.

Penetration Pricing

A penetration pricing strategy would be the preferable approach where:

* A low price is needed to discourage competitor entry due to no or insufficient entry barriers.

* Product demand can be expected to be highly elastic from

the start or become so shortly after introduction.

* The firm has no production capacity constraints.

* High volume production is likely to lead to scale and experience economies and a cost advantage for the firm.

* Large product usage will ensure that the innovator's technology will be adopted as the industry standard.

These two pricing strategies are not just theoretical abstractions but are being actively pursued by firms in diverse industries and markets. Two examples will illustrate how important it is to get the introductory price right. Getting it right can lead to phenomenal success in terms of sales and profits while not doing so result in a financial disaster.

The first case is a lesson in skimming and the firm the American chemical giant E.I. Du Pont.[4] When this long-established company launched its leather substitute Corfam in 1963, management predicted that in twenty years the new product would be the major component in 25% of American shoes. The reality was that Corfam had to be withdrawn from the shoe leather market in 1971 after Du Pont had invested $80-$100 million in the venture. Sales volume remained insufficient to produce the product profitably, it was explained.

What went wrong? It was not the product which was described as superior to leather in quality because it was porous. In pricing Corfam, Du Pont had used its traditional skim pricing strategy which involved initially pricing high with plans to drop the price as competitors with their own leather substitutes gained market entry. Consequently, Corfam was initially priced so high that Corfam shoes cost $25 which was two and one-half times the price of a leather shoe at the time. Despite subsequent discounting, the product never caught on. The lesson to be leaned was that skim pricing works only if demand is relatively inelastic but the American shoe market was highly price-sensitive at the time.

In a more recent example but with a happier outcome, in 1989 the Japanese automaker Toyota entered the luxury car market with its Lexus LS400 using a penetration strategy.[5] This was unusual for a luxury brand where skimming is the preferred pricing strategy. Management, however, knew that there was a large price-sensitive segment of the luxury car market that was not being served adequately and decided to compete in it with a quality vehicle. Excellent reviews in automotive magazines and *Consumer Reports*, heavy advertising and sales promotion, and positive word-of-mouth resulted in immediate market acceptance and a large surge in sales. Product demand was not only strong but became more inelastic so that five years after product introduction, the price of a Lexus LS400 had increased by nearly 50% from its original price of $35,000. Since then, Lexus has become well established successfully competing with older and more traditional luxury car brands.

8.2.2 The Growth Stage

Most products that come on the market fail for one reason or another in that they do not sell well or not at all or their financial performance in terms of sales revenue or profits falls significantly below expectations. Such products must consequently be withdrawn to conserve and redirect company resources to more profitable ventures. The number of new product failures is legion with the most famous marketing disaster of all time being the Ford Edsel automobile launched in September 1957. Production was halted just two years later after the company had lost roughly $350 million on the project. Many factors caused the new product's demise but faulty pricing was a major one. Products that survive the introductory stage are, according to the standard PLC model, ready for a sharp and rapid expansion of sales volume, revenue, and profits. The growth stage has therefore also been called the *takeoff stage*.

During growth, several important things take place. For one, target customers have become fully aware of the product's existence, started using it and, having had a positive experience, become repeat buyers. In the case of an innovation, competitors who have been developing a similar product now rush in to claim their own share of the expanding market. The innovator's demand curve for the product now becomes more elastic (horizontal) while the company's advertising effort shifts from developing primary demand for the product class to *selective demand* for the firm's brand. With increasing sales, more distributors and retailers are willing to carry and stock the brand. Also, with increasing sales and declining variable costs, unit profit margins tend to be high. In fact, they are likely to peak at the inflection point leading to the maturity stage.

Prices during the growth stage are likely to be unstable. Some products may keep their introductory prices but others may see significant shifts as managers gain more experience with the new product. Companies have been known to drastically cut new product prices during this stage when they realized the product was overpriced and they needed to reduce prices to get sales off the ground. Another situation calling for price cuts is where sales are below expectations resulting in overcapacity and large inventories of unsold product. On the other hand, price increases are warranted where sales are so brisk that a firm cannot keep up with demand.

8.2.3 The Maturity Stage

Successful products typically spend most of their lives in the maturity stage as indicated by the relative length of this stage in the hypothetical PLC curve of Figure 8-1. By now, market conditions have stabilized in that demand for the new product is nearly flat and the major objective is to maintain or attain incremental increases in market shares, sales revenues, and profits. To this end, firms will make proactive use of the four marketing strategy variables, including the price, to maintain brand loyalty and encourage buyers to switch from competing brands.

In maturity, customers have become increasingly sophisticated in that they have developed strong value perceptions of competing brands. Buyers have become sensitive to the purchase prices of the competing brands and models and the demand curves of all have consequently tended more toward the horizontal. This increased price sensitivity has encouraged competitors to use price as a major competitive tool. Price adjustments are therefore the rule rather than the exception with a price change by one firm often countered by one or more competitors designed to negate the hoped-for benefits.

Specifically, marketers of competing brands will *fine-tune* sell prices to reach contribution dollar objectives. Because of the relative stable conditions of the maturity stage, managers can, for the first time, gauge their products' price elasticities of demand with some degree of accuracy. As we know, the P.E.D. is an all-important metric not only for evaluating the relative profitability of various price change options but also for computing optimal sell prices for sales revenue and profit maximization.

At this point it might be useful to review the two rules of thumb for sales revenue and contribution maximization given in Chapters 6 (Market Demand) and 7 (Isoprofit Analysis), respectively, because it is in a product's maturity stage where these rules may be most effectively employed. These tell the marketer, given the product's present price-volume operating point (P_0, Q_0), whether or not its price needs to be adjusted and, if so, in which direction to either maximize sales revenue or total contribution (profit). These two rules are summarized in Table 8-1:

Table 8-1
General Pricing Rule of Thumb (1)

Sales Revenue Maximization	Profit Maximization	Required Change
If the P.E.D. is:	If the P.E.D. is:	-----------------
> 1.0	$> 1 / CM_0$ (%)	*Lower price*
= 1.0	$= 1 / CM_0$ (%)	*Hold price*
< 1.0	$< 1 / CM_0$ (%)	*Raise price*

For sales revenue maximization no price adjustment is necessary if the product's present price elasticity of demand (P.E.D.) equals 1.0. In the case of profit maximization, no price adjustment is needed if its present price elasticity of demand equals $1 / CM_0$. If, according to Table 8-1, a price adjustment is needed to maximize profit, isoprofit analysis, discussed in Chapter 7, can then be employed to determine the available pricing options.

Long before the once new product enters the final decline stage of its life cycle, companies typically have another model or version ready for launch. In fact, even before the new product comes on the market, management should plan for its eventual demise and be ready with *life extension* or *market stretching* strategies. With new versions or models, the decline stage shown in Figure 8-1 never materializes or is significantly delayed. Somewhere during the maturity stage another life cycle begins with a new S-shaped PLC curve superimposed on the old one. For a product such as the Apple iPhone, Samsung Galaxy or other smartphone this process can then continue indefinitely until a completely new technology evolves.

8.2.4 The Decline Stage

Eventually sales for the company's product enter a period of decline that even major product modification and drastic cost and price cutting is unable to halt. The product has now arrived at the decline stage of its PLC. During this stage, once loyal customers have lost interest in the product, drifted away, and begun buying competing brands. Typically, costs rise and profits decline along with sales revenue. To deal with this situation, three different strategies can be identified, namely, retrenchment, harvest, and exit.

Retrenchment

A retrenchment strategy involves a continuing long-term commitment to the product combined with a partial market withdrawal. Specifically, target-market segments not well served in that sales and profits are below par, are abandoned and freed resources reassigned to more profitable segments. This strategy presupposes, of course, that the product is being sold in different versions to different customer groups with their own price-volume schedules and price sensitivities and that one or more of these is sufficiently profitable to justify keeping the product alive.

Harvest

With a harvest strategy, management has decided to gradually withdraw from the market but do so in a manner that will generate maximum total contribution dollars over the product's remaining life. Prices are kept relatively high but major promotional and other marketing costs curtailed. As a result, unit contribution margins continue to be high even as market share is surrendered to competitors. The company essentially treats its product as a *cash cow*. This strategy works best in cases where there remains a loyal customer base for the product or brand that can be profitably served for some time in the near future.

Exit

Where there is insufficient life left in the product and losses are mounting, management may decide to cut these losses by abandoning the market altogether. Production of the product is halted and the remaining inventory sold off at reduced prices. With the bargain basement prices, directly competing products may also be withdrawn unless managements are willing to hold on expecting to raise their prices again after their competitor has left the scene.

8.2.5 PLC Summary

Keeping track of the number of units sold over time from the time of product introduction is a simple and cost-effective means for obtaining useful pricing and other marketing information. In fact, such PLC curves should be available for each brand, model, and product-market served. These curves are not likely to have the shape of the idealized PLC curve shown in Figure 8-1. The maturity stage, in particular, is likely to shows peaks and valleys like a camel's back (of the Bactrian kind) due to temporary price and sales promotions and other factors affecting product demand over time. Nevertheless, the product's progress and especially the onset of the critical decline stage should be clearly observable to alert management to needed remedial efforts as outlined above.

8.3 Industry Structure and Pricing Strategy

The term industry, as previously noted, is applied to a group of manufacturers or service providers selling into the same market. Examples are the airline, automobile, banking, construction, entertainment, hospitality, fashion, fast foods, restaurant, and retail industries. Each of these industries is uniquely structured in terms of:

i) The number of competitors that comprise it;

ii) the relative market power of the competitors in terms of market share, growth rates, profitability, financial resources, etc.;

iii) the entry barriers to new competitors including investment requirement, cost structure, patents, trademarks, and preemption, if any, of scarce resources or distribution channels.

The reason marketers are interested in industry structure is that it much influences the primary pricing strategy prevalent in a particular industry. Understanding industry structure helps the marketer explain and predict the pricing behavior of competitors and understand the pricing limitations and opportunities facing his or her firm.

Figure 8-2
Market Organization and Product Demand

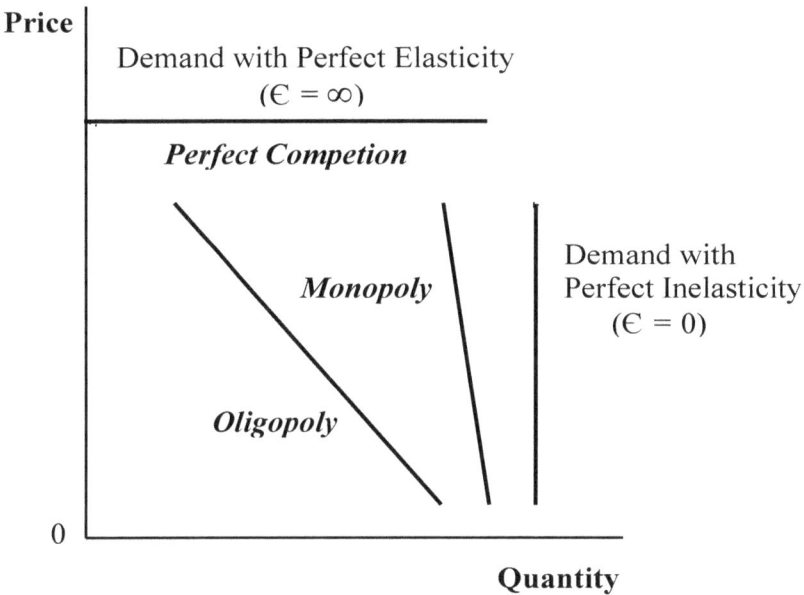

One defining element in industry structure and market organization is the level of competition. Economists view competition as a continuum that extends from *perfect competition* to *pure monopoly*. Few industries fit into either of these two extreme categories but they serve as good starting points for understanding market organization and pricing behavior. The three major forms of market organization are, according to microeconomic theory, perfect competition, monopoly, and imperfect competition the latter of which includes monopolistic and oligopolistic competition.[6]

8.3.1 Perfect Competition

Perfect or pure competition is an economic model describing a market in which there are many firms selling an identical product with none of them large enough relative to the entire market to influence the market price. In fact, each firm supplying this market is a *price taker* in that there is a market price for the usually undifferentiated product and the firm has no choice but to sell at that price. The demand curve for a firm in a perfectly competitive market is a horizontal line at the market price as shown in Figure 8-2.

The firm cannot sell above the prevailing market price because there would be no buyers and to sell for less would be imprudent since this would not increase demand. Since a firm maximizes its profits when marginal revenue equals marginal cost and since marginal revenue in the case of perfect competition is the market price, a firm under these conditions would produce and sell at a quantity level where its marginal cost of production equals the market price.

Many companies manufacture and market undifferentiated products, commonly known as *commodities*, either for reasons of choice or their products are not easily amenable to differentiation. The most often cited example of firms in a purely competitive market are farmers growing wheat, corn, or some other crop. No farmer will be so dominant as to be able to influence the price and each can sell his or her product only at the prevailing market price.

8.3.2 Pure Monopoly

A market situation in which a single firm sells a product for which there are no good substitutes is called pure monopoly. It is the exact opposite of perfect competition and for a firm it is by far a more favorable position to be in since the monopolist can charge monopoly prices and earn monopoly profits without greatly affecting market demand for his or her product. Pure monopolies are very rare with public utility companies, such as electric, gas, water, cable, and public transportation, being examples but these are prevented from earning monopoly profits by being heavily regulated by local governments. A monopolist's demand curve is nearly vertical, as shown in Figure 8-2. In the private sector, monopolies and monopolistic practices are subject to scrutiny under a country's antitrust laws and violations prosecuted but sometimes exceptions are made.[7]

8.3.3 Monopolistic Competition

Monopolistic competition is characterized by the presence in the market of a large number of firms which vigorously compete with each other for sales and profits by offering differentiated and unique products and services. Generally speaking, these entities function *independently* of each other without tacit or overt collusion among them. Due to product and brand uniqueness, usually based on product innovation, advertising and promotion, branding, and other non-price marketing strategy variable, they manage to achieve various degrees of market power. Most business firms, big and small, fit into this broad category. The product demand curves facing a firm under monopolistic competition typically have the standard downward-sloping form with slopes depending on their relative competitive advantages vis-à-vis similar products on the market.

8.3.4 Oligopoly

An oligopolistic industry is one in which the number of sellers is small enough for the activities of a single seller to affect the other firms and for the activities of the other firms to affect that firm in turn. Typically, an oligopoly is characterized by strong *interdependence* among the firms regarding all product-market activities including the price. The demand curve of the *dominant* firm in an oligopoly is downward sloping as for monopolistic competition but somewhat steeper and more inelastic so that it approaches that of a monopolist as shown in Figure 8-2 above. The reason for the relatively inelastic demand for their products and services is that, being few in number, oligopolistic firms have much of the market to themselves and manage to avoid overt price competition.

Table 8-2
Oligopolistic Market Structure - Selected Industries

Industry	*Companies*
Airlines	American, Delta, JetBlue, Southwest, United
Athletic shoes	Adidas, New Balance, Nike, Puma, Skechers
Banks	Bank of Am., JPMorgan, Wells Fargo, Citigroup
Book publishers	Hachette L., HarperCollins, Penguin R. H., Wiley
Book sellers	Amazon Books, Barnes & Noble, Powell's Books
Breakfast cereals	General Mills, Kellogg, Post H., Quaker Foods
Broadcast networks	ABC, CBS, FOX, NBC, PBS
Car rental companies	Alamo, Avis, Budget, Enterprise, Hertz, National
Commercial aircraft	Airbus, Boeing, Bombardier, Embraer
Credit cards	American Express, MasterCard, Visa, Citi
Defense contractors	Lockheed M., Boeing, General Dyn., Northrop G.
Delivery services	DHL, FedEx, Purolator, UPS, USPS
Foods	Kraft Heinz, Nestlé, Smithfield, Unilever
Gasoline stations	Chevron, Exxon, Mobil, Shell, Texaco
Grocery chains	Albertsons, Costco, Kroger, Walmart
Home builders	D.R. Horton, Lennar, NVR, PulteGroup
Jet engines	CFM, GE Aviation, Pratt & Whitney, Rolls Royce
Movie studios	Disney, Universal, Warner Bros., 20th Cent. Fox
Pharmaceuticals	Johnson & Johnson, Merck, Novartis, Pfizer, Roche
Poultry processors	Pilgrim's Pride, Perdue Farms, Tyson Foods
Pulp & paper	International Paper, Kimberly-Clark, Weyerhaeuser
Railroads	BNSF, CSX, Norfolk Southern, Union Pacific
Smart phones	Apple, Huawai, Nokia, Samsung
Wireless carriers	AT&T, Dish Wireless, T-Mobile, Verizon

Many industries and markets in the United States, Europe, and Asia are highly concentrated with just a few major firms, say three to five, sharing at least 50% and sometimes as much as 90% of the total market. A number of industries and the dominant players in each in terms of sales revenue and market share are listed in Table 8-2. Some of these firms are foreign-based but they all have a major presence in the American market as suppliers and purchasers of products and services. This list is far from definitive or inclusive and presented primarily to illustrate the point that in most of these industries the number of participating firms is relatively small.

Firms of an oligopoly have a strong incentive to stay ahead of their competitors in terms of sales, market share, and profits. Most of them are equity financed and owned by private or institutional investors, or investment companies which are all keenly interested to have the value of their investments rise. Not surprisingly, oligopolistic companies proactively use most of the marketing tools available to them to reach their goals. Continuous product innovation is one characteristic of oligopolistic industries. Indeed, these firms are typically large and financially strong enough to fund the costs involved in financing technological breakthroughs and product innovations on a large scale.

Oligopolistic firms typically spend millions of dollars yearly on advertising and sales promotion in order to stimulate selective demand for their products and services and turn potential customers into buyers. All firms in the industry are more or less obliged to participate with each firm trying to outdo the others in the originality and intensity of print and television advertising. Because of their interdependence, firms in an industry with an oligopolistic market structure are characterized by some unique behavioral patterns in terms of pricing including:

i) Price fixing: This pricing practice involves collusion in the form of an agreement among the members of an oligopoly to establish uniform prices to avoid price competition. Negotiations are usually conducted in secret because price fixing is the most egregious of antitrust violations. It will be more fully treated in Chapter 15.

ii) Predatory pricing: Another pricing practice associated with oligopolies is predatory pricing by which a dominant firm may temporarily charge exceedingly low prices, often below its products' direct variable costs, with the intent of driving one or more competitors from the market leaving it in a monopoly position. This practice too is proscribed by federal law.

iii) Price wars: Price wars among members of an oligopoly are a persistent danger and may erupt for a number of reasons. They can be destructive of an entire industry because the depressed prices may substantially shrink its size and force some members into bankruptcy. Price wars are discussed in Chapter 11.

iv) Leadership pricing: Price leadership and cooperative pricing is a form of tacit collusion among firms in an oligopoly that avoids direct price competition. The practice is not illegal because there is no verbal, written, or implied agreement among the firms. Because leadership pricing is very common, it is discussed first.

8.4 Leadership Pricing

Leadership pricing is an old concept but despite its importance and prevalence, it receives scant attention in the pricing and marketing literature of the day.[8] It is, however, well known to economists. Perhaps the most unique feature of oligopolistic competition is the *absence* of strong competition in one very important area—the price. Most real competition is confined to the non-price strategy variables in the marketing mix. As Gould and Ferguson noted: "Practically speaking, active price competition is seldom if ever observed in oligopolistic markets. To be sure, price wars occasionally erupt; but this does not indicate price competition. A price war indicates that the (probably implicit) communication channels among firms in the market are temporarily out of repair. In the normal course of events, the pre-price-war situation is quickly restored."[9]

Price competition is avoided by a practice known as *price leadership* in which one dominant firm in the industry sets the price and all others are expected to follow its lead.[10] In microeconomic theory, the dominant firm uses an estimated market demand curve for all competing products to set an optimal price that maximizes its own profit. The price leader's optimal price becomes the market price for all competing products especially in the absence of effective product differentiation, i.e., if customers view the competing products as commodities or close substitutes.

The price leader typically not only sets the price but initiates price changes which the other firms are expected to follow. Once the price leader has set the price, each of the other competitors of the oligopoly faces a highly elastic demand curve for its product meaning that it can sell all it wants at that price but little above it. If a company tries to sell its product significantly below this price, it is subject to sanctions by the price leader who may retaliate by dropping its price even further. The situation becomes more complicated when there is more than one dominant firm in the market and one of these tries to challenge the price leader and assume its role. Other difficulties may arise when the price leader attempts to initiate a price change and the others refuse to follow with similar changes or a firm other than the price leader initiates a major price change. The result may be either a short pricing skirmish or an all-out price war.

How does a firm in an oligopolistic industry become its price leader? Typically the price leader is the largest firm in terms of sales revenue and market share and the most profitable. The reasons for its leadership position vary. Sometimes the price leader was the first in the industry and established its brand as the standard of comparison. It may be the firm with the greatest technological prowess that brings out a continuous stream of advanced new products unmatched by its rivals. At other times the price leader has a significant cost advantage so that it can produce more economically and efficiently and set its prices accordingly. Other possible competitive advantages may lie in a superior distribution network or a more effective advertising and promotional effort. More often than not, it is a combination of all.

It should be noted that not all or even most industries with an oligopolistic market structure follow the practice of price leadership or other forms of tacit collusion especially where the competing products are highly differentiated. They not only vigorously compete using all the non-price marketing strategy variables available to them but also on price. It is only that firms that are part of an oligopoly are more susceptible to collusive practices and therefore face more scrutiny from state and federal agencies concerned with competition or the lack thereof.

8.5 Pricing Strategies with Cost Economies

In certain industries companies base their pricing strategies on cost advantages they enjoy over their marketplace rivals. Large companies benefit from *economies of scale* which result from the well-known fact that in almost every business activity including manufacturing, distribution, marketing, and purchasing, direct incremental and fixed costs tend to decline with increasing volume. These cost advantages can lead to *price leadership* in oligopolistic industries and the ability to set prices and terms most profitable to the price leader and which smaller firms are obliged to follow.

Another cost advantage comes from so-called *economies of experience* first popularized in the early 1970s by the Boston Consulting Group.[11] Unlike economies of scale which depend on cost reductions due to current output volume, experience economies are the result of cost reductions due to the *accumulated* volume of output. The effect results from experience—the more a company produces the more it learns to do so more efficiently. Specifically, Boston Consulting found that due to the experience effect, every doubling of accumulated output results in a predictable percentage decrease in a product's total unit cost in constant dollars. A graph of this cost reduction as a function of cumulative volume (on a logarithmic scale) is known as an *experience curve* and the practice of pricing products along an experience curve in form of continuous price reductions as *experience curve pricing*.

Like all cost-based pricing strategies, experience curve pricing is no longer a preferred pricing method. Nevertheless, all forms of cost reductions including those due to economies of scale and economies of experience continue to be very important for increasing the profitability of products and services.

8.6 Combination Strategies

This chapter has focused on the most important pricing strategies but firms obviously use others to reach their goals and price may be just one of the four marketing strategy variable employed. Many consumer high-tech firms including Alphabet (Google), Amazon, Apple, Meta (Facebook), and Microsoft have become enormously successful and profitable by a strategy of aggressive product innovation resulting in a continuous stream of must-have products and services. These products enjoy steep demand curves, i.e., demand is relatively insensitive to price so that these firms can successfully employ skim pricing with high profit margin and at the same time achieve the large volumes sales and market shares typically associated with penetration pricing.

In the retail and fast foods industries a combination strategy that may be called a *saturation strategy* is evident. Under this strategy, firms seek a monopoly position in their product markets but, unlike monopolies, do so in a perfectly legitimate manner by continuous expansion. Firms using this business model come to completely saturate their markets with huge numbers of retail outlets around the globe. Thus, as of this writing, McDonald's, Starbucks, and Walmart operate over 36,000, 33,000, and 10,000 retail outlets world-wide, respectively. While a saturation strategy is not illegal, it nevertheless includes strong anticompetitive elements because they drive out the smaller mom-and-pop shops by their sheer numbers and financial resources.

The business models employed by some of these firms, including the franchise concept, have been successfully exported overseas where it has even changed lifestyles. European coffee aficionados used to sit in locally owned cafés hours at a time over a can of gourmet coffee while reading or people watching. Starbucks has much changed that culture. Sometimes the standard model had to be modified. Thus, McDonald's was obliged to sell beer or wine in its European restaurants while in Asia the company had to redo its standard menu to make its system work.

In some cases the standard corporate model has not worked at all. Thus, Walmart, the world's largest retailer, had to withdraw from Germany and South Korea. As Kotler and Keller noted: "Walmart's tried-and-true formula of low prices, tight inventory control, and big selection doesn't always pay off in markets where consumers have different shopping habits, discount competitors are already entrenched, and employees and suppliers are less subservient."[12] The company left Germany, Europe's largest economy, in 2006 after ten years of continuous losses estimated at $3 billion.

8.7 Yield Management

Yield management, also known as *revenue management*, is a variable pricing strategy for the service sector developed under the direction of Robert L. Crandall, who was then Chairman and CEO of American Airlines (he coined the term), soon after the ruinous fare wars of 1992 (See "Price Wars" in Section 11.4 of Chapter 11). Its purpose was to address the industry-specific capacity management, pricing, and profitability problems faced by airlines. This innovative new strategy was soon adopted by other airlines and transportation companies and has since become enormously successful as a revenue and profit generator.[13]

In the airline industry, the seats available on a flight are referred to as *inventory* and whenever a flight leaves the gate with empty seats sales from those unoccupied seats are lost and cannot be replaced. The inventory is thus said to be *perishable* much like fresh produce. Yield management was designed to ensure that all seats on each flight are filled on take-off and that each seat has been sold at the maximum obtainable price.

An airline's objective is to maximize sales revenue on each flight by astute management of seating capacity and ticket prices for all three or four flight classes (economy, business etc.) the airline has chosen to offer. In the context of our previous analysis (see Figure 6-2 in Chapter 6), the goal is to cover the entire area under the linear demand curve P_M-Q_M and thus the total sales revenue achievable from each flight. Since for airlines, the total direct variable costs are minimal (carrying an additional flyer does no significantly add to cost) in comparison to the fixed costs, maximizing sales revenue is equivalent to maximizing total contribution to fixed costs and profits.

Yield management is made possible by use of high speed digital computer systems and special software that can track historical bookings for all flights and instantly adjust fares on upcoming flights accordingly. In fact, for any given flight the airline knows at any time of day prior to flight time how many passengers it had booked the previous year (or years) and compare this bookings rate with that for the next scheduled flight. If fewer flights have been booked for, say, economy class, when the request for ticket price information is received than in the previous year, it will indicate a drop in demand and, if more, an increase. Based on this information, the airline is able to instantly adjust the number of seats made available in each class and the corresponding ticket costs.

While yield management's advantages in terms of load factor and profits are apparent, it is still not a perfect system. For example, once a flight has been booked it cannot be resold later when some travelers would be willing to pay more to get on that particular flight. There is also much opportunity for customer alienation. In order to deal with flight cancellations and no-shows, airlines typically overbook, i.e., they sell more tickets than there are seats available. This can be bad news for someone whose seat has been resold because of a later than required appearance at the gate. The typically large disparity in ticket prices can also be a source of customer discontent and is only mitigated by the fact that flyers do not normally ask the person in the seat ahead or behind them how much they paid. Fare differences among comparable seats can be surprisingly large depending when or where the flight was booked.

Yield management is ideally suited to certain firms operating in the service sector. Not surprisingly, in addition to airlines the system has also been adopted by large hotel chains, car rental and cartage companies, parking garages, cruise lines, and even some private hospitals. According to Simon and Fassnacht the prerequisites for successful yield management implementation are:[14]

* The service supplier's capacity is fixed

* The variable costs of service performance are low and the fixed costs for capacity expansion high

* The capacity (inventory) is perishable

* The service is purchased in advance

* Demand can be divided into separate market segments allowing fencing

* Demand fluctuates and is uncertain

Clearly, these conditions are met by airlines and the other service providers mentioned.

8.8 Competitive Bid Pricing

An interesting pricing and profit opportunity area is competitive bid pricing which comes into play when the buyer is a government entity or other regulated body although large business firms sometimes use this practice as well. It assures the buyer that the product, service, or project requirements are fully met at the lowest possible price. Competitive bidding is a specialized field and beyond the scope of this book. However, a few words about it appear in order.

A buyer may issue a *request for quotation* (RFQ) for purchases involving just a few thousand dollars such as in the case of a government agency or firm buying its yearly requirements of office supplies, or millions in the case of a state for the building of a new highway or bridge or similar construction project, or billions in the case of an airline buying a new fleet of airplanes. For certain companies, such as those in the defense industry, competitive bidding may represent the only type of sales and purchase transaction legally engaged in.

Competitive bid contracts can be a very profitable source of sales revenue and profits for businesses in diverse industries and markets. Nevertheless, many firms shun it because of the costs involved in getting on a buyer's *approved bidders list*, in processing bid requests, and in administering the contract in the case of a successful bid. The purpose of the approved bidders list is to ensure that only qualified firms submit bids while any bids by spurious suppliers who may not be able to fulfill the contractual obligations are eliminated at the outset. An item often overlooked by potential bidders in competitive bidding is the very large cost savings that can accrue such as from the diminished need for advertising and sales promotion.

In *fixed-price* competitive bidding it is assumed that the low bidder is awarded the contract and, furthermore, that the bidding firm seeks to maximize its profit. Due to the costs in preparing a bid and fulfilling the contract plus the uncertain outcome of the bidding process, firms typically rely on probabilistic models and other statistical methods to assist them in preparing bids. Bidders also keep careful track of the bidding history of other firms on the approved bidders list for similar projects. For determining the best bid, a simple formula is available:[15]

$$E(B) = (B - C) \times P \qquad \text{Eq. (8.1)}$$

where, $E(B)$ = Expected bid value
  B = Bid price (\$)
  C = Direct project cost (\$)
  P = Probability of a winning bid

The bidding firm's objective is to maximize the expected value of its bid. To do so, different probabilities are assigned to each bid expressing the likelihood that it will be the winning bid. Then the expected value $E(B)$ for each bid is tabulated and the one with the highest expected value chosen for the bid price. For example, by Expression (8.1) above, if $B = C$ and $P = 1.0$, then $E(B) = 0$. In other words, if the firm does not mark up its cost it will likely be the winning bidder but its bid will be unprofitable.

Notes

1. Thomas Nagle and Georg Müller, *The Strategy and Tactics of Pricing*, 10.

2. Joel Dean, "Pricing Policies for New Products," *Harvard Business Review on Pricing*, 101-131.

3. Theodore Levitt, "Exploit the Product Life Cycle," *Harvard Business Review*, Nov.-Dec. 1965, 1-15. (www.harvard.edu/product/65608-PDF-ENG). See also Theodore Levitt, "Exploiting the Product Life Cycle," *The Marketing Mode*, 28-52.

4. Gerd Wilcke, "E.I. du Pont Plans a Halt To Production of Corfam," *New York Times*, 17 March, 1971, 61, 71.

5. Robert Dolan and Hermann Simon, *Power Pricing*, 278-279.

6. Ross Eckert and Richard Leftwich, *The Price System and Resource Allocation*, 208-222.

7. At least one pure monopoly exists with its government's approval and support, namely, Taiwan Semiconductor Manufacturing Company (TSMC). Reportedly the company makes over 90% of the world's most sophisticated chips that, among other applications, run the 1.4 billion smartphones in use world-wide. In 2020 the company reported profits of $17.6 billion on sales of 45.5 billion or nearly

40%! See Yang Jie, Stephanie Yang and Asa Fitch, "The Chips That Run the World," *The Wall Street Journal*, June 19-20, 2021, B1.

8. For a rare mention of price leadership in a marketing text, see George Risley, *Modern Industrial Marketing*, 195.

9. J. P. Gould and C. E. Ferguson, *Microeconomic Theory*, 342.

10. For a discussion of the economic theory behind price leadership see, for example, J. P. Gould and C. E. Ferguson, supra at 338-342, and Ross Eckert and Richard Leftwich, supra at 409-411.

11. See, for example, Chapter 13 (Experience Curve Pricing) in Kent Monroe, *Pricing*.

12. Philip Kotler and Kevin Keller, *Marketing Management*, 619. The problems encountered by Walmart in Germany involved the presence of a well-established discounter named Aldi which has dominated the German discount foods business for decades. This company, owned by two branches of the Albrecht family, also owns and operates Aldi stores in the U.S. (Aldi Süd) and Trader Joe's (Aldi Nord). Incidentally, in a sure sign that deep discounting based on cost advantages and distribution efficiencies can be highly profitable to its owners, both the Albrechts of Aldi and the Waltons of Walmart are quite wealthy with personal fortunes in the billions.

13. For a detailed treatment of yield management in the airline and other industries see Robert Phillips, *Pricing and Revenue Optimization*.

14. Hermann Simon and Martin Fassnacht, *Price Management*, 459.

15. Kent Monroe, supra at 557.

CHAPTER

9

Value Pricing

The only valid pricing objective in today's uncertain environment is to ask the customer to pay for the "perceived value" of what he is buying. That holds for products or services, consumer or industrial goods.[1]

Market oriented and specifically *perceived value pricing*, or simply *value pricing*, with its focus on the customer's perception of a product's value is a radical departure from the cost-plus approach in which the focus was on the product's cost of manufacture. For marketers, value pricing has opened up entirely new vistas for proactive and creative pricing methods and techniques which help to significantly expand growth and profit opportunities for their firms. Witness, for example, the enormous profits being generated by some high-tech consumer products and services companies in the field of wireless communications which would have been unimaginable by firms using the traditional cost-driven pricing methods of the past.

This chapter opens with a discussion of the concept of perceived value including a customer purchase model and the seller's response in the products and services offered. The psychological aspects involved in a potential buyer's purchase decision, such as the reference price, price-quality and other effects, are covered next. This is followed by some common pricing practices and techniques used by market and value oriented pricers.

9.1 Customers and the Perception of Value

Before a company can effectively price a product or service it must know what value the customer, and more specifically, the target group of customers, places in that product or service. Since individual customers and customer groups have their own value systems, value is a very subjective quantity and marketers speak of the *perceived value* rather than the more definitive value.

What then is perceived value? Dan Nimer, a former business executive turned pricing consultant and one of the earliest and best-known proponents of perceived value pricing, defined it simply as "what the customer is willing to pay for the 'bundle' of benefits offered by the supplier." The term bundle is to emphasize that the customer is evaluating not only the physical product or service but many other factors that go into the purchase decision. A justified price, according to Nimer, is "one that represents the value the buyer puts on what he buys."[2] The larger the product's perceived value, the higher should be the asking price.

A buyer's purchase decision is a complex one that may be simplified somewhat if one looks at the mental exercise she or he typically performs to arrive at it. Specifically, the customer is expected to weigh the benefits of owning and using the product or service against the total cost likely to be incurred. This evaluation may be expressed thus:

Perceived value = Perceived benefits – Perceived costs

It is only when the perceived benefits outweigh the perceived costs yielding a positive customer perceived value (CPV) that a purchase transaction will take place. Again, it is the perceived benefits and costs and not necessarily the real ones from the standpoint of a disinterested observer.

Consider, for example, some of the factors the buyer of a new automobile is likely to weigh before reaching a decision to buy or not to buy a particular make and model.

i) Perceived benefits: Brand image, engine performance (acceleration), gas mileage or range (in the case of an alternative fuel vehicle), interior roominess and décor, reputation for reliability, resale value, safety features, standard and available accessories, financing options, repair and service availability, warranty terms, location and reputation of dealership, competence and persuasiveness of sales staff, and other factors.

ii) Perceived costs: Net purchase price after applicable dealer discounts and trade-in value of present car, operating expenses, maintenance costs, financing costs (if any), insurance premiums, and state registration expenses.

Sometimes the customer has made up her or his mind on which make and model to purchase to the exclusion of any others from further consideration. In most situations, however, the buyer is likely to visit other car dealerships offering similar models of interest and make this mental assessment:

$$\frac{\text{Perceived Value Product A}}{\text{Perceived Value Product B}} = k$$

If the customer were to rate the perceived value of each make or model from 1 to 10, then a purchase of Product A is likely only if the *perceived value index* $k > 1.0$ and especially if this index is much larger than 1.0.

For the seller, this buyer model suggests a series of steps to profitably engage the target market including value assessment, value creation, value communication, and value recoupment.

9.1.1 Value Assessment

Value assessment for a new product or service should begin even before the development stage. Management must select a target market and determine the wants and needs of that market segment. This requires that the value system of these target customers become known. In other words, what design, performance and other factors are important to these buyers and what are not. This assessment must include a range of possible prices the product or service should be offered at. Next a feasibility analysis is required to determine whether, based on anticipated manufacturing and marketing costs and sales volume, the firm can profitably develop and market the new product or service. If not, another product-market segment may be more suitable or else the project may have to be abandoned. The following chapter discusses market segmentation, especially price segmentation, in more detail.

9.1.2 Value Creation

Business firms exist to create value. They create value for their owners and equity holders in the profits they earn, their employees in salaries and wages paid, their suppliers in products and services purchased, and their communities in taxes paid. Most importantly, companies create value in the products and services they develop and market. As previously mentioned, this value goes beyond the physical product and includes the entire package offered their customers. Firms differ in their relative success in value creation with the most profitable ones continuously creating the highest perceived value in terms of innovative new products and services or in terms of cost reductions that make their products and services more affordable.

9.1.3 Value Communication

An important part of value pricing is to convey a *value message* to potential customers of a product or service. The most popular and effective way for conveying such a message is through advertising and sales promotion. One way this marketing strategy variable may be used is to enhance a firm's image and raise the perceived value of all its products and services. Not surprisingly, the most successful companies and brands also are the ones most prolific in using this important tool. The value message must be complete and convincing or else the purchase decision will default to the price variable. Price competition is generally not conducive to maximizing contribution and profits.

There is a strong social component to buyer behavior. An often overlooked bonus of advertising, especially in a much-read magazine or one or more of the major television channels, is that the product or service promoted tends to get authenticated and legitimized. The reason is that readers and viewers are subconsciously aware that they are not the only ones seeing the advertisement but are in the company of millions of others and infer that the product must perform as advertised and the offer be legitimate because the seller would not be brazen enough to make claims to a national audience that are not true. This removes the fear from the purchase decision especially in the case of a new and untried product. It is one reason retail stores featuring the merchandise often carry a sign saying "As advertised on national television" or "As advertised in such and such magazine."

An especially powerful form of advertising is *word-of-mouth*. A satisfied or dissatisfied customer, especially one close to the potential buyer or one whose judgment and veracity can be trusted, can have a very profound influence on a potential buyer's value perception and purchase decision. Firms are well advised to follow up on any product or service complaints because word will get around. By word-of-mouth one must also include the Internet and especially the social media such as Facebook and Twitter.

9.1.4 Value Recoupment

A firm recoups its expenditures in value creation and communication by way of the purchase prices for its products and services. This is where the firm gets rewarded for its efforts on behalf of the customers it serves. Unlike cost-plus pricing, value pricing has no simple rules and formulas to follow. In theory, the firm's *price discretion* extends from the price floor, which we have previously identified as the product's average unit variable cost, to the product's or service's perceived value expressed in monitory terms.

A business does not have the market to itself, of course, and if it does, it is not likely to be for long. It must content with rival firms which puts an upper limit on the prices it can charge. It is also true that the customer typically does not want to pay the full price at which she or he values the product or service. Like the seller, the buyer seeks to make a profit on the transaction and do so by paying a price below her or his perceived value price wherever possible.

9.2 Psychological Aspects of Pricing

There is a strong human element in peoples' perception of value and the prices they are willing to pay for certain products and services. These emotional factors can exert a strong influence on their behavior especially if the purchase is a major one in terms of financial commitment or social status. Buyers show certain repetitive behavioral patterns in their evaluation of product and service offerings and marketers must take these into account to be able to price profitably. Specifically, these factors strongly impact demand curves and price elasticity of demand levels and thus sales and profits.

Pricing experts and authors Nagle and Müller have identified nine so-called *effects* that influence buyer behavior: Competitive-Reference Effect, Switching-Cost Effect, Difficult-Comparison Effect, End-Benefit Effect, Price-Quality Effect, Expenditure Effect, Shared-Cost Effect, Transaction Value Effect, and Fairness Effect.[3] All are important and five of these effects have been incorporated in the list below with this author's own interpretations and illustrative examples. To these two more have been added for a total of seven:

The Reference Price Effect

Except in the case of an entirely new product, buyers normally enter a purchase situation with a reference price on their minds. It may be a price they have paid in the past or the price of a competing product offering. This has been called the *reference price effect*. Thus, the buyer of groceries is likely to know the approximate prices of a number of items and expects to pay these prices on subsequent purchases. Prices that are out of line with these reference or expected prices are likely to be questioned and even rejected with the customer looking for alternatives. This puts strong limits on a retailer's pricing discretion.

Marketers can and do influence reference prices in a number of ways. For example, a reference price may be raised by adding a premium-priced product to the line which will make a mid-priced product more acceptable. They may also use their skills to encourage buyers to *trade up* to the more expensive model. Retailers try to influence reference prices by advertising manufacturers' suggested retail prices or the higher prices of competitors along with the lower store prices. The behavioral finding that the first price buyers see or hear mentioned becomes the reference price has given rise to *top-down selling*. Here, the seller of a product or service quotes a higher price first which is followed by a price more acceptable to the buyer.

The reference price effect also has important ramifications for new product pricing. Once the product is on the market and made available at a specific price, that price is likely to become the reference price unless it is made known to potential customers that the price is a special introductory price which will be raised to its normal level on a future date.

The Switching Cost Effect

Buyers are known to tire of products they have used for some time making them ready to try another make or brand. For consumer products the costs involved in a switch are usually minimal but for commercial and industrial buyers these costs and the risks involved can be substantial. These costs are known as switching costs and their influence on buyer behavior called the *switching cost effect*. The significance of this effect is that if these costs are high, price becomes less of an issue, i.e., buyers become less price sensitive and may not make the switch despite the attractiveness of the competing offer.

The switching cost effect is especially strong in the commercial and industrial markets where the risks of a bad management decision can be far-reaching. Suppose an automobile manufacturer has for years been using robots of a certain make to assemble its car frames and is now eager to replace these with more up-to-date designs. Now suppose that the present vendor has developed a new series of robots that is more efficient and has offered it to the auto company. Furthermore, suppose another robot builder is also primed to offer the company a new line of machines that do the work even more efficiently than the old vendor's new machines and at a lower price.

Will management make the switch? It may be very reluctant to do so after considering the additional costs involved such as the longer down-time (stopping the assembly line while the robots are exchanged), the retraining of maintenance technicians, the replacement of a large parts inventory, and the operational risks involved in case these machines should not be as robust and reliable as the product the company is used to and requires. Clearly, the present vendor has a clear advantage over its rival which will allow it to charge a premium price for the replacement robots.

The Price-Quality Effect

Where the prospective buyer is unfamiliar with a class of products or services, the purchase decision will likely depend on a specific product's relative price level. The reason is that customers intuitively believe this price to be fair and equitable and that it is a reflection of its worth and quality. In other words, the higher the price of a product or service the higher must be its quality. This notion finds expression in the old adage "you get what you pay for." To marketers, this in known as the *price-quality effect*. It can work for or against a product or service. If a product or service is premium-priced it may convey a message of high quality but a price perceived too low may signal shoddy quality and be rejected even though the two products or services may be of comparable quality.

In fact, Gabor has suggested that a potential buyer for a given product or service enters the market with two price limits in mind, namely, an upper and a lower limit.[4] A price beyond the upper limit will be viewed as too expensive and the product or service eliminated from further consideration. If, however, the price falls below the lower limit, the customer will suspect the quality and he or she will again reject the product or service. Both limits are quality assessments, of course, in that a price above the upper limit is viewed as a quality level that is higher than required. Customers, therefore, operate within a *price band* of acceptable prices beyond which no purchase will take place.

The price-quality effect is especially important in the pricing of services because, unlike material goods, these cannot be inspected before the purchase.[5] Examples of such specialized professional services are accounting, advertising, health care, legal, and management consulting. The size of the retainer or hourly fee is perceived as a strong indicator of quality. The price-quality effect is of less importance in the case of standardized services such as car washes, laundries, and dry cleaning. Here the customer has a fairly good notion of the quality level of the service ahead of time and does not need to rely on the price as an indicator.

Scenario A

Monica is a successful regional sales manager for an up-and-coming high-tech consumer products company and hopes to be considered for the newly created position of vice-president of marketing and sales. To smooth the way she and husband Craig have decided to invite the company's president and wife, Tom and

Walfrieda, to dinner. They would like to serve a good wine with the meal but neither knows anything about wine. At their favorite supermarket, which carries a large selection of French wines, Monica spots an especially pricey bottle labeled Châteauneuf-du-Pape and says to Craig "Get a load of this, this must be really good stuff."

The couple picks up a couple of bottles of their discovery and take them home. Neither is aware that this particular wine, known as the wine of the popes, has a very rustic, tannic character that is not to many people's taste and its alcoholic content is rather high. During the meal both couples take only a few sips before switching to mineral water. After dinner, the guests, trying to be polite, complement their hosts on their excellent choice of wine. Monica and Craig were, unfortunately, misled by the wine's high price tag and quality perception.

The Expenditure Effect

It should come as no surprise but the cost of a purchase in relation to the funds available strongly influences buyer behavior in both the consumer and business markets. The grocery buyer for a large family on a limited budget is more sensitive to the price of individual food and household items than the affluent professional couple for whom these purchases represent a much smaller percentage of its income. Similarly, the owners of a small business they have just started and which is struggling to survive are more sensitive to the price of office furniture than the managers of an established and profitable company. The purchasing agent for an automobile company will be more sensitive to the cost of components intended in the manufacture of one of their low-priced models than for their more pricey brands because unit variable costs must be kept to a minimum to ensure that sales are profitable at the low prices of these cars.

Generally, buyer price sensitivity for a product or service is large whenever a purchase represents a major portion of the funds available. The larger this percentage, the higher will be the buyer's sensitivity to the price. This is known as the *expenditure effect*. Especially important is the fact that all buyers are most price-sensitive in the purchase of big-ticket items and sellers must keep a close eye on their competition because potential customers will be shopping around for the best deal that includes not only the physical product but, in addition, all the other parameters that go into the purchase decision.

The Shared Cost Effect

People are more likely to purchase a product or service and are less sensitive to its price when they pay only part or none of it. Examples of this *shared cost effect* abound and companies in the transportation and hospitality industries such as airlines, car rental companies, hotels, restaurants, and travel bureaus take full advantage of it. When important company executives or high government officials and their entourages travel around the country and overseas they do not fly economy class, stay in one-star hotels, or dine at McDonald's. Only the best will do and the prices paid are of minor concern to them because their employers are picking up the tab. Similarly, when an insurance company pays for all or most of the cost of health care or reimburses policy holders for damage suffered to a home or automobile, service providers are able to charge more than would otherwise be possible.

Many other examples abound. Major business firms routinely send key employees to seminars and executive training programs to improve their business skills. This is beneficial to both companies and employees but is normally fully paid for by the employers. In particular, business schools at major universities offer accelerated MBA programs that are considerably more expensive per semester hour than for regular students. Trade fairs, exhibitions, congresses, conventions, and seminars paid for by other than the attendees are a boon to many businesses especially hotels and restaurants. Finally, many professionals are required to keep current in their field to retain their state licenses. Such expenses are tax deductible which means that these people too will not be overly cautious regarding their expenditures.

The Captive Customer Effect

Accessories typically command premium prices because if a customer has already purchased the basic product she or he is not likely to buy another brand to accessorize it. Thus, if a customer of a certain brand of camera is in the market for an interchangeable lens, he or she is most likely to buy it from the camera's maker and not from some other source especially if she or he is not very knowledgeable in the field. Needless to say, the lenses and other accessories will cost the customer considerably more than if they had been part of the original purchase. Countless other examples may be cited for what may be called the *captive customer effect*.

Replacement parts and tie-in products are other examples of the captive customer effect. Manufacturers and dealers charge considerably more for replacement parts because the price sensitivity for these is relatively low unless the identical part is available from another vendor at a much lower price. An example of a tie-in product would be the ink cartridge for a printer. Thus, Hewlett-Packard is known to use penetration pricing for its printers but skim the market for the ink cartridges it recommends for use with its printers. In fact, an HP machine recognizes the replacement cartridge as being a genuine Hewlett-Packard product.

The service industry is well-known for taking advantage of the captive customer effect. Banks and credit card companies obtain a substantial part of their income from overdraft charges, late payment fees, and similar fees and charges. For airlines, charges for checked baggage and flight schedule changes are a large source of profits. Movie theaters typically make as much or more money on their concession operations than on the tickets they sell and discourage or forbid patrons from bringing their own snacks and drinks onto the premises. Vacationers traveling in Western Europe know that whenever one of the numerous trade shows or conventions is in town, the prices of hotel rooms skyrocket as hoteliers cash in on the temporary surge in demand for accommodations. In each of these cases the customer has no or very limited alternatives to paying the going rate because the supply is limited.

The Social Benefits Effect

What may be called the *social benefits effect* (or *prestige* or *snob effect*) is quite different from the price-quality effect discussed above in that in this case the product or service is well known to the customer and he or she can come to a purchase decision without speculating on its quality. Here the customer chooses a product or service not for its intrinsic value but for the social benefits and prestige it confers on its owner. Because of the product's usually lofty price tag, its perceived value is very high to a select group of customers who find satisfaction in its exclusiveness and in knowing that few others can afford it.

Many luxury brands such as Armani, Cartier, Coach, Dior, Gucci, Hermes, Louis Vuitton, and Rolex benefit from this effect and their owners tend to be exceptionally wealthy. One reputedly said that the reason he entered the business was because "only in luxury goods can you make luxury profits." This is why, for example, an Armani T-shirt may cost a few hundred dollars, a Louis Vuitton handbag over a thousand, a Cartier watch several thousand, and a Leica camera over ten thousand dollars when other brands that are equally functional, stylish, and high-quality may be had for a fraction of these prices. The demand curves for these sought-after luxury brands are typically very steep allowing marketers extensive price discretion.

Scenario B

Sadie is director of marketing research at her healthcare company in downtown Boston and on the way to work she stops by a Starbucks restaurant to pick up a pricey cup of café latte plus a pastry. On the way she passes a Dunkin' Donuts restaurant and, although she prefers their coffee, enjoys fresh-baked donuts, and likes their prices, she never gets breakfast there. That is because Sadie highly values that Starbucks logo on her paper cup. To hold a Dunkin' Donuts coffee cup around her coworkers drinking Starbucks coffee would not be the in-thing for someone in her position, she feels, and so she keeps to her daily early morning routine.

Scenario C

Henry Blitzinger is a retiree from the U.S. State Department where he specialized in Chinese-American relations. After writing a couple of books on the subject which brought him critical acclaim and much publicity, he was contacted by a member of the staff of the Harry Walker Agency, reputedly the country's largest lecture bureau, to join its roster of speakers. The company's clients include former U.S. presidents, captains of industry, Noble laureates, bestselling authors, sports and Hollywood stars, and many other celebrities. Speaking fees are typically in the 4-5 figure range with the agency taking about a one-third cut for its services.[6] Henry did not hesitate to accept the proposal. He was fairly well off financially but could use the extra money. He also felt that by his talks he would be making a real contribution by educating the American public about an ascendant China and the pivotal role it is destined to play in the twenty-first century.

Henry had never been known for an extravagant life style. He had been wearing Brooks Brothers suits, Arrow shirts and ties, Florsheim shoes, a Timex watch, and driven an older model Toyota Corolla. With his new position, income, and the audiences he would be addressing, Henry realized he had to reinvent himself and project an image of affluence and sophistication. Henry now sports Armani suits, Charvet Place Vendôme shirts and ties, Gucci shoes, and a Cartier watch. He arrives at his speaking assignments in a chauffeured limo. Henry's new attire does not fit or look much better than what he had been wearing before nor does his new watch give better time. What he has gained are symbols of status in line with the expectations of his discriminating audiences. The luxury brands he has chosen to wear and the limo service legitimize the fees he is being paid since they demonstrate success made possibly by other businesses and organizations which highly value his lectures as well.

9.3 Setting an Initial Price

While it is a fact that value-based pricing has no specific rules or formulas to offer by which an initial price that is both profitable for the firm and acceptable to the buyer may be determined, some guidelines do exist for the case where a similar product or service is already on the market. The general approach is to use a competitor's price for a similar product or service as a reference and adjust that price to account for differences in the features and benefits of the two competing brands or models. In other words, the marketer adds positive differential values to the reference price and subtracts negative ones to obtain a net differential value which, when converted to a dollar figure, will give at least a ballpark estimate for an appropriate price point for the new product. A number of price-setting models have been suggested by various pricing consultants and authors.

Nagle and Müller recommend a 6-stage price setting process consisting of:[7] i) Defining a reasonable price range, ii) making strategic choices, iii) doing a breakeven sales analysis, iv) gauging price elasticity, v) accounting for psychological factors, and vi) communicating the new price to the market. In this model the most difficult stage will be the first on defining a reasonable price range because it requires the marketer to put a dollar value on the positive and negative attributes that differentiate her or his company's product from that of the closest competing model.

Take the customer deciding on what new car to purchase. Let us assume that one model accelerates to 60 m.p.h. ("zero to 60") in 8 seconds while the closest competing one takes 20 seconds. How would one translate the difference in a buyer's perceived value to economic value in dollars between the two models? The same goes for all the other variables the buyer will consider in her auto purchase decision.

The second of these, making strategic choices, relates to choosing among the major pricing strategies—skim, penetration, and neutral pricing. (Chapter 8). Step three calls for a breakeven analysis to address profitability issues. (Chapter 7). Next, the product's price elasticity is to be estimated so see if the price moves suggested by the breakeven sales analysis are achievable. (Chapter 6). The psychological factors that go into a purchase decision are to be considered next. (See above). The final step requires effectively communicating the new price to the market. (Chapter 10).

Pricing consultant Mark Stiving recommends the following five-step approach:[8] i) Identify your customer's second-best option to your product, ii) determine the price of the second-best option, iii) list your advantages and disadvantages relative to the second-best option, iv) estimate in dollars and cents the value of each advantage and disadvantage, and v) calculate your price:

$$Price = Price \text{ of second-best option} + Value \text{ of}$$
$$advantages - Value \text{ of disadvantages}$$

Regarding the fourth step, i.e., estimating the dollar value of each advantage and disadvantage, "This is hard," the author admits. "Not only is it subjective, it's difficult to convince a marketer to be honest about this." Stiving suggests use of some statistical techniques such as conjoint analysis or, more simply, asking potential buyers how they value the different features and benefits of the product or service.

A third approach to setting a value-based price is offered by pricing consultant Rafi Mohammed who recommends a four-step technique:[9] i) Identify the next-best alternative and use it as a base price, ii) determine a product's differences, iii) create a demand curve, and iv) undertake a "profit maximizer analysis." The most difficult step in this approach is obviously the third—the demand curve. Estimating a demand curve showing the trade-off between price and sales volume for a new product is probably one of the most challenging assignments in marketing. The author suggests market research, experienced judgment, or one-on-one pricing (average customer valuation). The profit maximizer analysis consists of using the demand curve and computing the sales revenue, total cost, and profit at various price points and selecting the price at which the profit is maximized.

Summarizing, none of the above procedures and techniques is without serious flaws. However, the basic premise of all, namely, that prices must be market and value oriented and tailored to specific market segments is valid. For a new product or service that must compete with those already on the market, the price of the closest alternative can serve as useful reference price. The firm's price must be adjusted up or down to take into account the perceived value difference between the firm's product and the competing one. Translating this perceived difference into a monetary value to arrive at a price will be a major challenge.

With these difficulties in mind, Utpal Dholakia, a behavioral scientist, has suggested a simpler pricing method he calls good-better-best.[10] "Instead of targeting specific segments the idea behind good-better-best pricing is to allow customers to self-select into the segment they want." In this scheme three versions of a product are offered with "good" being low in quality and price, "better" of medium quality and price, and "best" the top quality version with the highest price. One of the benefits of this method is that it allows the marketer to motivate customers to trade up from good to better to best with increasingly higher prices and profit margins. He tells the story of a jewelry designer who offered two versions of jewelry—a bracelet and a combo set at a much higher price. Of these only the bracelet sold. The minute she added an outrageously high-priced second combo set, sales for the first combo set soon exceeded those of the bracelet alone.

9.4 Multiple Products Pricing

When a product is introduced to the market it is usually done by offering different models or versions to appeal to different market segments. For pricing a line of products Monroe has recommended use of the so-called Weber-Fechner law.[11] It is based on the findings of two behavioral scientists, Ernst Weber and Gustav Fechner, who studied how changes in a stimulus are actually perceived by people. Specifically, Fechner showed that the relationship between the magnitude of a stimulus S and the magnitude of the resulting response R takes this form:

$$R = k \log S + a \qquad \text{(Eq. 9.1)}$$

where k and a are constants. Equation 9-1 is known as the *Weber-Fechner Law*. In a pricing context, S would be the seller's price and R the buyer's response to that price. This law can be interpreted to mean that a buyer's price perception follows a logarithmic rather than a linear scale. In other words, price differentials between different versions of a product or service should become wider as one approaches the highest priced model. Monroe gives two formulas by which the price of any model or version j may be computed based on the Weber-Fechner law:

$$P_j = P_L \, k^{\,j-1} \qquad \text{(Eq. 9.2)}$$

where P_L is the price of the lowest-priced model or version and k the ratio to be applied for the price of each succeeding one. The ratio k is obtained from this relationship:

$$\log k = \frac{1}{n-1} (\log P_H - \log P_L) \qquad \text{(Eq. 9.3)}$$

where n is the number of models in the line and P_H the price of the highest-priced model. The low and high end prices anchor the product line price-wise and must be chosen carefully and preferably for maximum sales revenue or contribution dollars.

Illustrative Example: Droneco Ltd. (I)

Droneco Ltd. was founded to manufacture and market surveillance drones for governmental and private use and the first line of five Droneco products is now ready for market introduction. During the product planning stage, seven target markets were identified: i) Large municipalities for managing traffic flow, ii) major sporting and entertainment event sponsors for crowd control, iii) diverse construction contractors to monitor work progress, (iv) national parks and state forestry services for spotting wildfires, v) western cattle ranchers for keeping track of their livestock, vi) governmental agencies to patrol their countries' borders, and vii) African game reserves to protect endangered elephants or rhinos from poachers.

Droneco's market study revealed that potential customers across the seven market segments were willing to invest anywhere between $5,000 and $25,000 per vehicle. These drone versions differ mainly in the materials used in their construction, their durability and reliability, their speed and maneuverability, their range of operation, the length of time they can stay afloat, and the complexity of their sensor systems. Management decided to limit the number of versions offered to just five. In the absence of adequate volume-price information that would let him compute the optimal prices for the five models, the marketing manager decided to use the Weber-Fechner findings to price the Droneco line.

By Equation (9.3) he computed:

$\log k = 1 / 4 \times (\log 25{,}000 - \log 5{,}000) = 0.25 \times (4.3979 - 3.6990)$
$\log k = 0.25 \times 0.6989 = 0.1747$
$k = 1.496$

Using this ratio in Equation (9.2) for the five models he obtained:

$P_1 = \$5{,}000$
$P_2 = \$5{,}000 \times 1.496 = \$7{,}480$
$P_3 = \$7{,}480 \times 1.496 = \$11{,}190$
$P_4 = \$11{,}190 \times 1.496 = \$16{,}740$
$P_5 = \$16{,}740 \times 1.496 = \$25{,}000$

The actual prices would be slightly modified so that P_2, for example, would be offered at $7,499 instead of $7,480. A comparison of prices based on a regular interval and the Weber-Fechner schemes is shown in Figure 9-1 below.

Marketers normally do not use equal price differentials for different product versions because customers' perceived value and price differentials are usually much out of line. As for the Weber-Fechner approach in this example, the two low-priced versions are so close in price that it may lead to cannibalization between the two while the price of the premium version is so disproportionately high that it may find too few buyers. Most likely, Droneco's management will further limit its product offering to three or four versions and space their prices more equitably but generally in keeping with the Weber- Fechner findings.

Figure 9-1   Pricing of Five Droneco Product Versions

a. Regular Interval

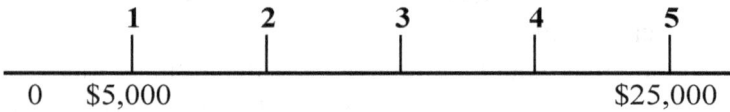

b. Weber-Fechner

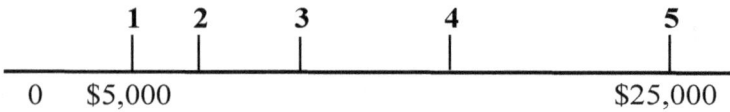

9.5 Pricing Practices and Techniques

Market oriented pricing has given rise to a number of pricing practices and techniques the most common ones of which are discussed below.

9.5.1 Price Bundling and Unbundling

Price bundling, also known as *product bundling*, is popular in every type of industry or market and for both consumer and industrial products and services since it is beneficial to sellers and buyers alike. With bundling a firm offers two or more of its products or services at a total price that is lower than if the customer purchased each product or service separately. For the firm, bundling increases sales revenue and strengthens brand loyalty by encouraging the purchase of additional products and services the customer may not have purchased at all or elsewhere while the customer benefits from lower prices. *Unbundling* is the reverse practice where products and services previously offered only as bundles, a practice known as *pure bundling*, now become available separately.

Sometimes pure bundling makes good sense in the case of an innovative and complex new product where the potential buyer may have difficulty in putting all the elements of a working system together. A case in point was IBM's successful introduction in 1964 of the System/360 digital computer for business use by offering lease or sales contracts that included hardware, software, systems engineering, maintenance, and employee training as one bundle. This marketing strategy was very successful for about five years when the U.S. Department of Justice sued IBM alleging attempts to monopolize the digital computer system market in violation of the Sherman Antitrust Act. Later that same year (1969), IBM decided to unbundle by charging for hardware, software, and services separately. Most bundling today goes by the term *mixed bundling* where the customer has the choice of buying either a bundle or each component separately.

Bundling is part of most peoples' everyday experiences. In restaurants, the diner can purchase individual food items à la carte or a complete meal including entrée, dessert, and soda for a lesser price. McDonald's sells hamburger and chicken products individually or as a "meal deal" including French fries and a soft drink that costs less than the sum of the individual items. Hotels may bundle breakfast and some services with the room price at a discount. Cable companies usually offer cable, telephone, and Internet services at a special bundle price. Insurance companies allow their customers a special discount if they purchase both homeowners and auto insurance. Travel bureaus put together special packages that may include the flight or cruise ticket, hotel accommodations, meals, and travel guide expenses. Many other examples of bundling could be cited.[12]

In a price-sensitive market when price competition becomes fierce, companies may decide that unbundling of previously bundled products and services is more profitable. Air travel provides the perfect example. A complimentary meal used to be included on most long distance flights. To reduce costs and improve profitability, this practice has been largely discontinues and meals are now available at an extra charge. Similarly, all of a traveler's baggage used to be checked in free while now only one piece of luggage is so treated. Interestingly, in line with our previous discussion on oligopolies and their coordinated behavior, practically all the air lines follow these same practices in what antitrust lawyers call conscious parallelism.

9.5.2 Private Label and Store Brands

National brands are typically marketed to the whole country. Because they are heavily advertised and obliged to meet high quality standards, such products tend to be relatively expensive. To appeal to a more price-sensitive market segment, private label brands, also known as *store brands*, have become a major part of the retail scene and are believed to now account for at least twenty percent of supermarket sales. Store brands are typically priced below the national brands which they are designed to imitate. According to Gabor, offering store brands can be a successful policy where i) the national brands are burdened by high marketing costs, ii) the quality of the national and store brands are comparable, and iii) the store has a favorable image in the eyes of the customer.[13]

Like price bundling, the use of private label or store brands brings benefits to all parties in the sales chain from producer to user including manufacturers, distributors, retailers, and customers. For customers the benefits are obvious in the cost-savings involved in buying a lower-priced store brand of good quality. For the retailer it has the benefit of drawing more price-sensitive shoppers into the store who are then likely to also buy from the more standard product offering carrying higher markups.

The benefits for the manufacturer of private label brands are also significant. It allows manufacturing at peak capacity thereby holding unit variable costs to a minimum. While sales at the lower prices and margins may not be very profitable, a steady stream of contribution dollars will help cover the firm's overhead costs. Where overcapacity exists, this is one way of dealing with it. A number of cost savings will accrue as well. Thus, since private label products are not advertised on a national level, the firm need not budget for this item.

Some companies employ private labels as *fighting brands* against price-aggressive competitors.[14] Consider a manufacturer of high quality, large-margin leather goods whose best seller is Product A. Suppose further, that an import from a low-cost manufacturer, Product B, has become available that not only simulates the company's product A in looks and style but is of a comparable quality and, most importantly, costs significantly less. The company may answer the challenge by offering a Product C under a private label to directly compete with Product B. Its low price may not make sales of Product C profitable but it will protect Product A by preventing the competitor from drawing price-sensitive customers away from Product A to Product B. Competition will now take place between Products B and C which the company can turn in its favor by positively differentiating Product C from Product B to raise its perceived value vis-à-vis its competition.

9.5.3 Price Lining

Price lining is the practice of offering an entire inventory of a class of products at a number of specific but limited prices.[15] It is not uncommon for a department store or other retailer to have a policy to carry merchandise only at specific price points. For the retailer, this tends to simplify the purchase, inventory, and pricing process. For these retailers the normal pricing procedure is reversed in that the store's buyers search only for merchandise that can be sold at the set prices. To make the method work, a minimum of three basic price points is recommended which should roughly correspond to "good," "better," and "best." Also, these should be sufficiently far apart to suggest differences in quality. For example, a clothier's inventory of men's neckties might be sold at $20, $30, and $50 depending on type of material and quality.

The main argument for *price lining* for shoppers is that it makes it easier for them to make their selections since there are only a limited number of merchandise categories and associated price points to choose from. This pricing model could be especially useful for certain specialty retailers such as gift and jewelry shops since shoppers will normally have a price range for the intended gift in mind and price lining would make it easier to zero in on a suitable item. The drawback to price lining is, of course, that merchandise that shoppers may want to buy is often not available.

9.5.4 Odd Pricing

Another pricing technique popular with businesses, especially retailers, is to use a price that ends with an odd number because it is believed this is more attractive to buyers than an even one. The practice is known as *odd pricing*. This number should be slightly less than the closest round number. That is why most prices end in a 5 or 9 but never in a 6, 8 or 0. Thus, bananas may be priced at 59 cents a pound and not at 60 cents, a Kindle e-book at $9.99 instead of $10.00, a paperback novel at $19.95 rather than $20.00, and a television set at $499.95 rather than at $500.00. Customers undoubtedly focus on the left-most, the most significant, figure in the price and pay less attention to the remainder.

The practice must have a very beneficial impact on sales or it would not find almost universal favor with sellers of both products and services. It is not confined to the U.S. but practiced around the globe. To the average shopper, merchandise priced at $9.95 is perceived to be a much better deal than something priced at $10.00 and a product priced at $995.95 is more attractively priced than the same product at $1,000.00. In either case, the customer perceives the lower price to be a bargain even though the actual price differential is negligibly small. A price ending in less than a full dollar would also signal to the price-sensitive shopper that it has been cut to the bare bone further reinforcing the bargain message.

An exception is made in the case of luxury goods. A bargain message is something the makers of such merchandise definitely do not want to convey and it is the reason why odd pricing is almost never used here. In fact, luxury products clearly identify themselves by carrying prices that end in zeros. Thus, one would never see a Louis Vuitton handbag listed at $4,999 but always at $5,000 or a Rolex watch at $39,999 in lieu of $40,000. Another practice in use, especially in gourmet restaurants and fashionable resorts, is to leave the dollar sign off menu items. Listing items, for example, as 30 in lieu of $30 has been shown to encourage patrons to spend significantly more than with the dollar prefix at such venues.

9.5.5 Raising the Price Without Overtly Doing So

Raising prices for consumer or industrial products to adjust for cost increases or some other reason is as unpopular with sellers as it is with buyers. This is especially true where demand for the product is highly price elastic and the product is frequently purchased so that any price change will be instantly noticed. In such situations firms often "raise prices without raising prices" by such techniques as:

* Changing the physical characteristics of the product

* Revising the discount structure

* Changing the payment terms

* Charging for delivery

* Raising the minimum acceptable order size

* Charging for special services such as rush orders

* Collecting interest on delinquent accounts

There are obviously many other creative ways by which prices may effectively be raised without the necessity of having to announce a price increase.

Notes

1. Daniel A. Nimer, "Pricing The Profitable Sale Has A Lot To Do With Perception," *Sales Management / Special Report*, 1971,13.

2. Daniel A. Nimer, "Developing a Strategy for Pricing," *Management Review*, November 1971, 43.

3. Thomas Nagle and Georg Müller, *The Strategy and Tactics of Pricing*, 64-73.

4. André Gabor, *Pricing*, 254.

5. André Gabor, supra at 195.

6. Stephen Solomon, "Speech is Golden on the Lecture Circuit," in Ross Eckert and Richard Leftwich, *The Price System and Resource Allocation*, 380-381.

7. Thomas Nagle and Georg Müller, supra at 135.

8. Mark Stiving, *Impact Pricing*, 43, 49.

9. Rafi Mohammed, *The 1% Windfall*, 14-18.

10. Uptal Dholakia, *How to Price Effectively*, 124-125, 250-252.

11. Kent Monroe, *Pricing*, 402-404

12. Some creative examples of bundling may be found in Dale Furtwengler, *Pricing for Profit*, 101-132.

13. André Gabor, supra at 166.

14. Robert Dolan and Hermann Simon, *Power Pricing*, 213-214.

15. André Gabor, supra at 158-162.

CHAPTER

10

Marketing and Pricing Dynamics

*The key to profitable pricing is building
and sustaining competitive advantage.[1]*

Businesses thrive when customer oriented marketing and market oriented pricing come together in a synergistic union that is the envy of competitors and the delight of owners and shareholders, customers, employees, suppliers, and the public at large. This chapter focusers on the marketing and pricing dynamics necessary to achieve such results. A key component of modern marketing is market segmentation and that topic is covered first. It will be shown how this practices, and especially price customization, can significantly increase sales revenue and profitability. This is followed by a discussion on how a firm may consistently outperform its competitors and achieve optimum results by a number of means all designed to reduce the price sensitivity of products and services and thereby increasing their profit potentials.

10.1 Market Segmentation

Manufacturers have historically treated their markets as an undifferentiated *mass market* of buyers with uniform needs and wants. The object was to produce a standard product at the lowest possible cost, mark it up to cover overhead and profit, and sell it. All business activity was essentially company-, production-, and product- oriented. Modern marketing did not yet exist and the term, if used at all, meant selling what the company had to offer.

Even as late as the early 1970s, Professor Philip Kotler in his classic *Marketing Management* called market segmentation "a relatively recent and revolutionary concept in business circles." He defined *market segmentation* as the "subdividing of a market into homogeneous subsets of customers, where any subset may conceivably be selected as a market target to be reached with a distinct marketing mix."[2] This still serves as a good definition for this now conventional marketing concept. The focus has clearly shifted away from the needs and wants of the seller (the firm) to the needs and wants of the buyer (the customer).

Kotler and Keller give four criteria for segmenting consumer markets—geographic, demographic, psychographic, and behavioral.[3] *Geographical* segmentation is based on such factors as region of the country, urban or rural area, city size, and climate. *Demographic* segmentation takes into account a customer's age and life-cycle stage, gender, marital status, education, income, occupation, race, religion, and social class. In *psychographic* segmentation customers are divided according to psychological and personality traits such as lifestyle, core values and whether they are culture oriented or sports fans. *Behavioral* segmentation involves the relationship between buyers and the product such as product knowledge, benefits, usage rate, and attitude towards the product. The authors list a total of twenty-five of these variables for segmenting consumer markets. Additionally, they present seventeen variables that can be used to segment business markets.

Market segmentation has become the norm in most industries and markets. In automobiles, some manufacturers operate in the luxury segment, others market more low-priced designs while still others offer a complete line of vehicles that appeals to different market segments from busy singles to style- and comfort-oriented family folks to status-conscious corporate executives. Some hotels cater only to the most discriminating patrons while others seek out business travelers, families with children, or budget-minded tourists. Department stores and shopping centers may carry only brand name luxury goods or offer merchandise of more traditional appeal. Numerous specialty retailers and boutiques cater to the needs and wants of select groups of buyers.

10.2 Target Markets

An important marketing function after dividing these larger markets for goods and services into market segments is choosing that segment or segments which the firm can most profitably serve. These become the firm's *target markets*. Choosing these should be based on the firm's resources and capabilities, the size, sales and profit potential of each segment, and the competition in each segment. Instead of using a shotgun approach to marketing, companies now can focus on their target markets and channel their efforts and limited human and financial resources to serving these in the most efficient and profitable manner possible. Sellers are the biggest winners of market segmentation because the most important marketing mix variable to drive profit, the product's price, can now be customized for optimum results.

Take, for example, an industrial product such as a fastener in form of a nail of a certain shape and dimension. A building contractor will buy it by the bagful, a carpenter or cabinetmaker may need a few hundred, while a hobbyist just a few. Each of these three buyers represents a target market and the firm may choose one, two or all to serve. While the packaging may be different it is essentially the same nail. The difference is in the price with each target market paying a different one with the hobbyist most likely paying the most per nail. The reason for the price differences is that the demand curve for each of the three target markets is different. With the demand curve being different so will be its surrogate pricing metric, the price elasticity of demand.

The most important characteristic of a target market for pricing purpose is that target market's demand curve and the price elasticity of demand (P.E.D.) at the present price-volume operating point, i.e., the expected change in sales volume in response to an incremental price change. This is the number the pricer is called on to estimate with a high degree of accuracy either by intuition, experience, or research. Each target market for a product or service has its own unique demand curve. In other words, this important metric cannot be just any P.E.D. but one that specifically applies to the target market being served. It is therefore important to note that wherever the term ϵ_0 appears in a mathematical expression throughout this text it refers to the price elasticity of demand of a product or service at the present price-volume operating point (P_0, Q_0) prior to the price change in a *specific target market* in which this product or service is being offered.

10.3 Versioning and Price Customization

The term *versioning* has come into general use by which is meant the practice of offering the same or slightly modified product or service to different customer groups. Often these different versions do not involve any differences in the manufacturing or marketing costs. While this practice of charging different buyers different prices for essentially the same product or service may appear questionable and as *price discrimination* even be illegal under certain circumstances, it is nevertheless a fact of life. As will be shown below, the practice is the only way a firm can capture the full sales potential for that product or service and thereby optimize sales revenue or total contribution.

Versioning and *price customization* requires a special mechanism by which more affluent and so-called "price buyers" can be kept apart. Otherwise all of them would buy at the lowest possible price and the company would forego more profitable sales. This mechanism is known as a *price fence*. Price fences are criteria set by the seller which a buyer must meet in order to qualify for a lower price. Nagle and Müller identify four main price fences— buyer identification fences, purchase location fences, time-of-purchase fences, and purchase quantity fences.[4]

Some of the more common price fences are based on age or status. Thus, seniors and school-age children typically do not pay the full price on public transportation, in museums, or movie theaters and similar venues as adults and may be readily identified as belonging to that special price-sensitive class. If the market is segmented by family income, for example, a mail order firm may do one mailing to high income ZIP codes with one set of prices and another with lower prices to less affluent areas even though the products in the two catalogs are identical. If the company mailed out just one catalog, the high income customers would buy at the lower prices meant for the more price-sensitive buyers and the company would forego additional sales revenue and profits.

Airlines erect price fences by charging different prices for the same seats depending on the day and time of travel. Business travelers fly on Monday morning and return home on Friday evening and since they are the least sensitive to the ticket price, flying on those days and times is more expensive. Restaurants may have lunch and dinner menus offering similar meals but the evening one will be more expensive because dinner is usually more leisurely and service-oriented and diners expect to pay more. Electric utilities will charge more for energy usage during weekdays between certain hours when demand is highest than for off-peak energy usage during the rest of the week. In the business-to-business (B2B) sector, a firm may qualify for a quantity or order size discount only if it meets the dollar or purchase quantity criteria.

Needless to say, price fences are not always perfect barriers. How could one, for example, keep a Warren Buffett or Bill Gates from seeing a movie at a local theater during matinee hours designed for the price sensitive market such as seniors or school-age children? That is not to say, of course, that either would be inclined to do so!

The benefits of price customization are best demonstrated on hand of Figure 10-1. The drawing shows a *linear price response curve* (PRC), the downward sloping line Q_M–P_M, which is a version of the typical Marshallian demand curve but with the price and quantity axes reversed. As previously noted, Q_M represents the maximum quantity customers will take if the price is reduced to zero while P_M is the maximum price customers are willing to pay, i.e., the reservation price. As usual, [P] and [Q] represent the optimal price and quantity for *sales revenue* maximization, and P* and Q* the optimal price and quantity for *total contribution* maximization, respectively. P_F is the price floor and Q_F the quantity taken at that price. Price customization can be analyzed in terms of whether a product's sales revenue or total contribution is to be maximized.

Figure 10-1
Optimal Prices for Maximum Revenue and Contribution

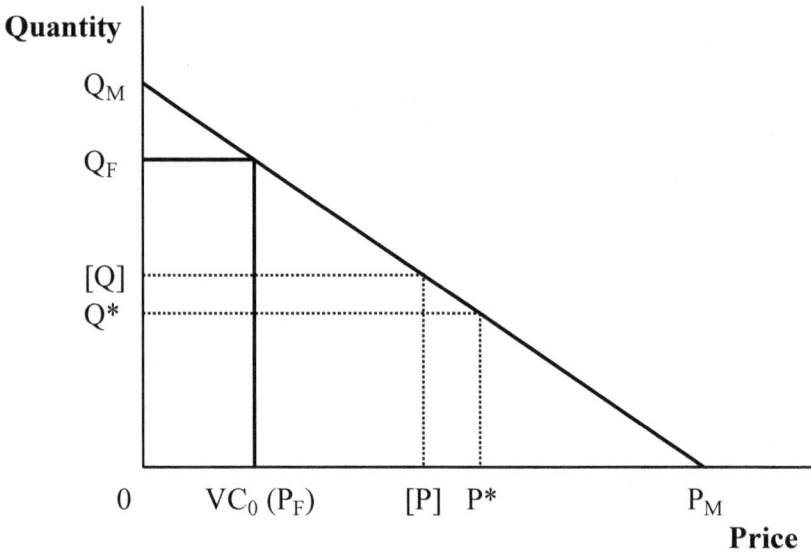

10.3.1 Customizing for Maximum Revenue

The reader will recall that sales revenue for a product or service is obtained by multiplying the price by the quantity sold. The PRC shows the quantity that can be sold at each price during some unit of time. In fact, the area under this curve (the right-triangle P_M–Q_M) is the maximum sales revenue that can be generated from this particular product or service. This sales potential is given by $R_P = \frac{1}{2} \times P_M \times Q_M$.

Let it be assumed that the firm offers just one product at one price. What will be its best price to capture the maximum amount of this potential sales revenue? As may easily be shown, it is the price [P] which lies midway between 0 and P_M.[5] Projecting upward from [P] to the PRC, we note that it bisects this curve, i.e., it lies at its midpoint where the price elasticity of demand $\in$ for the product or service equals one ($\in$ = 1.0). Projecting left from there to the quantity axis, we find [Q] which is the quantity for sales revenue maximization. The area [R] = [P] × [Q] represents the largest rectangle that can be enclosed within the right-triangle of the PRC and is the maximum sales revenue achievable with just one price point.

The area of this rectangle and therefore the maximum sales revenue [R] is seen to be only one half (50%) of the potential sales revenue R_p. The other half of potential sales revenue R_p is lost to the firm for two reasons. Sales represented by triangle Q_M-[Q]-[P] do not materialize because at the combination of price and quantity in that region no buyers may be found since their value perceptions of the product falls below these price-volume levels. Triangle [Q]-[P]-P_M similarly represents lost sales because potential customers who would take the quantities at the associated higher prices cannot do so because the product is available at only the lower price of [P]. In other words, their value perception of the product is significantly higher than that of the other groups of potential customers.

A business must obviously find another way to increase sales revenue and capture the one-half of potential sales it is missing. This other option is to add two more *versions* of the product or service with price points midway between O and [P] and midway between [P] and P_M, respectively. This three-product, three-price solution will add another 50% to the sales revenue achievable and bring the total to 75%. The following illustrative example will further clarify the point.

Illustrative Example: Roboco Enterprises

Roboco Enterprises is the brainchild of Emily Bolingbroke, a retired robotics engineer. Emily designs and markets costumed action robots for the amusement of young children. Her present customers are mostly the parents of small boys but she would like to appeal to little girls as well to stimulate their interest in science and technology. Her toys are constructed from plastic components and include a microprocessor, a battery-run motor, and a remote control unit. Emily's latest design, the Model EB7, is a miniature robot dressed as a circus clown that can do all sorts of gymnastic exercises including rollovers, handstands, pushups, sit-ups, and somersaults.

Emily would like to sell the Model EB7 to some toy stores in her area for around $80 to $100 each. She has been told that the maximum she can hope to get for the toy is about $160. Maximum monthly sales are estimated at about 200 units at an extremely low price near zero. What advice can one give Emily? Should she sell just one version and at what price or should she offer additional versions and, if so, at what prices? The cost differences between models would be negligible. Her goal is to maximize sales revenue.

Figure 10-2
Sales Revenue Without and With Versioning
for Roboco's Model EB7 Toy Robot

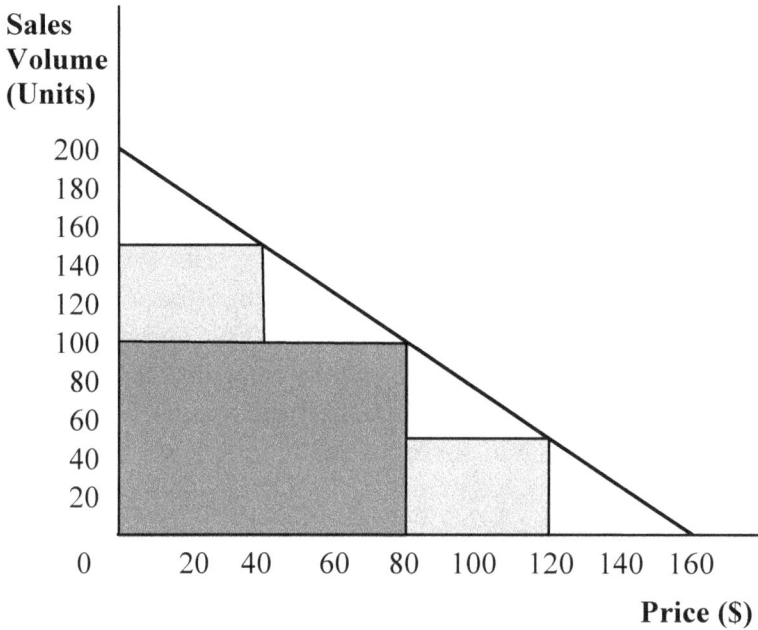

With the maximum possible sales volume Q_M given as 200 units and the maximum price P_M as $160, one can draw the price response curve as shown in Figure 10-2. The optimal price [P], which is one-half the maximum of $160, is therefore $80. This is the price Emily must charge for maximum sales revenue [R]. Thus, [R] = $80 × 100 or $8,000 which corresponds to the darkly shaded area in Figure 10-2. This revenue is just one-half of the potential sales revenue of $R_p = \frac{1}{2} \times \$160 /$ unit $\times 200$ units = $16,000.

Suppose Emily added two more versions of the Model EB7, with one at half the price of the $80 version and the other at $120, which is halfway between $80 and $160. This would add another 2 × $40 / unit × 50 units or $4,000 to sales revenue. (See the lightly shaded rectangles in Figure 10-2). Total sales revenue would now be R = $8,000 + $4,000 = $12,000. Clearly, by adding two more versions, an economy and a premium one with each model differing in looks and performance capabilities, Emily would have added another 50% to sales revenue bringing the total to 75% of the potential sales revenue of $16,000. This process could be extended, except that too many versions with only minor differences between them could confuse customers and be detrimental to overall sales. Emily could, however, sell other versions through different channels.

10.3.2 Customizing for Maximum Contribution

Returning to Figure 10-1 above, the reader will recall that total contribution K is the difference between sales revenue R and the total direct variable cost V where V is given by the area $VC_0 \times Q_F$. Therefore, the right-triangle bounded by Q_F, VC_0, and P_M represents the maximum total contribution K_p achievable with this product. The question again is, What price must the firm charge to capture the maximum of this potential contribution?

It can be shown that the optimal price P* for contribution maximization lies at the midpoint between VC_0 and P_M.[6] As in the case of sales revenue maximization above, this price yields just 50% of the potential contribution K_p. The other half is again lost because potential customers are either not willing to purchase the product in the quantities required by the PRC below the optimal price P* while others would pay more than P* if the firm offered the product at a higher price.

The company will again meet this challenge by adding two more product versions with two more price points to the line. These three products will roughly correspond to "good," "better," and "best" and might be called "economy," "standard," and "premium" models. The two additional prices will lie midway between VC_0, the product's unit variable cost, and the optimal price P* for contribution maximization, and between P* and the maximum price P_M, respectively. These additions will add another 50% to contribution bringing total contribution to 75% of the maximum potential contribution K_p.

A three-product offering, or rather, three-class seating has become standard in the airline industry. This makes intuitive sense because of the different needs and wants of travelers. The leisure passenger will book long in advance of the flight, is more interested in the price than any amenities, and is more likely to cancel out. For this customer *economy class* is the answer. The corporate executive traveling in *business class* is likely to book shortly before a scheduled flight, is less interested in the ticket cost because her or his employer is paying the fare, and wants to travel in relative comfort. The *first-class* passenger can afford and is willing to pay for all the amenities the airline has to offer. Clearly, the price sensitivity and willingness to pay differs much among the three market segments. The following analysis will further clarify these points.

Illustrative Example: Jubilee Airlines

Jubilee Airlines is a charter air service which specializes in transporting seniors from their retirement homes in the United States and Canada to various places around the globe that are of special cultural and historical interest. The airline has recently added three Boeing 787-8 Dreamliner wide-body, fuel-efficient jets to its fleet but has not yet decided whether to fly these in a one-class configuration or have the traditional three-class seating arrangement of regular commercial airlines that includes economy class, economy plus (business) class, and first class.

The Boeing 787-8 Dreamliner seats about 240 in a three-class seating arrangement.[7] The incremental variable costs of transporting each additional passenger are small, here assumed to be just $100, while the maximum price a senior would pay for a round-trip ticket to the intended destination is estimated to be $1,300. Jubilee Airlines' goal is to maximize the dollar contribution from each trip. From this information the PRC of Figure 10-3 can be drawn.

Figure 10-3
Contribution With Single and Three Class Seating
for Julilee Airline's Boeing 787 Dreamliner

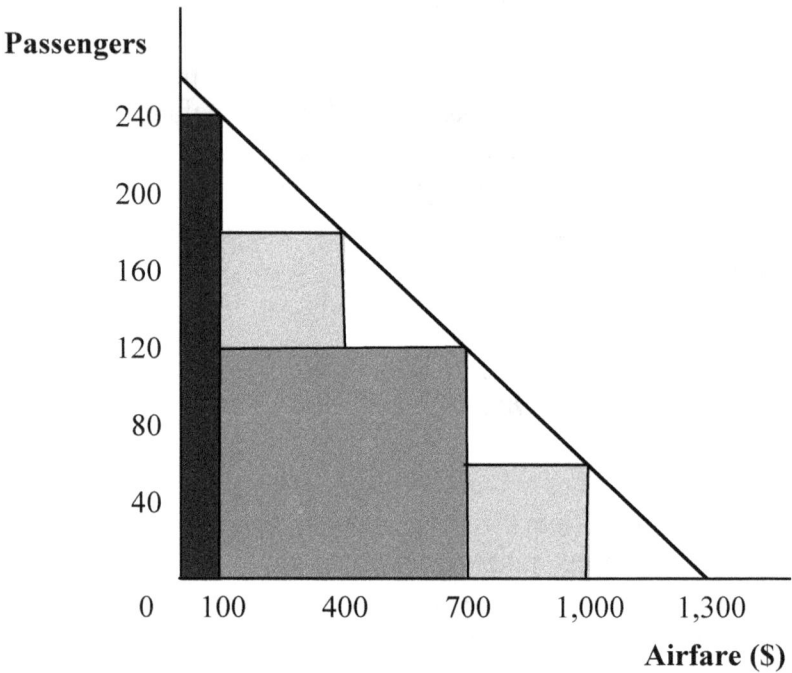

The maximum potential total contribution from this particular flight would be $K_p = \frac{1}{2} \times (\$1,300 - \$100) \times 240 = \$144,000$. If the airline set its price at $700, which is halfway between $100 and $1,300, it would maximize its contribution at $K = (\$700 - \$100) \times 120 = \$72,000$. This area, indicated by the large dark square, represents just 50% of the maximum potential contribution K_p. Thus, the "load factor" which is the percentage of capacity utilization is just 0.50. Adding two more classes priced at $400 and $1,000 would add another $K = (\$400 - \$100) \times 60 + (\$1,000 - \$700) \times 60 = \$18,000 + \$18,000 = \$36,000$. (See the two lightly shaded areas in Figure 10-3). Total contribution would therefore be $K = \$72,000 + \$36,000 = \$108,000$ which is 75% of the maximum potential contribution K_p of $144,000 giving a load factor of 0.75.

While the above analysis is useful for demonstrating the advantages of a three-tier seating arrangement, it is not totally realistic because more than the 240 seats would become available if Jubilee flew just one (economy) class. In fact, maximum seating for the 787-8 is about 380 passengers. Thus, the maximum potential contribution from this flight with economy class only would rise to $K = \frac{1}{2} \times (\$1,300 - \$100) \times 380 = \$228,000$. Yet the actual total contribution would be $K = \$600 \times 190 = \$114,000$ which is just $6,000 more than with 3-class seating. The load factor would still be only 0.50 meaning one-half the seats would remain empty.

10.4 "Raising the Flagpole" (RTF)

The reader will recall the discussion in Chapter 8 on pricing strategies and specifically Figure 8-2 showing the demand curves faced by different firms based on industry and market structure. Specifically, a demand curve labeled *monopoly* is shown which is very steep approaching perfectly inelastic demand where the P.E.D. for the product or service is, by definition, perfectly inelastic ($\epsilon = 0$). It was pointed out that while this condition is very desirable because of the very high profits achievable, it was rarely met in practice because of competition and other factors. In fact, firms in a monopoly position often face government scrutiny for possible antitrust violations. There are, however, perfectly legal means by which near-monopoly positions may be achieved.

First of all, let us focus on why such a monopoly position is so desirable. Consider the four linear demand curves of Figure 10-4. These are for different products with the same maximum quantity Q_M that can be sold when the price approaches zero and the same unit variable cost VC_0. The only difference between the four lines is their different price elasticities of demand resulting from the different maximum prices P_M that customers are willing to pay. The four linear curves are in ascending order of inelasticity and labeled P_{M1}-Q_M, P_{M2}-Q_M, P_{M3}-Q_M, and P_{M4}-Q_M so that the first and last are the most elastic and least elastic, respectively.

Figure 10-4
Contribution Maximization by "Raising the Flagpole"

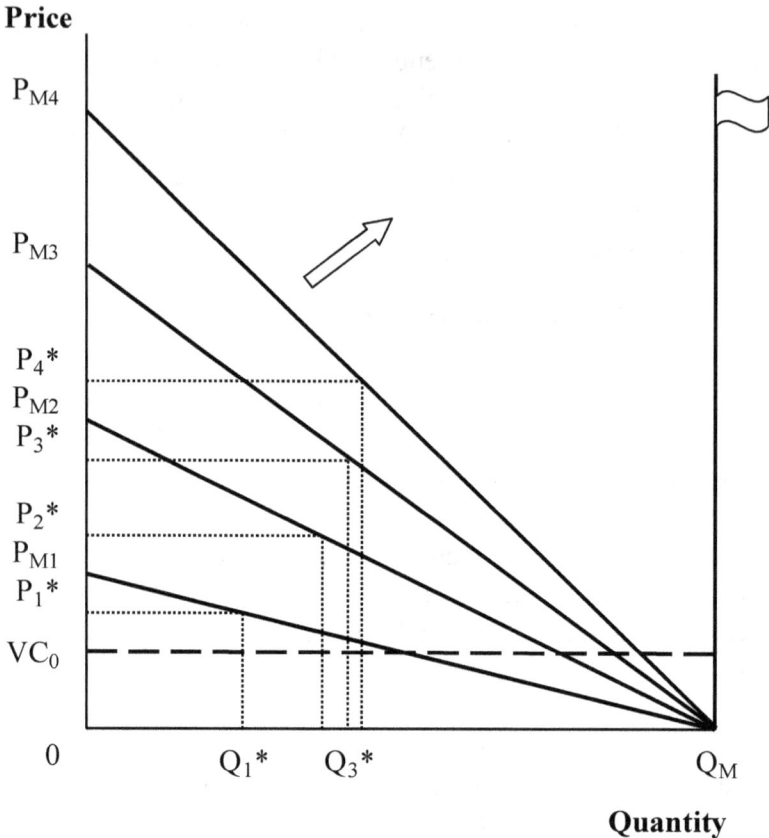

Referring to Figure 10-1, we know that the maximum total contribution achievable for a particular product or service is the area of the triangle formed by its linear demand curve and its unit variable cost line VC_0 and that the optimal price P^* for contribution maximization lies at the midpoint between VC_0 and P_M of each curve. These optimal prices appear in Figure 10-4 as P_1^* through P_4^*.

Clearly noticeable in Figure 10-4 is the fact that as the linear demand curve gets steeper, i.e., rises towards the vertical indicating more inelastic demand, the optimal sell prices also increase from P_1^* to P_4^* meaning that the firm is entitled to charge higher prices.

At the same time, the triangle under each linear demand curve above the unit variable cost VC_0 gets larger as well meaning that the total contribution potential increase proportionately. If one were to look on the linear demand curve as a "flagpole" (for raising the profit banner) one could speak of *raising the flagpole* (RTF).

10.5 Pricing Guidelines (V)

Based on Figures 10-1 and 10-4, the analyses of price optimization for sales revenue and profit maximization, and the illustrative examples, these further generalizations can be made.

Pricing Proposition 6

The optimal prices for sales revenue and profit maximization:

a. The optimal price for revenue maximization will be different from the optimal price for profit maximization so that it is not possible to achieve both sales revenue and profit maximization at the same time.

b. The optimal prices that will maximize both sales revenue and total contribution (profit) are equal only in the special case where the product's unit variable cost is zero.

Pricing Proposition 7

The optimal price for profit maximization is always higher than the optimal price for sales revenue maximization.

Pricing Proposition 8

Sales revenue and profit will be significantly improved when a product or service is offered in two or more versions and associated prices rather than just one version at one price.

Pricing Proposition 9

The more inelastic and steeper (more vertical) the demand

curve for a product, the higher is the optimal price for total contribution maximization and the larger the achievable total dollar contribution (profit) to fixed (overhead) cost and profit.

10.6 RTF Implementation

How then does one "raise the flagpole" to attain these superior results in terms of improved margins and more contribution dollars? Among the measures managers and marketers will want to pay special attention to are such marketing activities as market segmentation, product innovation, product differentiation, patenting, branding, and advertising and sales promotion. Each will be briefly discussed in turn.

10.6.1 Product Differentiation

Historically, differentiating products and services from those of competitors has been the traditional means of meeting buyers' diverse needs and wants, value perceptions, and price expectations. The technique is well-established and profitable and predates some other marketing concepts like market segmentation and value pricing. The object is to make the product or service as unique and different as possible from other products and services on the market. Product differentiation is a more general and less focused approach than found in market segmentation where products and services are developed and marketed specifically for the firm's target market or markets.

Product differentiation became necessary after the same core products became available from different manufacturers. An undifferentiated product is much like a *commodity* with a horizontal demand curve such as the one labeled *perfect competition* in Figure 8-2 of Chapter 8 on pricing strategies. For a business firm it is not an enviable position to be in because it leaves its management with few if any pricing options. Since homogeneous commodity products are viewed as being essentially the same, buyers simply use price as the primary selection criterion.

Products and services differ in their abilities to be differentiated. Some are natural commodities with little opportunity for differentiation such as aspirin, potatoes, or salt. Yet even here, manufacturers attempt to differentiate their products from others on the market. Thus, aspirin maker Bayer (which developed the "wonder drug") promotes "Bayer aspirin" as the real thing. Potatoes are labeled "Idaho potatoes" if they come from that state and it's "Morton salt" that contains the nutrient Iodine. Most products and services, however, are readily differentiated by design, style, size, packaging, and many other factors to ensure that they have steeply downward-sloping rather than more horizontal demand curves.

10.6.2 Market Segmentation

Market segmentation, more fully discussed in Section 10.1 above, plays a central role in how well a firm does in the marketplace. If marketing is all about finding a need and filling it at a profit, then finding a segment of the market whose needs and wants have not yet been met and targeting it with an effective marketing mix of strategy variables can be very profitable. Relatively large enterprises are very good at this exercise because they have the marketing and financial resources for identifying new market segments and target markets. Often overlooked by the larger firms are the many market niches made up of customers with special needs and wants that are not part of the mainstream

Niche marketing is very much the province of smaller firms both in the consumer and industrial goods sectors. These often family owned and bank financed businesses are found all over this country, Europe, and Asia. Each has found a small part of the market with specialized needs and wants and has the expertise to develop innovative and unique new products to fill them. Niche markets are often difficult to find and identify but they are there and can be a way for young entrepreneurs to get a start in the business world. *Internet niching* has become a popular way for them to go.

10.6.3 Product Innovation

Strictly speaking, to be called an innovation a product or service should be so unique and different that there is nothing comparable on the market when it is introduced. Among the most successful and popular digital consumer product innovations of the recent past have been the Apple-1 (1976), the videocassette recorder (1976), the digital camera (1976), the compact disc (1979), the camcorder (1981), the cell phone (1984), the Internet (1985), Windows (1985), the digital video disc (1993), high-definition television (1996), the iPhone (2007), and the iPad (2010). Similar developments are found in many other industries and markets.

For most of these products the innovators envisioned a potential market long before the general public expressed any need for or desire to own one. In the case of the personal computer for example, the major computer makers at the time were focused on the business community and long rejected the notion of a computer for home use until Steve Jobs and Steve Wozniak appeared on the scene to prove them wrong. Their innovations opened up huge new markets with billions of dollars in sales and employment opportunities for tens of thousands. Successful innovations typically have the steepest demand curves as customers buy them in large quantities despite the premium prices they command.

More commonly, the term product innovation is applied to the process of bringing out new models and versions of products already on the market. In that sense, innovation has become an imperative for survival for many firms especially in industries and markets of rapidly changing technologies. Product life cycles are getting ever shorter and companies must innovate or risk losing out to more aggressive competitors. Thus, to keep a competitive edge both Apple and Samsung continuously introduce new models of the iPhone and Galaxy smartphones, respectively, while companies in diverse industries serving both the consumer and industrial sectors keep modifying their product offerings to keep up with changes in technology and/or customer wants and tastes.

Not surprisingly, among the world's most successful and profitable companies are also the most innovative including Apple, BMW, Disney, Google, IBM, Microsoft, Proctor & Gamble, Samsung, and SAP. In general, product innovation ensures that demand curves remain inelastic allowing manufacturers and marketers the maximum amount of pricing discretion.

10.6.4 Patents and Trademarks

Patents, trademarks and other intellectual property rights have been called "the crown jewels" of a company. For many firms, especially in the high-tech field, they are the source of most of their economic power. In order to promote inventions and innovation, the United States and most foreign governments grant their citizens an exclusive right to exploit their inventions commercially for a given number of years. In other words, the inventors are granted monopoly powers that would otherwise be violations of the antitrust laws.

In the United States the patent law (Title 35 of the United States Code) is administered by the U.S. Patent and Trademark Office (USPTO). The term for a utility patent is 20 years from the filing date and, in the case of a design patent, 15 years. For the marketer, a product protected by a patent can have a very steep demand curve meaning that it is amenable to premium pricing if there are no close substitutes available on the market.

A trademark is a sign, design, or phrase used to identify and distinguish a particular seller's products or services from those of others. (In the case of a service, it is called a service mark). Trademark law is covered under Title 12 of the United States Code. Trademark registration is not required by law but highly recommended in case of trademark litigation especially in claims of trademark infringement.

In order to qualify for registration, a mark must be *distinctive*. This means it must be i) *arbitrary* or *fanciful* or ii) *suggestive* of the product. A *descriptive* mark may be registrable under certain circumstances but a *generic* mark cannot be. A trademarked product may carry the symbol ™ or, if registered with the USPTO, the symbol ®. A firm is entitled to use a trademark if it was first to use the mark in commerce or was the first to register it. In the highly completive environments firms are commonly in, a trademark can be a valuable asset especially if the company and product or service enjoys a reputation for quality.

10.6.5 Branding

Brands and trademarks are complementary concepts in that a brand is a marketing tool used in promoting a product or service while a trademark is an intellectual property right allowing brands to be bought, sold, or licensed and defended against infringement. While the practice of branding goes back to antiquity such concepts as branding, brand equity, and brand marketing are relatively new.

Branding has been defined as endowing products and services with the power of a brand while *brand equity* is the value added to a trademark as a result of the brand name. Brand names should be i) memorable (easy to remember and recognize), ii) meaningful (relate to the product), iii) likeable (pleasurable), iv) transferable (to other products), v) adaptable (to changing tastes), and vi) protectable (by intellectual property law).[8] The first of these is especially important and the ancient adage *nomen est omen* often applies.

Companies use different strategies in selecting brand names. Some firms simply rely on the company name to identify their products such as Campbell does for its soups. Others choose a brand name for each product category such as Sears which used Kenmore for its appliances and Craftsman for its tools before selling the brands. Still others use individual brand names for their major lines.

Table 10-1

Top Global Brands

Rank	*Forbes*	*Interbrand*
1	Apple	Apple
2	Google	Amazon
3	Microsoft	Microsoft
4	Amazon	Google
5	Facebook	Samsung
6	Coca-Cola	Coca-Cola
7	Disney	Toyota
8	Samsung	Mercedes-Benz
9	Louis Vuitton	McDonald's
10	McDonald's	Disney
11	Toyota	BMW
12	Intel	Intel
13	Nike	Facebook
14	AT&T	IBM
15	Cisco	Nike
16	Oracle	Cisco
17	Verizon	Louis Vuitton
18	Visa	SAP
19	Walmart	Instagram
20	GE	Honda
21	Budweiser	Chanel
22	SAP	J.P. Morgan
23	Mercedes-Benz	American Express
24	IBM	UPS
25	Marlboro	IKEA
26	Netflix	Pepsi
27	BMW	Adobe
28	American Express	Hermés
29	Honda	GE
30	L'Oreal	YouTube

In the luxury segment of the auto industry, for example, General Motors has its Cadillac, Ford its Lincoln, Toyota its Lexus, and Volkswagen its Audi brands. Table 10-1 is a recent listing of the top thirty brands as compiled by *Forbes* magazine and *Interbrand,* a brand consultancy, with each using its own rating criteria.[9] While there are some differences as to the exact ranking of each brand, there is nevertheless a general consensus on which brands are the most popular and powerful.

Both the owners of brands and customers benefit from branding. Recognized and popular brands can create intense emotional bonds with customers leading to strong brand loyalties. Since buyers are familiar with and trust a favorite brand, the risk is substantially reduced.

In summary, branding is a powerful means of gaining a competitive advantage because brand loyalty effectively creates a barrier to competitor entry when buyers consider their options among competing brands. Most importantly, in a pricing context, brand-loyal customers are willing to pay premium prices. From pricing studies and everyday experience we know that these price differentials can be very substantial.

10.6.6 Advertising and Sales Promotion

A strong and popular brand supported by an imaginative and effective advertising and sales promotion effort is a winning combination that can result in an unusually strong competitive advantage. The reason is that this third element in the mix of marketing strategy variables can substantially increase perceived value in the brand and the underlying products and services and help "raise the flagpole" which we have decided is the gateway to higher profits. Advertising and sales promotion are two communication platforms that are part of *marketing communication* which also includes special events, public relations, direct and interactive marketing, word-of-mouth, and personal selling.

Advertising is by far the most important of these platforms and includes various media types each with its own advantages and limitations. Kotler and Keller identify eleven of these:[10] Newspapers, television, direct mail, radio, magazines, outdoor, yellow pages, newsletters, brochures, telephone, and the Internet. Newspapers are cited for their timeliness and good market coverage but suffer from a short life and a small "pass-along" audience. Magazines have the advantage of a long life and good "pass-along" readership but are disadvantaged by long ad purchase lead times.

Television and the Internet are especially important. Television, the most popular advertising medium, combines sight, sound and motion to attract attention but has the limitation of only fleeting exposure and a high absolute cost. The Internet, according to the authors, benefits from relatively low cost plus interactive possibilities but suffers from a still low usage rate in some countries.

All marketing communication efforts are designed to guide a prospective buyer through the various stages of the buying process from unawareness of the company's brand or brands to awareness, to liking, to preference, to purchase intention, and finally to actual purchase. As companies attempt to rise above the din of the marketplace with thousands of brands vying for buyer attention, they are willing to spend huge amounts on advertising their products and services. Companies around the globe, especially those in consumer products industries, spend billions of dollars annually advertising their products and services. These expenditures my range from 1% to over 5% of annual sales revenue with 3% being an average.

Managements are reluctant to divulge their advertising expenditures mostly for competitive reasons. Another reason may be an attempt to promulgate the idea that their products and services are so sought-after and desirable that they practically sell themselves. That is, of course, not the case by far. In fact, a look at Table 10-1 of the top brands above also identifies the biggest advertisers. Among these are Amazon, Disney, Google, McDonald's, Mercedes-Benz, Samsung, and Toyota. Each has an annual advertising budget estimated at anywhere from $2 to $5 billion.

Undoubtedly many of these advertising outlays produce no or only marginal benefits for anyone except for the advertising agencies themselves. John Wanamaker, an early marketing pioneer, once lamented, "I know half the money I spend on advertising is wasted but the trouble is I don't know which half." Most managements find themselves in a similar situation.

With the huge amounts of money involved, it behooves corporate executives and managers to closely monitor their advertising agencies so that their advertising budgets are not used as a slush fund to be spent as the agencies please. Managers should at all times know how much money is being spent and where and for what specific purpose. The planned and actual results should then be compared and, where necessary, changes implemented. It is important to remember that the yearly advertising budget is an indirect fixed (overhead) cost that directly impacts the bottom line.

Notes

1. Thomas Nagle and Georg Müller, *The Strategy and Tactics of Pricing*, 171.

2. Philip Kotler, *Marketing Management*, 165-166.

3. Philip Kotler and Kevin Keller, *Marketing Management*, 213-227.

4. Thomas Nagle and Georg Müller, supra at 95-103.

5. For a proof, see "Formula Derivations" in the Appendix.

6. Ibid.

7. See https://en.wikipedia.org/wiki/Boeing_787 Dreamliner.

8. Philip Kotler and Kevin Keller, supra at 246.

9. Forbes magazine publishes an annual list of the world's 100 most valuable brands. All brands must have a presence on the American market to be included. The brand value for first-ranked Apple is estimated at $241 billion, for tenth-ranked McDonald's $46 billion, and for last-ranked Volkswagen $8 billion. See "Forbes The World's Most Valuable Brands - 2020 Ranking" at https://www.forbes.com/powerful-brands/list/3/. Interbrand, the global brand consultancy, compiles a yearly list of the world's top 100 brands

based on brand value. According to the Interbrand listing, top-ranked Apple has an estimated brand value of $323 billion, tenth-ranked Disney comes in at $41 billion, and last-ranked Zoom at $4 billion. See "These Are The 100 Best Global Brands 2020 According to 'Interbrand'" at http://www.entertales.com/100-best-global-brands-2020-interbrand/.

10. Philip Kotler and Kevin Keller, supra at 507.

CHAPTER

11

Price Competition

Price-cutting—a price-setters nightmare...Once price-cutting starts, many firms usually get hurt and few, if any, benefit.[1]

In the previous chapter we considered the various options available to the marketer for improving the profitability of products and services already on the market as well as for increasing the likelihood that a new product or service will be profitable. It was proposed that these goals could be achieved by increasing the slope of the respective demand curves to reduce price sensitivity thereby allowing the marketer more pricing discretion. These measures are also designed to prevent price from becoming the dominant marketing strategy variable since direct price competition is known to lead to less than optimal results for most of the competing firms.

The focus of the present chapter is on competitors and competition including no-holds-barred price wars. Managers and marketers, unfortunately, often use price to achieve market share goals instead of paying more attention to the other well-known means to increase profitability. To gain more insights we shall examine the important relationships between price, sales revenue, market share, and profitability using quantitative techniques including some easy to understand graphs and formulas. The reasons for the fixation by managers on market share will be discussed as well as ruinous price wars that are often the outcome of extreme price cuts. The chapter ends with some price-based profit-enhancing methods in common use.

11.1 The Profit Impact of a Price Reduction

Marketers may decide to reduce the price of a product or service for any number of reasons but few realize how big the impact on profits can be even for relatively modest price drops of less than 10%. The actual impact depends on the product's price elasticity of demand and its percentage unit contribution margin. The impact for larger price reductions is proportionally higher and can reach astounding numbers.

Table 11-1 shows the profit impact of price reductions for unit contribution margins CM_0 of 20%, 50%, and 80% and five price elasticities of demand, P.E.D.s, from 1.0 to 5.0.[2] The table gives the percentage changes in total contribution (profit) as a result of three incremental price reductions, namely, 10%, 20%, and 30%. From this listing, it is apparent that price cuts for products with small percentage contribution margins in conjunction with low price elasticities of demand can significantly lower total contribution and profit. Thus, even in the case of a relatively high CM_0 of 50% and a P.E.D. of 2.0, the drop in total contribution dollars for the three price cuts amounts to 4%, 16%, and 36%, respectively.

Steep price cuts cannot only negatively impact the price-setting firm's performance metrics unless its contribution margins and price elasticities of demand prior to the cut are sufficiently high, they can have negative consequences for all the firms in the industry. As Nagle and Müller have noted: "Price competition is usually a negative-sum game, since the more intense price competition is, the more it can undermine the value of the market over which one is competing....Therefore, price competitors do well to forget what they learned about competing from sports and other positive-sum games, and to try instead to draw lessons from what are, hopefully, less familiar competitive games such as warfare."[3]

Table 11-1
The Impact of a Price Reduction on
Percentage Total Contribution

P.E.D.	CM_0	Price Reduction		
		10%	20%	30%
1.0	20%	(45.0)	(100.0)	(165.0)
	50%	(12.0)	(28.0)	(48.0)
	80%	(3.8)	(10.0)	(18.8)
2.0	20%	(40.0)	(100.0)	(180.0)
	50%	(4.0)	(16.0)	(36.0)
	80%	5.0	5.0	0.0
3.0	20%	(35.0)	(100.0)	(195.0)
	50%	4.0	(4.0)	(24.0)
	80%	13.8	20.0	18.8
4.0	20%	(30.0)	(100.0)	(210.0)
	50%	12.0	8.0	(12.0)
	80%	22.5	35.0	37.5
5.0	20%	(25.0)	(100.0)	(225.0)
	50%	20.0	20.0	0.0
	80%	31.3	50.0	56.3

Unlike price increases, consumers welcome price reductions and, provided these are not large and predatory, competitors do not generally respond aggressively with cuts of their own for comparable products especially if these price adjustments are meant for such benign reasons as retaining existing market share or to temporarily boost sales. The following sections will discuss some of these non-aggressive downward price adjustments.

11.2 Price Reduction to Retain Market Share

As mentioned previously, volume market share (VMS) is very important to automobile manufacturers especially in the United States and guarding this vital metric is often a top priority. Yet demand curves may suddenly shift for diverse reasons requiring immediate action. For example, the country's economy may have taken a downturn, or consumer tastes have changed in the type of

Figure 11-1
A Shift in Demand vs. Sales Revenue

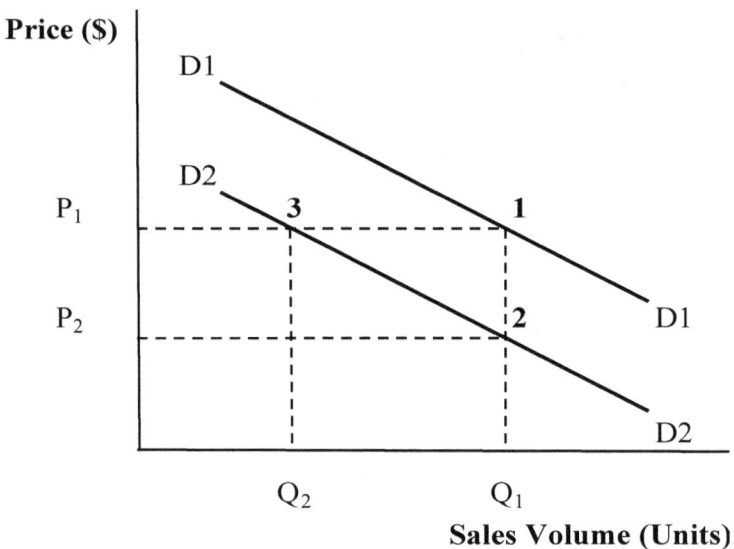

automobiles they buy, or sales have been taken away by a competing model car that recently entered the market. Figure 11-1 demonstrates this situation. The original linear demand curve for this model car, a 4-door sedan, is shown as D1-D1. At the original price-volume operating point (P_1, Q_1), the monthly sales revenue was $R_1 = P_1 \times Q_1$. When consumers demand shifted from sedans to sport utility vehicles the demand curve for this vehicle shifted to D2-D2. In order to maintain its VMS, the manufacturer had to drop its price from P_1 to P_2 for a new monthly sales revenue of $R_2 = P_2 \times Q_1$. Clearly, while sales revenue declined, the important VMS level was maintained.

This was not the only option available to the auto company, of course. If it had been a European one, and especially of luxury vehicles, the response would likely have been entirely different. European managers would have chosen the option indicated by price-volume operating point "3" in Figure 11-2 with a reduced monthly sales revenue of $R_3 = P_1 \times Q_2$. The reasons would have been: i) Fear that discounting their vehicles would result in long-term damage to their brand image, ii) less European concern with market share in lieu of profit margins, and iii) strict labor laws in the European Union that do not permit short-term hiring and laying off of workers to accommodate changes in demand.

Some of the comments coming from European auto executives on this issue are informative. Thus, the CEO of BMW is quoted as saying: "At no time are high discounts compatible with 'premium.' They are neither good for the brand nor good for the business. We have therefore decided to not defend our market share in Germany at any price. Profit comes before volume." The CEO of Porsche expressed similar sentiments: "We have a policy of keeping prices stable to protect our brand and to prevent a drop in prices for used cars. When demand goes down, we reduce production volume but don't lower our prices."[4] In early May 2021 Volkswagen announced that it would no longer compete with Toyota to be the largest car company by volume sales. Instead, the executive stated, the company would devote its efforts to developing electric vehicles.

11.3 Temporary Price Reductions

Temporary price cuts, also known as *price deals*, are benign price-based promotional efforts that are highly popular with marketers and consumers. One can distinguish between general, non-targeted and targeted sales promotions. In non-targeted promotions the product is made available to all buyers while targeted promotions are aimed at more specific ones. Coupon sales are an example of the latter. Both types are meant to appeal to the more price-sensitive segment of a larger product-market.

11.3.1 General Price Promotions

Sometimes sales promotions are run to quickly sell off excess inventory especially if a new model is ready to replace the model offered for sale. At other times price deals are meant to induce trial of a new product or service. In most cases, however, the motivating factor is to quickly boost sales and/or increase market share. Undoubtedly, promotional pricing creates excitement in the marketplace and focuses buyer attention on the product being promoted. These promotions are sure to increase volume market share and, if conditions are right, revenue market share as well. Assuming profitability is also important, the marketer is advised to determine the profit impact of each such promotion. This can be done by inspection of Table 11-1 above or by use of one of the methods previously described that allow the marketer to examine the profit impacts of various price change options, namely, in Chapter 5 (Contribution Analysis) or Chapter 7 (Isoprofit Analysis).

For reasons noted above, price promotions involving products with low unit contribution margins in conjunction with low price elasticities of demand, can be problematic. The higher the CM_0 and P.E.D., the better are the chances for favorable results from promotional price cuts. From the Table 11-1 it is also apparent that all contribution dollars are lost where the percentage price cut is equal to or larger than the product's percentage unit contribution margin regardless of the size of the price elasticity of demand. In other words, anytime the discounted product's price gets lower than the price floor, the unit variable cost, the firm will lose money on each sale of the product.

In some cases a company may willingly take the loss. An example would be if the firm had an obsolete product or excess inventory which it wanted to sell off in order to recoup its investment or save on future carrying costs. Another instance would be if the firm, usually a retailer, wanted to attract customers by selling a product below cost in a practice known as *loss leader pricing.*

Another important consideration concerns the long-term benefits of price promotions. In a well-known paper on the subject, its author found that the resulting benefits are usually as fleeting as the promotion itself. According to this researcher, quoting from an A. C. Nielson publication: "There is overwhelming marketplace evidence that the consumer sales effect is limited to the time period of the promotion itself. A price-off promotion causes sales to rise, but once the promotion stops, they return to their original level."[5] The author, an advertising executive, argued in favor of the long-term superiority of consumer advertising over sales promotions.

Frequent price promotions for the same product or brand are not recommended because these may negatively impact price *credibility* and integrity. It is important that prices not fluctuate too much or too often and remain credible. Otherwise, the promotional price will become the customer's new reference price and he or she will not buy until the next deal has come around. At that time the customer will buy in large quantities and stock up to have enough product on hand until the next promotion. This practice of hoarding promotional items is obviously inconsistent with a seller's need for consistent sales revenue and total contribution dollars.

11.3.2 Coupon Sales

Another popular type of sales promotion involves *coupons* which entitle a customer to buy a product or service at a discounted price when presented at the cash register during a sale. According to a study by a major consumer products company, over 7% of household goods by volume were purchased with a coupon.[6] Coupons are an effective segmentation technique because the time and effort required in searching for, clipping, organizing, and redeeming coupons will appeal only to the most price-sensitive segment of a larger product-market while less price-sensitive customers will continue to pay the full price. The marketer's challenge is to get the coupons to preferred target audiences, namely, present users who will hopefully buy more of the product as well as consumers who can be induced to buy the product for the first time.

Coupons have several advantages over on-shelf price cuts. The ability to target select customer groups through judicious media selection for coupon placement is one of them. Newspapers, magazines, flyers etc. are all targeted at different audiences and coupons should obviously appear where the target buyers are best reached. Another coupon advantage is that competitors are not as easily alerted to specific deals and therefore less likely to react. Thus, coupons represent a form of stealth price cutting that falls under the competitors' radar. In addition, the product's reference price is not likely to be affected because coupons are less conspicuous than an advertised or on-shelf price reduction. Customers will therefore not permanently associate the coupon price with the product. Finally, with coupon sales there is less opportunity for product hoarding because a coupon is normally good for one or a few items only.

11.4 Price Wars

A large-scale, across-the-board price cut by a firm, especially one that is part of an oligopoly, can lead to a price war among its members. Such cuts are sufficiently large to go beyond the customary proactive and reactive pricing practices engaged in between competitors to maintain or marginally increase sales revenue and profits for one or a limited number of products. It also does not concern companies which have adopted a penetration pricing strategy as a business philosophy and practice it, usually based on a cost or logistics advantage, on a consistent basis. In *severe price competition*, companies aggressively use price as a competitive weapon to substantially increase sales revenue and market share at the expense of one or more competitors.

The factors favoring severe price competition among firms serving the same market include these ten:

* The industry is part of an oligopoly in which a few firms control most of the market for a given product class.

* The industry has high fixed and small unit variable costs.

* Industry growth rate is low so that for an individual firm to grow its sales it must take market share from a competitor.

* Firms in the industry have excess inventory which they want to dispose of.

* The product is frequently purchased and a necessary staple or needed to maintain a certain lifestyle.

* Customers are highly price sensitive, i.e., the product's price elasticity of demand is high

* Customers perceive the product offerings of competitors to be homogeneous and not significantly differentiated from each other.

* Brand loyalty is at a minimum and switching between brands does not involve any risk or extra cost to the buyer.

* Company advertising and sales promotion focus on price to the exclusion of product features and benefits.

* In the case of commercial or industrial goods, quality and performance are assured by industry or national standards that require certification before being offered for sale.

In such situations, with depressed sales, market shares, and profits, marketers have often settled on the price variable as a quick and easy fix knowing that price cuts are easily implemented and, if necessary, reversed while the impact on performance is immediate and significant. More often than not, however, these actions have magnified rather than solved any problems. While a price cut will lead to an increase in sales volume for almost all products and an increase in sales revenue if conditions are right, profit is likely to suffer as was shown in Table 11-1 above.

Price wars among members of an oligopoly are an ever-present danger. Such contests can be ruinous not only to individual firms but to the entire industry as a whole. As Baker et al have noted: "Price wars rarely have any winners—and few survivors are as healthy as they were before the wars broke out. Their destruction is often so severe and long-lasting that the only reliable way to come out ahead is to avoid them altogether."[7] The reason is that the deteriorating price structure during a price war causes sales revenue and profits for the entire industry to shrink while individual firms may be forced into bankruptcy.

11.4.1 Major Historical Conflicts

Price wars often result when the mechanism of price leadership breaks down as was the case in two big contests that are often used as business school case studies. These involved the ready-to-eat (RTE) breakfast cereal and the commercial airline industries.

In the breakfast cereal case, the industry was highly concentrated and profitable when in 1996 a price war broke out among the "big three," namely, Kellogg, General Mills, and the Post division of Kraft Foods. At the time, the three firms had a combined volume market share of about 75% with the industry and price leader Kellogg accounting for 35% followed by General Mills at nearly 25% and Post at 15%. Industry sales were about $8 billion but had seen a steady decline due to wide-spread consumer dissatisfaction with the continual price increases and the rising popularity of substitute breakfast foods. Over a ten-year period food prices had gone up by 45% but cereal prices by twice that amount led by the price leader Kellogg whose management usually cited increasing costs as a justification.

The opening round in the cereals price war was fired in April 1996 when Post defied price leader Kellogg by unilaterally slashing prices by 20% across the board on all 22 of its brands.[8] Kellogg retaliated with a 19% price cut on two-thirds of its brands which was followed by a 11% cut by General Mills. A few months after its price move, Post had increased its market share by 4% while Kellogg had lost an equal share. While Post, according to a top Kraft manager, took a large hit on its profit margins, the company fared better earnings-wise than its competitors because cereals represented just one of

Kraft's 11 divisions. However, with the lower market prices, all competitors were left worse off because the size of the RTE cereals market along with industry earnings had shrunk considerably by the end of the price war.

What has been called "the mother of all price wars" took place in 1992 in the airline industry. Beginning with the Airline Deregulation Act of 1978, this industry saw some tumultuous times including steep fare discounting, high operational costs (jet fuel etc.), and mounting losses. Load factors were only about 60% of capacity and total industry losses in 1991 about $2 billion. In early April 1992, American Airlines, America's largest air carrier, announced a major strategic move designed to return the industry to profitability.

Under American's "value pricing" plan the hodge-podge of fare schemes then in use was replaced by a simple four-tier fare structure: Fist Class, Regular Coach, Discount Coach–7 Day Advance Purchase, and Discount Coach–14-Day Advance Purchase. The latter two, the discount coach fares, were not refundable. Prices were drastically slashed for all four tiers off published list prices and the carrier's number of fares reduced from ½ million to 70,000.[9]

American's management, led by Robert Crandall (see Sec. 8.7, Chapter 8), expected its competitors to follow its lead with similar fare structures. Initially American's two major competitors, Delta Airlines and United Airlines, reluctantly did so but two smaller ones, TWA and USAir, revolted by offering even larger price cuts. These were soon matched by other large carriers including Continental Airlines and Northwest Airlines. In October, American abandoned its version of value pricing after practically all carriers had returned to heavy discounting. The effort to stabilize prices had failed. As industry losses mounted, three of the smaller carriers were operating under Chapter 11 bankruptcy protection. This fare war cost the industry additional billions with American alone losing an estimated $1 billion in 1992.

The top airline executives blamed each other for starting the fare war with Mr. Crandall calling Northwest's response "a monstrous stupidity." "We tried to provide some price leadership but it didn't work, so we are back to death by a thousand cuts," he lamented.[10] John H. Dasburg, CEO of Northwest, saw it differently claiming that American's fare plan was predatory and designed to drive smaller rivals from the market. He did not think much of American's price leadership and found in its value plan "an element of arrogance" and an attempt "to dictate to customers" a long-term pricing structure. In fact, Continental and Northwest sued American in Federal district court under the Sherman Antitrust Act charging attempted monopolization and predation. The plaintiffs claimed damages of $1 billion but lost their suit in August 1993 after a short trial.

11.4.2 Preventing and Containing Price Wars

Price leadership is one of the primary means of preventing price wars but, as we saw in the case of the conflicts in the commercial airline and breakfast cereal industries above, this mechanism does not always work. More often than not, the problem is poor communication between the industry leader and its competitors. According to one paper on price warfare, item one on a company's agenda should be to prevent a war before it starts by revealing the firm's strategic intentions.[11] Accordingly, some time before the contemplated price change, the rationale behind it should be made known to the other members of the oligopoly.

Ideally, only the price leader should initiate major pricing moves and that only after testing the waters. By giving advance notice, the other industry members will have time to evaluate the proposal and respond to it. If the reaction is overwhelmingly negative, the price leader should reconsider. This communication, sometimes known as *signaling*, is not illegal if it does not involve direct communication between competitors but rather takes the form of announcements to the general public.

Rather than answer a competitor's challenge of a major price cut with a similar one, a more prudent approach would be to carefully examine all the price and non-price options available to the firm before acting. Among the factors to be considered are the size and nature of the price cut and whether it is temporary or permanent, the competitor's relative strength or weakness in terms of competitive advantage, the sales, market share, and profits that are put at risk by the price cut, and the benefits versus costs of a possible response. In short, because the stakes are high, the best advice that can be given a marketer is not to initiate price confrontation by predatory price cuts, avoid price competition wherever possible, and proceed with caution in responding to a challenge.

For customers, a price war is, of course, a boon. Is there anyone who does not want to see a significant prices drop especially when prices are perceived to be too high, the amount of discretionary funds available are small and getting smaller, and competitors are willing to part with their goods and services for ever less money? Probably not. However, the good times rarely outlive the price war. Once the dust has settled, the number of viable competitors is likely to have been reduced and those left standing will soon raise prices to pre-war levels to recoup some of their recently incurred losses.

11.5 Market Share and Profitability

One of the central issues in pricing has been the relationship between market share and profit. Specifically, the questions have been, Does an increase in market share in a product or service lead to higher profit for that product or service? More generally, Are firms with high market shares more profitable than ones with low shares?

11.5.1 The PIMS Project and Its Implications

Before we weigh in on this issue, let us begin by answering the question, What do we mean by market share? There are actually two ways market share may be computed. Often it is not specified which of the two is being used with the result that market share statistics often lead to faulty interpretations.

In *volume market share*, sometimes also known as *unit market share*, the firm's unit sales of a particular product, brand, or model are compared to the number of units sold by all competitors of similar products, brands, or models in the entire market served during a particular time frame. *Volume market share* is defined as:

$$\text{VMS (\%)} = \frac{\text{Company Sales (units)}}{\text{Total Market Sales (units)}} \times 100\% \quad \text{Eq. (11.1)}$$

VMS is popular in the automobile industry and others to assess the relative popularity of certain brands and models and the business pages of major newspapers often list monthly unit sales of these various brands and models together with their market shares. For example, in the month of June Ford Motor Company may have had a market share of x% of all passenger cars sold in the United Sates while in the sport utility vehicle (SUV) category, to which the particular vehicle belongs, the company's unit market share may have been y%.

Revenue market share, on the other hand, compares the firm's sales revenue for a product, brand, or model to dollar sales generated by all competitors of identical products, brands, or models in the market served during a specific time frame. Revenue market share is defined as:

$$\text{RMS (\%)} = \frac{\text{Company Sales (dollars)}}{\text{Total Market Sales (dollars)}} \times 100\% \quad \text{Eq. (11.2)}$$

For many industries, the denominators of Equations (11-1) and (11.2) are readily obtained from a number of sources including industry trade associations, business publications, Thomasnet, industry-specific researchers, and investment houses.

Volume market share cannot be used as a direct indicator of profitability because there is no direct relationship between the two. In fact, the VMS is entirely a function of the price elasticity of demand and can be raised by simply lowering the price. It can also be traded much like corporate stock—"bought" by lowering the price and "sold" by raising it. As the price is lowered to raise the VMS, the price floor, represented by the unit variable cost, is eventually reached and exceeded meaning that there are little or no contribution dollars generated and operations will become unprofitable. In other words, a high VMS for a product or service does not ensure that it is also profitable.

Unlike volume market share, *revenue market share* can be an indicator of profitability. Less apparent is whether the pursuit of RMS will necessarily lead to high contribution and profit. The prevalent belief that large market shares are a prerequisite to long-term profit is based on a major study done in the early 1970s and published in the *Harvard Business Review*. In that study researchers used the data base of the Profit Impact of Market Strategies (PIMS) project of the Marketing Science Institute and concluded that "There is no doubt that market share and return on investment (ROI) are strongly related." To support this assertion, the paper includes a chart showing a straight-line relationship between RMS (ranging from about 10% to 40%) and pre-tax ROI (10% to 30%).[12]

These researchers sought to explain "the high rate of return enjoyed by large-share businesses" by citing three primary factors: i) Economies of scale in procurement, manufacturing, marketing, and other cost components plus the "experience curve," ii) increased market power which allows firms to bargain more effectively and to "administer" prices leading to significantly higher ones, and iii) quality management because good managers are successful in achieving high market shares and skillful in controlling costs and getting maximum productivity from employees. According to the authors, "It is now widely recognized that one of the main determinants of business profitability is market share. Under most circumstances, enterprises that have achieved a high share of the markets they serve are considerably more profitable than their smaller-share rivals."

Predictably, when the news that high market share and company profitability are positively correlated began circulating among members of the business community, there was an immediate push by managers to gain market share in the product-markets they were in. The CEO of General Electric, Jack Welch, was quoted as saying that he would get out of any business in which GE could not attain the number one or two position in terms of market share. This drive to grow sales without regard to anything else in the hope of increased long-term profit was rarely successful and led many companies to utter ruin. Yet the fixation on market share persists to this day and is a recurring topic in the pricing literature.

Among the pricing experts, consultants, and authors who have dealt with this issue and specifically in relation to PIMS, the most prominent have been Nagle and Müller: "A common myth among marketers is that growing market share is the key to profitability... The source of this myth is a demonstrable correlation between market share and profitability. But as any student of statistics should know, correlation does not necessarily imply a causal relationship. A far more plausible explanation for the correlation is that both profitability and market share are caused by the same underlying source of business success: a sustainable competitive advantage in meeting customer needs more effectively or in doing so more efficiently."[13]

Simon and Fassnacht write: "In our view, what matters is not the absolute level of the market share but how a company achieves its market share. If that market share comes through aggressive prices without a correspondingly low-cost base, then a company has 'bought' that market share at the expense of its profit margins...If the company achieves its high market share through innovation and quality at appropriate prices, then margins and profits are healthy and aligned. The high profit in turn allows the company to make additional investments in innovation and product quality."[14]

11.5.2 Issue Resolution by Graphical Analysis

The Nagel and Müller contention that high market share and profitability are both the result of a competitive advantage finds support by examining the impact of a product's unit variable cost on the optimal prices for sales revenue and contribution maximization. This may be done by use of Figure 11-2, which is based on Figure

Figure 11-2
The Market Share and Profitability Relationship

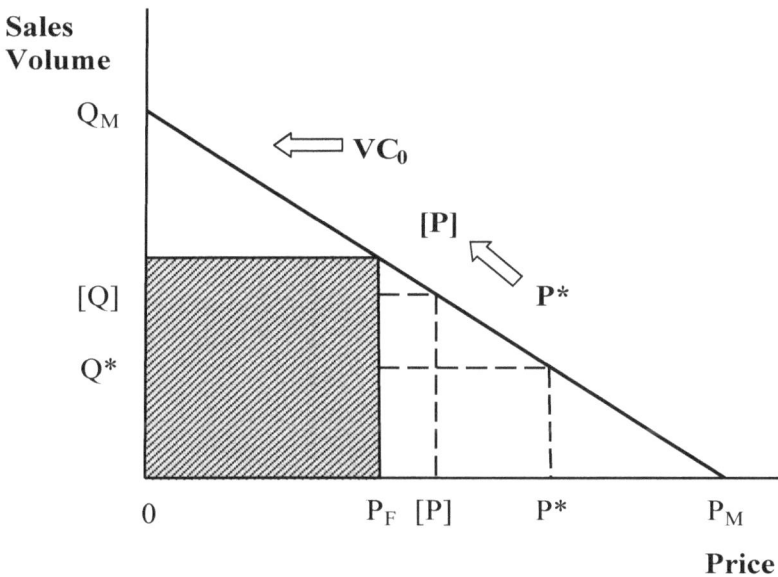

10-1 of Chapter 10. As previously shown, on the price response curve labeled P_M-Q_M the optimal price [P] for sales revenue maximization is located at the midpoint of the PRC. Similarly, the optimal price P* for total contribution maximization is found at the midpoint of that portion of the PRC to the right of the unit variable cost VC_0 (the price floor P_F) Clearly, as VC_0 moves toward zero (the origin), as indicated by the upper arrow, P* moves along the PRC towards [R], as indicated by the lower arrow, until the two price optima meet.

With [P] = P*, both sales revenue and total contribution have reached their peak values. Since a high sales revenue is equivalent to a high RMS for the product, it follows that when unit variable cost is zero, maximum sales revenue, maximum revenue market share, and maximum total contribution (profit) occur at the same price point. In other words, by reducing and holding down this product's unit variable cost, management will simultaneously achieve three maxima, namely, sales revenue, revenue market share, and total contribution (profit). Incidentally, a mathematical analysis leads to the same result as will be shown later in this book.

If the company is able to duplicate this feat with most of its product line, it will indeed be in the enviable position of enjoying both high market shares and superior profits. Clearly then, the relationship between company profits and market share the PIMS researchers found is not merely correlative but causal.

11.6 Pricing Guidelines (VI)

Based on Figure 11-2 and the foregoing analysis the following additional pricing proposition can be offered:

Pricing Proposition 10

Revenue market share and profitability,

a. As a product's unit variable cost decreases towards zero its optimal prices for sales revenue (market share) and total contribution (profit) maximization approach each other so that a product with a large revenue market share also tends to be highly profitable.

b. For products whose unit variable costs are near zero, efforts to maximize sales revenue will also maximize total contributions and profits.

c. A firm whose line of products enjoys high revenue market shares tends to be more profitable than a firm whose products have smaller revenue market shares.

A unit variable cost of zero is obviously an ideal that cannot be fully achieved in practice. What all this means, nevertheless, is that firms which can approach it can achieve both maximum market share and profit at the same time without sacrificing one for the other. Clearly, businesses with low direct and overhead costs enjoy an important competitive advantage over other firms in their industry.

In the American consumer retail business, Walmart and Costco are prime examples of cost-efficient operations. Each enjoys both exceptional market shares and profits. Besides its markup on costs, Costco charges an annual membership fee which brings in large sums of additional cash with little added cost. E-commerce giant Amazon, founded in 1994 to sell books online, had long been unprofitable but has become so by changing its business model. It is now using the huge amounts of data it collects to continuously adjust its prices to maximize profits. In early 2005, the company started Amazon Prime which is a paid subscription program for added services by which substantially more income is generated to add to the company's profitability.

11.7 Profit-Enhancing Measures

In business-to-business and consumer markets, a number of easily implemented techniques are available to improve the bottom line. Four among these involve effectively dealing with the pocket price waterfall, power buyers, ad hoc pricing, and sales force compensation.

11.7.1 Managing the Pocket Price Waterfall

Most every business-to-business sales transaction shows a significant variance between the *list* or *base price* which is the price the seller has set for the particular product or service and the *pocket price*, also known as the *transaction price*, which is the actual amount of money received by the seller. Separating the two prices is a series of discounts and rebates that result in significant amounts of lost revenue and profit. In a well-known study McKinsey's Marn and Rosiello have called this phenomenon the *pocket price waterfall*.[15]

Figure 11-3
The Pocket Price Waterfall

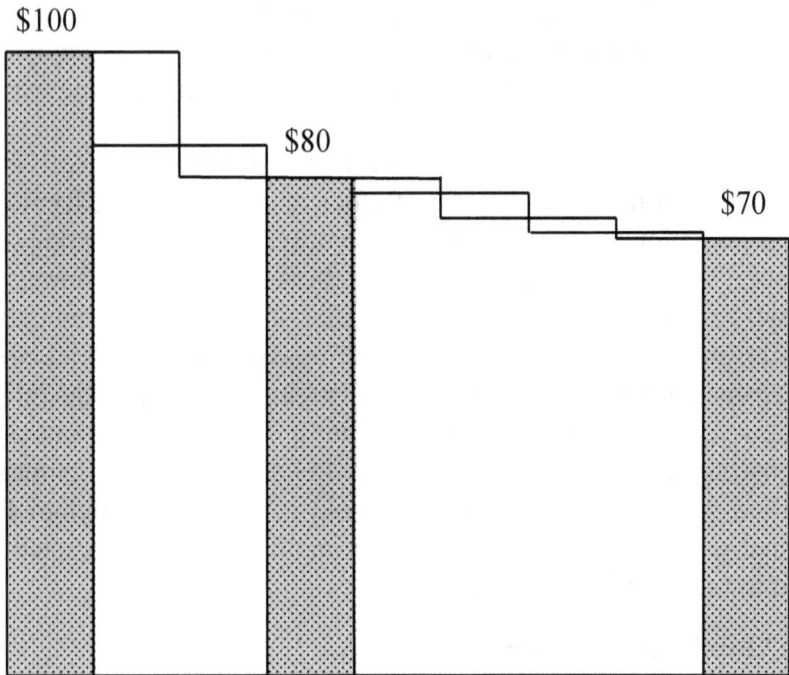

$100

$80

$70

| Base | *Dist.* | *Order* | Inv. | *Cash* | *Coop* | *Spec.* | *Shipm.* | Pocket |
| Price | *Disc.* | *Size* | Price | *Disc.* | *Adv.* | *Allow.* | *Allow.* | Price |

This writer's version of a pocket price waterfall is illustrated in Figure 11-3. In practice the size of the waterfall would, of course, depend on a firm's exact discount structure. The seller in this hypothetical example is a manufacturer of automobile components while the customer is one of its stocking distributors who, in turn, sells the merchandise to auto parts stores. The price of this auto part has been set at $100 which is here called the *base price*. This particular customer is entitled to a 15% ($15.00) distributor discount plus an additional order-size discount of 5% ($5.00) bringing the invoice price to $80.00. In addition, the distributor is allowed several off-invoice discounts and rebates, namely, i) a 3% ($2.40) discount for early payment, ii) a cooperative advertising allowance of 5% ($4.00) for local advertising, iii) a special merchandising discount of 3% ($2.40), and a 1.5% ($1.20) freight allowance. This brings the payable pocket price to $70.00. The total price reduction or *pocket discount* is therefore $30.00 or 30%.

Each of these discount and rebate elements represents a *revenue leak* according to the authors which should be fixed. Typically this auto parts manufacturer would have other customers and channels of distribution with each calling for a different pricing and discount structure. Among these would be original equipment manufacturers (OEMs), and specifically auto companies, as well as other large-volume buyers such as auto parts retail chains. Consequently, this particular part would not have just one pocket price but a whole range of such prices from close to the list price on one end to near the price floor, i.e., the product's unit variable cost, on the other. The authors have labeled this range of pocket prices the *pocket price band*. It can be surprisingly and unreasonably large. The authors found companies in diverse industries with pocket price bands ranging from 60% to 500%!

It is these authors' contention, as supported by many actual examples, that actively managing pocket prices and pocket price bands offers a unique opportunity for sales revenue and profit improvements which had hitherto received scant attention from managements. Specifically, they propose systematic transaction price management with the objective of achieving the best net realized price for every order or transaction.

In one case, a manufacturer of home appliances, changes in the discount structure to reduce leakage resulted in an increase in the average pocket price levels of 3.5% and a 60% operating profit gain. Some discounts and allowances needed to be repositioned on the discount chain, or reduced or eliminated altogether where they produced no significant benefits.

The authors recommend that top managements set quantifiable leakage reduction goals for each element in the pocket price waterfall and monitor the results for each major product line on a quarterly basis. Furthermore, according to the authors, pocket price should be the only yardstick employed in evaluating products, customers, and individual transactions and that all revenue and profitability calculations should be based on pocket prices. In *Pricing the Profitable Sale*, the unit contribution margin CM, expressed either in dollars or percentages, has been a cornerstone of our profitability analyses. Clearly, in computing this metric it is most important that an average *transaction* (final) price be used and not a list price, manufacturer's suggested retail price (MSRP), or invoice price. Otherwise the CM will be overstated, i.e., the product will seem more profitable than it is and the computed results wrong or misleading.

11.7.2 Dealing with Power Buyers

Power buyer is a term used by Nagle and Müller for a firm whose volume purchases give it sufficient leverage to extract the lowest prices and most favorable terms and conditions from its suppliers. [16] One purchase agent at such a power buyer reportedly told one of its suppliers that he expected him (the supplier) to sell him their products near cost and to find his profit elsewhere. Power buyers are prevalent in highly competitive industries such as the auto industry. Many mass-merchandisers such as Costco, The Home Depot, Lowe's, Target, OfficeMax, Staples, and Walmart fall into this power buyer category as well.

Buyers and purchase agents for power buyers tend to be highly sophisticated, skilled, and aggressive and often not above using bully tactics to get their way. Their information resources on competing suppliers and experience in dealing with these make them formidable adversaries. In short, power buyers tend to play hardball and supplier managements must learn to play the same game and not be overly intimidated. Dealing with power buyers calls for special strategies and tactics.

A question any company's management must ask itself is whether to deal with a power buyer in the first place. Unit contribution margins are sure to be low because the power buyer will not allow a firm to capture the full value its products or services represent to him. This does not mean, of course, that the supplier to a power buyer cannot ever make a profit. It is only more difficult.

This point can easily be shown by inspection of the contribution formula given originally by Equation 3.8 of Chapter 3:

$$K = (P - VC) \times Q = CM \times Q \qquad \text{Eq. (11.3)}$$

where K is the total dollar contribution, P the sell price, VC the product's unit variable cost, CM the unit contribution margin, and Q the number of units sold. Clearly, with a low price, the product's unit variable cost must necessarily be very small, the resulting unit contribution margin high, and the quantity also high, for significant contributions to fixed cost and profits to be realized. Successful suppliers to power buyers must consequently enjoy a cost advantage over competitors and have large production capacities.

Sellers are not completely at the mercy of such buyers, however, because they will have leverage over them in proportion to the uniqueness of their product. Most vulnerable to pricing pressures will be makers of undifferentiated commodity products because the power buyer will have multiple sources of supply. A prime example would be a standardized auto part. A maker of a more differentiated and unique product, on the other hand, would have some leverage while the supplier of a sought-after name brand product would have the most.

Consider, for example, a branded product such as a Braun electric shaver or coffee maker. Braun products are known for style and quality and can command premium prices. A firm like Braun would have considerable leverage in its sales to one or more power buyers because the brand adds prestige and luster to that buyer's product selection and the manufacturer would therefore not be subject to the oppressive tactics that a power buyer might employ with other firms. Interestingly, Braun appliances are not only sold at high-end stores but a number of discount chains as well. In order to avoid cannibalization of its own products, the company typically offers special product versions for this price-sensitive segment of the market reserving its premium lines for specialty stores where higher prices and contribution margins are achievable.

Where the firm is being squeezed on price to the extend that margins are disappearing, it is sometimes necessary to consider just walking away from such a buyer. Management should never let itself become so completely dependant on a power buyer's business that the company's survival is at stake if the relationship is broken. If the firm has other and more favorable options for generating revenue and total contribution, it should not hesitate to so inform the power buyer and stand its ground. More often than not, the power customer will accede to the seller's price proposal because it cannot get a better deal elsewhere, despite claims to the contrary, or the cost of switching suppliers will be unacceptably high.

11.7.3 Ad Hoc Pricing

Another means of enhancing profitability is by eliminating *ad hoc* or spur of the moment price decisions in response to price objections from customers. Such price concessions can significantly erode profit performance especially if it has become routine. The difference between reactive, ad hoc price negotiation and pro-active, policy-based price negotiation has been extensively treated by Nagle and Müller.[17] In a typical scenario, a buyer is unhappy with a price quotation and calls someone he or she knows at the seller to get a better deal. This may require several calls to ever higher management levels until the right individual is found.

The customer's purchasing agent is now a hero because of the clout he or she has demonstrated in getting the lowest price while the seller executive has been able to show clout in being able to overrule several lower levels of management. But business transactions should not be about clout and instead about basic economics. While personal relationships are undoubtedly very important in the business world, these should enhance profitability for the firms involved and not undermine it.

The answer to ad hoc pricing is a strong pricing policy that is adhered to throughout the organization. This policy should cover all contingencies including the criteria for price concessions, who may grant them and to whom, by how much a price may be lowered, and what conditions apply. Ideally, only one person in the organization should be authorized to give price concessions and that individual should be the one with overall profit and loss responsibility or a designated representative.

An effective pricing policy will shield all levels of management from outside pricing pressure and uphold the firm's price credibility and integrity so that customers will have no expectation of further price concessions as a result of their lobbying efforts. Most importantly, a pricing policy will help assure that quarterly and yearly sales revenue and profitability goals are met. Where a pricing policy consistently leads to loss of sales revenue and profits, it should obviously be revised and other options considered but ad hoc price concessions should never be among these.

11.7.4 Sales Force Compensation

Most pricing consultants and authors agree that one of the most effective ways for a business to make sure that its value message is delivered and implemented is by compensating its sales force not based on sales volume or revenue but at least in part on the profitability of such sales.

Profitability and the Sales Force

In his work as an early pricing consultant, Spencer Tucker found that "In client companies where commission is paid on contribution, there has been a complete turnabout in profits."[18] As the author noted, if a company pays a flat commission on sales revenue, it serves notice that all sales revenue has the same value. This is clearly not so—sales revenue with larger total contribution content is obviously more valuable to the firm than one with a smaller one. This being the case, why should the reward for high and low-margin sales be the same? Besides not optimizing profits, pushing sales revenue has the added disadvantage of skewing the mix of products sold due to a salesperson's natural inclination to concentrate on products whose sale requires the least amount of time and effort.

To Dale Furtwengler, a pricing consultant and author, product markets are composed of price buyers and value buyers. A price buyer asks for the price first while a value buyer asks the price after having first determined that the product is right for him or her. "A value seller likes to maximize revenue, or profit dollars, on each sale by getting higher prices for the value provided... Conversely, a price seller in a value environment will feel pressure to sell up— to get better prices. That goes against this individual's nature and creates performance expectations he or she isn't likely to meet."[19] This has ramifications, according to Furtwengler, on the type of sales force required and the relative costs involved in training and motivating personnel of different sales backgrounds.

A professional salesperson does not talk price but value. This means that the employee must be able to communicate value to the customer by convincing him or her that the product offering will meet that customer's needs better than a competing brand. For this to happen, salespeople have to understand not only their company's own product offerings and their uses but that of their major competitors as well and, additionally, be fully informed how the product is being used and valued by their customers. In other words, salespeople must be more than order takers and be able to think like their customers and, where possible, put themselves in their place. This takes time and effort which, in turn, should be encouraged by a suitable rewards system.

A New Compensation Formula

A program that encourages profit-oriented sales should be fair and equitable and also easy to implement. A number of formulas for this purpose can be found in the literature. One proposed by Nagle and Müller, for example, allows the computation of a *sales credit* for each sale that depends on the particular product's percentage contribution margin and the difference between the target and actual prices achieved.[20]

Another and more direct approach would have the firm compute a salesperson's incentive bonus or, in the case of straight commission earnings, the weekly or monthly commissions earned for all of her or his sales during a specific time period based on the salesperson's sales revenue and total contribution. In this yet untested proposal, for each salesperson and each sale two quantities would be recorded—the actual sales revenue and the total contribution generated by this sale. (Both sets of data should be readily available from the firm's accounting department). At the end of the commission period (week or month), the sum total of the salesperson's sales revenues and total contributions for all his or her sales would be determined and the following formula applied to these two totals:

$$E = (R + w \times K) \times k \qquad \text{Eq. (11.5)}$$

where,
E = Earnings (\$)
R = Sales revenue (\$)
K = Total contribution (\$)
w = Weighing factor ($w > 0$)
k = Scaling factor ($k > 0$)

Total contribution, it may be recalled, is the difference between sales revenue and total variable cost. The weighing factor "w" would allow the total contribution to carry more, the same, or less weight than the sales revenue. The scaling factor "k" would allow management to adjust the earnings rate from a small commissions bonus to all-commissions earnings in lieu of a salary.

Example

Peter and Elke are salespeople at Plunkett Home Furnishings. March sales revenue for Peter was $100,000 with $25,000 in total contribution dollars earned while Elke had the same sales revenue but $50,000 in total contribution. Using weighing and scaling factors of 2.0 and 0.002, respectively, in Equation (11.5) the March bonus dollars earned by Peter and Elke would be:

Peter: E = ($100,000 + 2.0 × $25,000) × 0.002 = $300
Elke: E = ($100,000 + 2.0 × $50,000) × 0.002 = $400

Thus, Elke would earn $100 more than Peter in March because of the higher profitability of her sales.

Suppose we wanted to determine March commissions rather than March bonuses using this formula. Raising the scaling factor to 0.025, for example, commissions would be:

Peter: E = ($100,000 + 2.0 × $25,000) × 0.025 = $3,750
Elke: E = ($100,000 + 2.0 × $50,000) × 0.025 = $5,000

Elke's March earnings would again be higher than Peter's because of the higher total contribution content of her sales. Earned commissions would typically go into each salesperson's individual commissions account from which each would receive a *draw* against commissions of a specific amount each payday. This is a common practice in retail to give an employee a consistent monthly income.

11.8 Marketing Intelligence

In an adversarial and competitive business environment good and timely information on competitors and consumers is essential for profitable operations and sometimes even for survival. The collection and evaluation of competitor information especially regarding products and prices is therefore an important business function that should be conducted in a systematic rather than a haphazard manner.

For each major competitor, needed information includes: Company strengths and weaknesses; marketing and pricing goals and strategies; present product and service offerings and associated prices; sales, market shares, and profitability by product; and imminent product and/or price changes. Other vital information concerns technological changes that could pose dangers or opportunities, and shifts and trends in buyer needs and wants.

One of the best sources of reliable marketing intelligence is the firm's own sales force. A company's salespeople are its frontline soldiers and as such among the first to see and hear about a competitor's new products and prices, impending product and/or price changes, quality or delivery problems, and much more. Salespeople should be encouraged to routinely furnish such information on their weekly call reports or in special reports to management.

Loyal customers and members of the firm's distribution chain represent another source of useful information especially if a good working relationship has been cultivated in the past. Trade organizations often collect and publish such statistical data as sales and market shares for the major companies that make up the industry. Much can also be learned at trade shows where competitors come together to showcase their new product offerings. Other sources for competitive information include:

* Statements by company executives

* Company news releases

* Catalogs and price lists

* Product advertisements

* Business newspapers and magazines

* Business sections of daily papers

* Federal and state government statistics

* Annual reports to stockholders

* Financial analysts and stock brokers

* Advertising agencies

Sometimes the same information sources can be used to feed back information to induce competitor conduct favorable to the firm. Care must be taken that it is done in a discrete and lawful manner. What is lawful and what is not is covered in Chapter 15.

Notes

1. Alfred Oxenfeldt, *Pricing Strategies*, 222-223.

2. Table 11-1 is based on the Profit Impact Formula given by Equation (14.1) in Chapter 14:

$$\blacktriangle K = \frac{1}{CM_0} \{- \mathcal{E}_0 (\blacktriangle P)^2 + (1- \mathcal{E}_0 CM_0) \blacktriangle P\}$$

For example, if the product's unit contribution margin before the price change (CM_0) was 20% and the price elasticity of demand at the present price-volume operating point ($\mathcal{E}_0$) was 2.0, a 10% price reduction would cause a 40% reduction in total contribution and profit:

$\blacktriangle K = 1 / 0.20 \times \{- 2.0 (- 0.10)^2 + (1 - 2.0 \times 0.20) (- 0.10)\} = - 0.40$

3. Thomas T. Nagle and Georg Müller, *The Strategy and Tactics of Pricing*, 153.

4. Herman Simon and Martin Fassnacht, *Price Management*, 345.

5. John Philip Jones, "The Double Jeopardy of Sales Promotions," *Harvard Business Review*, September – October 1990, 5.

6. Rafi Mohammed, *The 1% Windfall*, 91

7. Walter L. Baker, Michael V. Marn, and Craig C. Zawada, *The Price Advantage*, 133.

8. Nancy Millman, "Price Wars Spread Into the Cereal Aisle," *Chicago Tribune*, July 1, 1996.

9. Edwin McDowell, "Airlines Tally the Damage From Summer's Fare War," *The New York Times*, Sept. 12, 1992, A1.

10. B. O'Brian, "American Air Launches New Price Sortie," *The Wall Street Journal*, April 21, 1992, B1.

11. Akshay R. Rao, Mark E. Bergen, and Scott Davis, "How to Fight a Price War," *Harvard Business Review on Pricing*, 80.

12. Robert D. Buzzell, Bradley T. Gale, and Ralph G. M. Sultan, "Market Share—A Key to Profitability," *Harvard Business Review*, January 1975, 98, 104. (https://hbr.org/1975/01/market-share-a-key-to-profitability).

13. Thomas T. Nagle and Georg Müller, supra at 154-155.

14. Hermann Simon and Martin Fassnacht, supra at 35.

15. Michael V. Marn and Robert L. Rosiello, "Managing Price, Gaining Profit," *Harvard Business Review on Pricing*, 51-73. For a collection of actual pocket price waterfalls in diverse markets and industries see Walter L. Baker, Michael V. Marn, and Craig C. Zawada, *The Price Advantage*, 307-325.

16. Thomas T. Nagle and Georg Müller, supra at 123-125.

17. Thomas T. Nagle and Georg Müller, supra at 114-118.

18. Spencer A. Tucker, *Pricing for Higher Profit*, 270.

19. Dale Furtwengler, *Pricing for Profit*, 42-43.

20. Thomas T. Nagle and Georg Müller, supra at 278.

CHAPTER

12

Price Optimization

*In maturity, when the source of demand is repeat buyers
and when competition becomes more stable, a firm can
better gauge the incremental revenue from a price
change and discover that a little fine- tuning of price
can significantly improve profits.*[1]

Standard pricing texts do not normally discuss price optimization in any detail although it may receive some cursory coverage. The probable reason is that the topic cannot be gainfully discussed using a non-quantitative approach and a mathematical one could easily lead into a quagmire with complex derivations and formulas that may or may not be useful to a marketer for pricing purposes. Nevertheless, price optimization is important and, in line with the opinion of Simon and Fassnacht that a mathematical one is "the most elegant and precise form of price optimization," we proceed with it although using a less esoteric approach that is no less revealing and useful than that given by these authors.[2]

In this chapter we shall explore different mathematical and graphical techniques available to marketers that will allow them to optimize prices to reach their firms' sales revenue, market share, and profit maximizing goals for their diverse products and services.

What is meant by an optimal price? It is that price that will result in maximum sales revenue, market share, or total contribution (profit) for a particular product or service in a chosen target market. In prior chapters we have stated some of the conditions that must exist for either to occur and whether a price increase or cut is required to achieve these results. This information was summarized in the General Pricing Rule of Thumb (1) of Table 8-1 in Chapter 8 (Pricing Strategies). However, this prior material did not enlighten us as to how much a price must change to achieve optimal results. We are now in a position to answer this question. In other words, this and the two following chapters are about the "fine tuning" of established prices. Chapters 13 and 14 focus specifically on sales revenue and total contribution (profit) maximization, respectively.

12.1 Price Optimization and the P.E.D.

The key to effective price optimization is the point price elasticity of demand which is simply the percentage quantity change resulting from a percentage price change. Equation (6.4) of Chapter 6 (Market Demand) defines this quantity as:

$$\varepsilon = -\frac{\blacktriangle Q}{\blacktriangle P} \qquad \text{Eq. (12.1)}$$

where $\blacktriangle P$ is the percentage price change and $\blacktriangle Q$ the percentage quantity change. The negative sign, it may be recalled, is used to always keep the P.E.D. a positive number. More specifically, if the subscripts 0 and 1 represent the variables before and after a price change, respectively, one has:

$$\blacktriangle Q = \frac{Q_1 - Q_0}{Q_0} \qquad \text{Eq. (12.2)}$$

and $$\blacktriangle P = \frac{P_1 - P_0}{P_0} \qquad \text{Eq. (12.3)}$$

The P.E.D. plays such a crucial role in price optimization because it is the nexus between factors inside the firm such as product cost and profit margins and outside it as buyer perceptions and market demand for the product. It essentially represents the aggregate assessment of many buyers and potential buyers regarding their relative needs and wants to possess the product and their value perception of it in relation to all competing products on the market. This evaluation is reflected in the buyers' relative sensitivities to the product's price and specifically in the product's price elasticity of demand at any given operating point (P_0, Q_0) on the product's demand curve. Furthermore, as mentioned before, the P.E.D. represents a useful surrogate for a demand schedule or curve which is almost never available to a pricer.

The price elasticity of demand is not without problems. While not quite as difficult to come by as a demand schedule or curve, it too requires some effort and care to determine with any degree of precision. The various techniques available for estimating the price elasticity of demand before a contemplated price change were covered in Section 6.5 of Chapter 6 (Market Demand). As was shown there, determining a product's P.E.D. often involves a complicated and costly effort that may or may not yield useful results.

A more fundamental problem with the P.E.D. was pointed out by Tucker and later writers.[3] This is the fact that the elasticity factor is not linear in any amount or direction. As Tucker noted, in some cases a 5% price increase can cut volume by 30% but a similar price cut may raise volume by only 8%. However, Tucker's scenario is undoubtedly an extreme case. That the P.E.D. is not linear should not be surprising since the demand curve is, as the name implies, a curve. In estimating the P.E.D. we use a linear approximation to it which necessarily departs from the true curve.

As noted earlier, to effectively deal with this nonlinearity issue, only small (incremental) price increments should be considered. In fact, price adjustments should, as a rule of thumb, not exceed 15-20% of the original price in either direction. Results from sales revenue and total contribution computations for larger price changes are highly suspect and should be used only to establish trends.

12.2 Price Optimization Techniques

In this section we consider five techniques for determining optimal prices for maximum sales revenue and total contribution (profit) each of which has its unique advantages and disadvantages. An example at the end will demonstrate use of the various techniques.

12.2.1 General Pricing Rule of Thumb (1)

Application of the General Pricing Rule of Thumb (1) for Price Optimization as given in Table 8-1 of Chapter 8 (Pricing Strategies) is the simplest and quickest way to determine the direction of a required price changes to achieve either maximum sales revenue or total contribution and profit. Restated for convenience it is:

i) For sales revenue maximization:

Lower the price if the product's P.E.D. is larger than 1.0, *hold* it if it equal to 1.0, and *raise* it if it is less than 1.0.

ii) For total contribution (profit) maximization:

Lower the price if the product's P.E.D. is larger than $1 / CM_0$, *hold* it if it is equal to $1 / CM_0$, and *raise* it if it is less than $1 / CM_0$.

This decision rule, based on standard microeconomic theory, does not, however, give the magnitudes of the required price changes.

12.2.2 Linear Demand Curve

Using the estimated P.E.D. for the product, a linear demand or price response curve can be drawn and the optimal prices for sales revenue and total contribution (profit) maximization obtained in two ways:

i) By Inspection

Referring to Figure 10-1 of Chapter 10 (Marketing and Pricing Dynamics) and the Appendix (Formula Derivations), the optimal price for sales revenue maximization is one-half of the product's maximum (reservation) price P_M. For total contribution and profit maximization, the optimal price lies midway between the product's unit variable cost and the maximum (reservation) price. Specifically, it is one-half the sum of the reservation price P_M and the unit variable cost VC_0.

ii) By Formula

This more formal procedure requires that the equation of the linear demand or price response curve be determined. For a linear demand curve, for example, it will take the form $P = a - (a / b) Q$ where "a" is the vertical (price) axis intercept, "b" the horizontal (quantity) axis intercept, "a / b" the line's slope, and "P" and "Q" the y-axis and x-axis labels, respectively. Using this equation, the expressions for sales revenue R and total contribution K can be derived which will both have the shape of a parabola. The first derivative of each expression yields a second equation which gives its slope at all points. Since at the apex of a parabola this slope is zero, one need only set this second equation equal to zero to obtain the price and quantity points where R and K reach their maximum values.

12.2.3 Incremental Search

In what may be called the *incremental search technique*, use is made of Equation (12.1) above and the standard incremental relationships to construct a table of sales revenue and total contribution. For obtaining the optimal price for sales revenue maximization [P], four steps are required for each point on the sales revenue curve:

$$\text{i) } P_1 = P_0 (1 + \blacktriangle P)$$
$$\text{ii) } \blacktriangle Q = - \epsilon_0 \blacktriangle P$$
$$\text{iii) } Q_1 = Q_0 (1 + \blacktriangle Q)$$
$$\text{iv) } R_1 = P_1 \times Q_1$$

For obtaining the optimal price P* for total contribution (profit) maximization, two more steps are added:

$$\text{v) } V_1 = VC_0 \times Q_1$$
$$\text{vi) } K_1 = R_1 - V_1$$

In practice, small price increments such as ±1%, ±3%, or ±5% are chosen and a series of computations made using steps i) through vi) and tabulated. This table will identify the price points at which sales revenue and total contribution are maximized.

12.2.4 Graphical

In this approach the formulas for the price response curve, sales revenue, and total contribution are developed and then plotted on graph paper or the incremental technique described above is extended to the entire range of prices and plotted. From these three curves the optimal prices for sales revenue [P] and total contribution P* may simply be read off. This technique requires the most effort but has the advantage of displaying all the price-quantity options for the entire price range from zero to the reservation (maximum) price.

12.2.5 Formula

In Chapters 13 and 14 special formulas are presented by which optimal price changes may be computed directly knowing just two parameter values, namely, the price elasticity of demand at the present price-volume operating point ϵ_0 and the product's unit contribution margin CM_0 (%) at that point. These four formulas for maximization of sales revenue [R] and total contribution K* are, respectively:

$$[\blacktriangle P] = \frac{1 - \mathcal{E}_0}{2\,\mathcal{E}_0} \qquad\qquad \text{Eq. (12.4)}$$

$$[\blacktriangle Q] = \frac{\mathcal{E}_0 - 1}{2} \qquad\qquad \text{Eq. (12.5)}$$

$$\blacktriangle P^* = \frac{1 - \mathcal{E}_0\,CM_0}{2\,\mathcal{E}_0} \qquad\qquad \text{Eq. (12.6)}$$

$$\blacktriangle Q^* = \frac{\mathcal{E}_0\,CM_0 - 1}{2} \qquad\qquad \text{Eq. (12.7)}$$

where $[\blacktriangle P]$ and $\blacktriangle P^*$ are the optimal price changes for sales revenue and total contribution (profit) maximization, respectively, while CM_0 is the percentage contribution margin in decimal form. As usual, the right-hand sides of the equations are to be multiplied by 100% to obtain the actual percentages.

12.3 Application

The following illustrative example will demonstrate use of these five techniques for price optimization.

Illustrative Example: Wein♦Glas Ltd.

Claudia Chianti has been operating a small import business from her home for the past two years. Her customers are wine aficionados who highly value her selection of wine glasses, decanters, cork screws, bottle storage racks, and similar items. One of her products is a set of stemware which costs her, inclusive of freight and import duties, a total of $50 and which she sells online for $100 plus shipping. Her monthly sales are 50 sets. Three months ago, Claudia charged just $80 for the set and shipped 100 sets a month. Then, at a trade show she heard that most mail order businesses use a simple rule of thumb by which a product's sell price should be at least double its cost. After her return, she raised her prices accordingly. While this price increase was just 25%, Claudia was surprised to find her sales volume plummet by 50%. She now wonders what went wrong.

To obtain some clarification Claudia went to see her friend Rosalind Riesling who teaches Marketing at nearby Champaign Community College. On hearing about the results of the recent price change, Rosalind determined that this product's P.E.D. was 2.0 (50% / 25%) meaning that demand for it was highly elastic. Rosalind told Claudia that when she raised her price, many customers presumably decided it was too steep for them after finding a less costly substitute elsewhere. Rosalind then proceeded to show her friend how to determine the optimal prices for sales revenue and contribution (profit) maximization for her stemware product.

Rosalind established these initial conditions for Claudia's product:

$$P_0 = \$80 \quad Q_0 = 100 \quad P_1 = \$100 \quad Q_1 = 50 \quad VC_0 = \$50$$

From these facts she obtained the following basic information:

$\blacktriangle P = (\$100 - \$80) / \$80 = \$20 / \$80 = 0.25 \text{ or } 25\%$

$\blacktriangle Q = (50 - 100) / 100 = -0.50 \text{ or } -50\%$

$\mathcal{E}_0 = \blacktriangle Q / \blacktriangle P = 50\% / 25\% = 2.0$

$CM_0 = (\$80 - \$50) / \$80 = 0.375 \text{ or } 37.5\%$

12.3.1 General Pricing Rule of Thumb (1)

In our example, for maximizing sales revenue Claudia must drop her original price of $80 since the P.E.D. was larger than 1.0. Since the original total contribution margin CM_0 was 0.375 and its reciprocal is 2.67, she must raise her price to maximize profit. This is because the actual P.E.D. (2.0) is less than the required P.E.D. of 2.67. As previously mentioned, our pricing rule of thumb can only tell us the direction but not the amount of the required price change.

12.3.2 Linear Demand Curve

Using the available data, Rosalind next drew a traditional liner demand curve for Claudia's stemware by labeling the vertical axis "Price" and the horizontal axis "Quantity," entering the two known price-volume points, and connecting these as shown in Figure 12-1 (solid line). She then extended this line in both directions (broken lines) to obtain the price and volume intercepts which are seen to be $120 and 300 units, respectively.

i) By Inspection

On Figure 12-1 Rosalind noticed that at the midpoint of the product's linear demand curve the price was $60. Similarly, she found that one-half of the sum of the reservation price ($120) and the product's unit variable cost ($50) came to $85. These, Rosalind told Claudia, were her optimal prices for sales revenue and total contribution (profit) maximization, respectively.

Figure 12-1
Linear Demand Curve for Wei▲Glas Ltd.

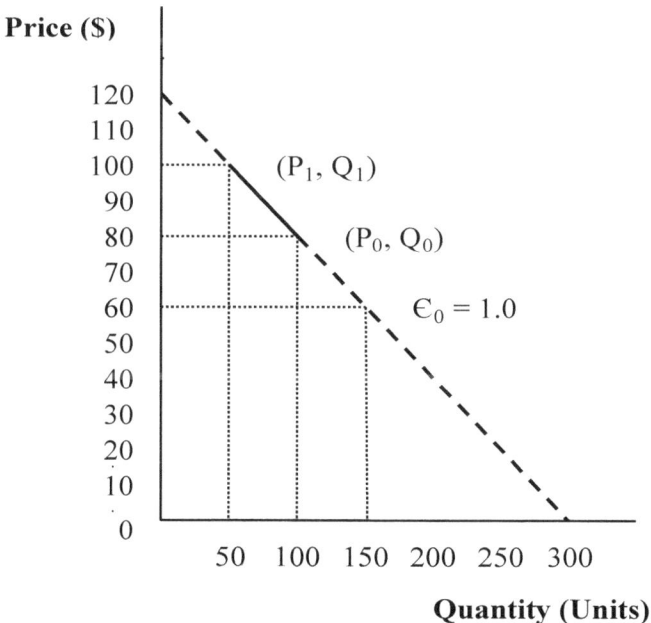

ii) By Formula

Rosalind continued her analysis by finding the equation for this linear demand curve. Using the two axes intercepts and slope of Figure 12-1, the equation for the linear demand curve is:

$$P = 120 - (120 / 300) \, Q = 120 - 0.40 \, Q$$

The sales revenue function is therefore:

$$R = P \times Q = 120 \, Q - 0.40 \, Q^2$$

Differentiating R w.r.t. Q and setting the result equal to zero yields the optimal quantity for sales revenue maximization [Q]:

$$\frac{\partial R}{\partial Q} = 120 - 0.80 \, Q = 0$$

$$[Q] = 150$$

The optimal price and maximum sales revenue are therefore:

$$[P] = 120 - (0.40)(150) = \$60$$

$$[R] = [P][Q] = (\$60)(150) = \$9,000$$

Following the same procedure, Rosalind now obtained the optimal quantity Q* and price P* for total contribution maximization, and the maximum total contribution K*:

$$K = (P - VC_0) \, Q = (120 - 0.40 \, Q - 50) \, Q = 70 \, Q - 0.40 \, Q^2$$

$$\frac{\partial K}{\partial Q} = 70 - 80 \, Q = 0$$

$$Q* = 87.5$$

$$P* = 120 - 0.40 \, Q* = 120 - (0.40)(87.5) = \$85$$

$$K* = (P* - VC_0) \, Q* = (\$85 - \$50)(87.5) = \$3,063$$

Thus, Rosalind explained, a price cut to $60 would have resulted in a 12.5% sales revenue increase while a price increase to $85 would have caused a contribution increase but of just 2.1%.

12.3.3 Incremental Search

Since Rosalind already knew the optimal prices [P] and P*, she could narrow her search to just a few price points and decided to confine the price range of her search from $50 to $100 with price increments of $\blacktriangle P = \pm 0.05$ or $\pm 5\%$. Starting with the price-volume operating point prior to the price change, she computed a second one following the six steps given above and letting $\blacktriangle P = -0.05$:

$$P = \$80 \,(1 - 0.05) = \$76$$
$$\blacktriangle Q = -2.0 \,(-0.05) = 0.10$$
$$Q = 100 \,(1 + 0.10) = 110$$
$$R = (\$76)(110) = \$8,360$$
$$V = (\$50)\,(110) = \$5,500$$
$$K = \$8,360 - \$5,500 = \$2,860$$

Rosalind computed a third point by letting $\blacktriangle P = -0.10$ and continued incrementing until she arrived at $52 when she reversed direction by letting $\blacktriangle P = +0.05$ and so on. From her tabulation as shown, Rosalind was able to determine that the maximum sales revenue was achieved at a price of [P] = $60 with a sales revenue of $9,000 while the maximum total contribution occurred near P* = $84 for a total contribution of about $3,060.

▲P	P ($)	▲Q	Q	R ($)	V ($)	K ($)
0	80.00	0	100.0	8,000	5,000	3,000
-0.05	76.00	0.10	110.0	8,360	5,500	2,860
-0.10	72.00	0.20	120.0	8,640	6,000	2,640
-0.15	68.00	0.30	130.0	8,840	6,500	2,340
-0.20	64.00	0.40	140.0	8,960	7,000	1,960
-0.25	60.00	0.50	150.0	9,000	7,500	1,500
-0.30	56.00	0.60	160.0	8,960	8,000	960
-0.35	52.00	0.70	170.0	8,840	8,500	340
0.05	84.00	-0.10	90.0	7,560	4,500	3,060
0.10	88.00	-0.20	80.0	7,040	4,000	3,040
0.15	92.00	-0.30	70.0	6,440	3,500	2,940

The value for maximum sales revenue agrees with the previous result while that for maximum total contribution is slightly off because the 5% price increments used were a little too large.

Figure 12-2
Sales & Total Contribution for Wein♦Glass Ltd.

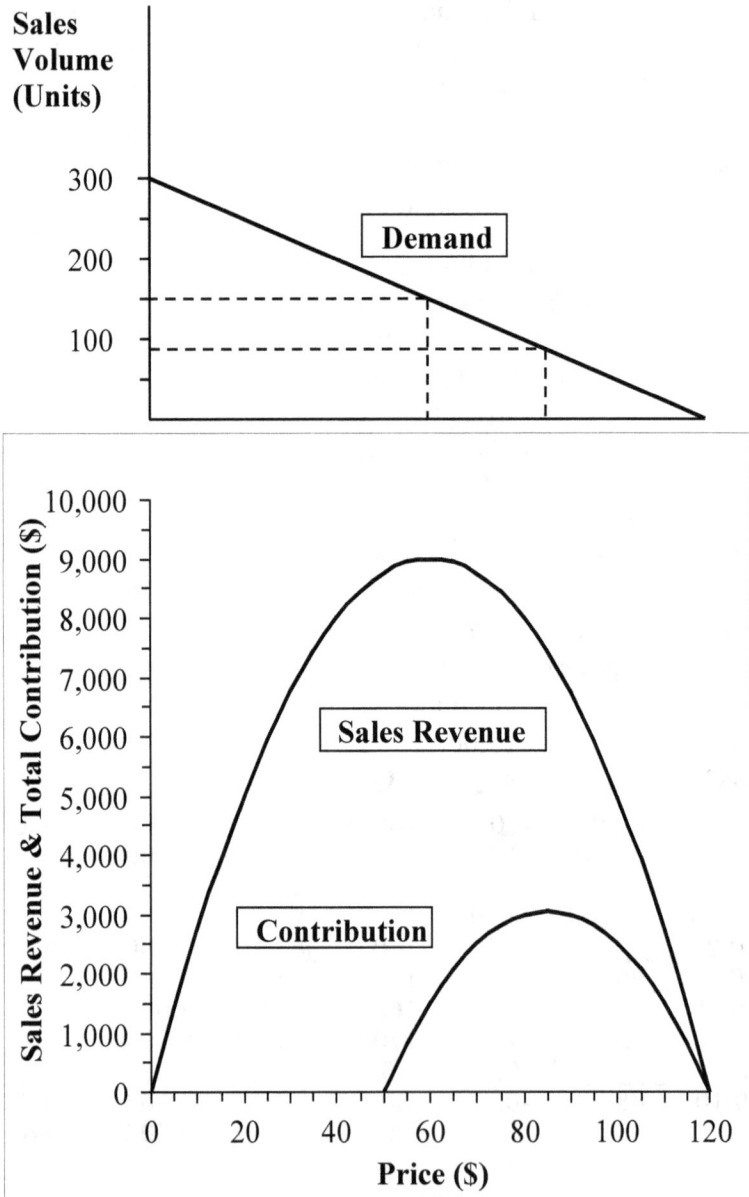

12.3.4 Graphical

To show Claudia the complete array of pricing options with the associated sales volumes Q, sales revenues R, and total contributions K, Rosalind decided to plot all three curves in the price range from zero to the reservation price of $120. Using the PRC format, she placed P on the horizontal axis and Q, R and K on the vertical axis. The equation for this PRC was found to be:

$$Q = 300 - 2.5\,P$$

The expression for sales revenue was therefore:

$$R = P\,Q = -2.5\,P^2 + 300\,P$$

Similarly, the total contribution now became:

$$K = (P - 50)\,(300 - 2.5\,P)$$

$$K = -2.5\,P^2 + 425\,P - 15{,}000$$

These three expressions are plotted in Figure 12-2. Sales revenue and total contribution are again seen to peak at the optimum prices of $60 and $85, respectively, with the actual values being about $9,000 and $3,000, respectively. As Rosalind expected, no contribution dollars were generated at and below a price of $50 because that is the product's unit variable cost. As we learned earlier, no contribution dollars are earned at or below that cost which we have labeled a product's price floor. The two lower curves also demonstrate the important fact that even small price variances from the optimal prices can severely impact sales revenue and total contribution.

12.3.5 Formula

The price adjustment formulas given by Equations (12.4) through (12.7) above present the most direct and accurate means of determining the optimal prices for maximum sales revenue and total contribution. Using the given data, Rosalind computed these values for revenue maximization:

$$[\blacktriangle P] = (1 - 2.0) / (2 \times 2.0) = -0.25 = -25\%$$

$$[P] = (1.0 - 0.25)\,(\$80) = \$60$$

$[\blacktriangle Q] = (2.0 - 1) / 2 = 0.50 = 50\%$

$[Q] = (1 + 0.50) (100) = 150$

$[R] = (\$60) (150) = \$9,000$

For contribution maximization, Rosalind made these calculations:

$\blacktriangle P^* = (1 - 2.0 \times 0.375) / (2 \times 2.0) = 0.0625 = 6.25\%$

$P^* = (1 + 0.0625) (\$80) = \$85$

$\blacktriangle Q^* = (2.0 \times 0.375 - 1) / 2 = -0.125 = -12.5\%$

$Q^* = (1 - 0.125) (100) = 87.5$

$K^* = (\$85 - \$50) (87.5) = \$3,063$

These formula results were identical to those found by the previous techniques but here Rosalind arrived at the solution directly using only the product's P.E.D. and unit contribution margin.

12.3.6 Recommendation

Rosalind recommended to her friend Claudia that she reduce her price for this stemware set from the present $100 to $84.95 even though the contribution increase was only minimal. This would be a return to close to her original price of $80 and bring back at least some of her lost customers. Per Rosalind, since she was operating out of her home and her overhead cost was minimal, this contribution of a little over $3,000 would be close to her monthly profit as well. Rosalind also suggested to Claudia that she search for and offer more unique and differentiated products for which substitutes are not as readily available. She might even invent some exotic names for her different sets which would enhance their uniqueness and appeal. According to Rosalind, such products would be less price sensitive (have steeper demand curves) allowing her to charge higher prices and achieve larger margins and profits.

12.4 A Special Note

The following two chapters are dedicated to price optimization for maximizing sales revenue and maximum total contribution (profit) for products and services based on a linear demand curve. They go beyond of what has already been covered in this and previous chapters and include additional formulas and pricing propositions. The approach used in this book is for the solution of the simplest pricing issues but also the most instructive and useful. Most other approaches are based on various hypotheses and presumptions, usually accompanied by some very advanced and esoteric mathematical manipulations, as pricing theorists try to express in mathematical terms pricing practices used by sellers and the behavior patterns exhibited by buyers neither of which are readily quantifiable.

As already mentioned in the Preface to *Pricing the Profitable Sale*, the equations and formulas of the following two chapters are presented without detailed proof. Their derivation is fairly simple using basic algebra and the interested and mathematically skilled reader can easily fill in the gaps. A step-by-step derivation of each formula appears in the Appendix of the author's *Pricing for Profit*. As previously stated, however, the most important part of these chapters is not the formulas themselves but the series of pricing guidelines and propositions which are based on the formulas presented.

It should also again be pointed out that the figures and graphs for sales revenue and total contribution shown in this chapter, the two chapters to follow, and the Appendix are idealized in that they are perfectly symmetrical parabolas. This is because the underlying equations presume a linear demand curve which is an approximation of an actual curve. (See Figure 6-1 of Chapter 6). In a real situation these curves would appear somewhat skewed. This does not, however, affect the validity of any of the pricing propositions and rules of thumb presented.

Another important point that again needs emphasis is that the price elasticity of demand (P.E.D.) as used in this and the following two chapters is not just any P.E.D. but the one directly associated with the firm's chosen target market for a particular product or service. The pricer must establish this target-market-specific pricing metric with as high a degree of accuracy as possible. To assist him or her, it will be shown that this difficult hurdle can be overcome by simply choosing different P.E.D. levels and noting their relative impacts on optimal prices and maximum revenues and profits.

Notes

1. Thomas T. Nagle and Georg Müller, *The Strategy and Tactics of Pricing*, 246.

2. Hermann Simon and Martin Fassnacht, *Price Management*, 185.

3. Spencer Tucker, *Pricing for Higher Profit*, 13.

CHAPTER

13

Pricing for Maximum Revenue

*Growth which fails to fulfill its promise of profitability
can spell disaster and has in fact brought ruin to many
a company whose executives were guided by the mistaken
belief that growth was its own reward.[1]*

Not every firm sets prices for its products and services to
maximize contribution and profits. Many business managers focus
on revenue and market share goals instead believing that being a
strong force in the market will eventually lead to price leadership
and increased profitability. For other firms, such as those with
high indirect fixed and small unit incremental costs, as found in
public transportation and other industries, it is more common and
meaningful to talk about revenues rather than profits. The more
tickets a public transportation company sells, the more contribution
dollars it generates to cover continuing operating expenses.

This chapter is intended to show marketers and pricing
practitioners how to compute sell prices that lead to maximum
revenue and revenue market shares for their companies' diverse
products and services. First the necessary formulas to make these
computations are developed. Next, a reference table is presented
which the busy marketer can use to look up the needed information
without having to use the formulas. Then some of the formulas are
"normalized" to make them independent of the original conditions

with another associated reference table. An illustrative example is worked out to show how this optimization procedure may be applied. The chapter concludes with some additional pricing propositions. In the Appendix the interested reader will find another hypothetical example from the public transportation industry.

13.1 The Revenue Maximizer Formulas

The following twelve "revenue maximizer" formulas are based on Equation (3.3) of Chapter 3 whereby revenue R is the product of the net sell price P and the quantity Q sold at that price:

$$R = P \times Q$$

If one lets the subscripts 0 and 1 designate the parameters before and after an incremental price change, respectively, and Δ the dollar change resulting from such a price change, one obtains:

$$\Delta R = R_1 - R_0 = P_1 Q_1 - P_0 Q_0$$

13.1.1 The Revenue Impact Formula (RIF)

By some basic algebraic manipulations it can be shown that the relationship between the incremental percentage price change $\blacktriangle P$ and the resulting percentage revenue change $\blacktriangle R$, given the product's price elasticity of demand $\mathcal{E}_0$ at the present price-volume operating point (P_0, Q_0), is:

$$\blacktriangle R = - \mathcal{E}_0 (\blacktriangle P)^2 + (1 - \mathcal{E}_0) \blacktriangle P \qquad \text{Eq.(13.1)}$$

Because the expression gives the impact of a price change on sales revenue, one may call it the *revenue impact formula*.

If one places $\blacktriangle P$ on the x (horizontal) axis and $\blacktriangle R$ on the y (vertical) axis, and plots Equation (13.1), the result is a parabola which rises from zero to a maximum value at $[\blacktriangle P]$, the optimal price change for revenue maximization, and drops back to zero.

13.1.2 Revenue after a Percentage Price Change

Since the revenue after a percentage incremental price change is the original revenue plus the percentage incremental revenue change from the price change, Eq. (13.1) becomes:

$$R_1 = R_0 (1 + \blacktriangle R)$$

$$R_1 = R_0 \{1 - \text{\Large€}_0 (\blacktriangle P)^2 + (1 - \text{\Large€}_0) \blacktriangle P\} \qquad \text{Eq. (13.2)}$$

where, $\qquad \blacktriangle P = (P_1 - P_0) / P_0$

This expression too is a parabola.

13.1.3 The Optimal Percentage Price Change

By differentiating Equation (13.1) w.r.t. $\blacktriangle P$ and setting the result equal to zero ($\blacktriangle P = 0$) the optimal percentage price change to achieve maximum revenue can be shown to be:

$$[\blacktriangle P] = \frac{1 - \text{\Large€}_0}{2\, \text{\Large€}_0} \qquad \text{Eq (13.3)}$$

It is interesting to note that the optimal incremental price change for revenue maximization depends on only one quantity, namely, the product's price elasticity of demand. Nothing else matters.

13.1.4 The Optimal Condition

Conditions are optimal when no price change is required to achieve maximum revenue. Microeconomic theory informs us that for this to happen, the price elasticity of demand at the present price-volume operating point must be 1.0: [2]

$$\text{\Large€}_0 = [\text{\Large€}] = 1.0 \qquad \text{Eq. (13.4)}$$

This is precisely the result obtained when one sets Equation (13.3) for the optimal percentage price change equal to zero. We also know (see Table 8-1 of Chapter 8) that if the P.E.D. is less than 1.0, the price must be raised for revenue maximization, lowered if it is larger than 1.0, and held if it is equal to 1.0. Equation (13.3) lets the marketer not only determine the required direction of the incremental price change but compute the exact amount.

13.1.5 The Price Range for Positive Revenue Changes

By setting Equation (13.1) equal to zero we obtain its roots, i.e., the two price points at which the parabola described by this equation crosses the x ($\blacktriangle$P) axis:

$$\blacktriangle P = 0; \quad \frac{1 - \mathcal{E}_0}{\mathcal{E}_0} \qquad \text{Eq. (13.5)}$$

Hence, the curve crosses the x-axis at 0 and a point which is twice the optimal price change given by Equation (13.3). The favorable price range therefore extends from $\blacktriangle P = 0$ to $\blacktriangle P = 2 \times [\blacktriangle P]$.

13.1.6 The Optimal Price

The optimal price is simply the original price P_0 plus the optimal percentage price change as given by Eq. (13.3):

$$[P] = P_0 (1 + [\blacktriangle P])$$

$$[P] = \frac{P_0}{2\,\mathcal{E}_0} (\mathcal{E}_0 + 1) \qquad \text{Eq. (13.6)}$$

The optimal price is thus dependant on only the present price P_0 and the P.E.D. at that price.

13.1.7 The Revenue Price Range

The range of prices over which revenue can be generated under the given conditions extends from zero to twice the optimal price [P] as given by Equation (13.6):

$$0 < P_1 < \frac{P_0 (\mathcal{E}_0 + 1)}{\mathcal{E}_0} \qquad \text{Eq. (13.7)}$$

13.1.8 The Optimal Percentage Quantity Change

The optimal percentage quantity change follows directly

from the definition of the P.E.D. and Equation (13.3):

$$[\blacktriangle Q] = -\epsilon_0 [\blacktriangle P]$$

$$[\blacktriangle Q] = \frac{\epsilon_0 - 1}{2} \qquad \text{Eq. (13.8)}$$

13.1.9 The Optimal Quantity

The optimal quantity is the original quantity Q_0 plus the percentage quantity change as given by Eq. (13.8):

$$[Q] = Q_0 (1 + [\blacktriangle Q])$$

$$[Q] = \frac{Q_0}{2} (\epsilon_0 + 1) \qquad \text{Eq. (13.9)}$$

13.1.10 The Maximum Revenue Change

Inserting Equation (13.3) for the optimal percentage price change into the revenue impact formula, Equation (13.1), one obtains the maximum sales revenue change:

$$[\blacktriangle R] = \epsilon_0 [\blacktriangle P]^2 \qquad \text{Eq. (13.10)}$$

This expression together with that for $[\blacktriangle P]$ of Equation (13.3) are the two key formulas for revenue maximization.

13.1.11 The Maximum Revenue

The product of the optimal price, Equation (13.6), and optimal quantity, Equation (13.9), yields the maximum sales revenue achievable under the given conditions:

$$[R] = [P] \times [Q]$$

$$[R] = \frac{R_0}{4\,\epsilon_0} (\epsilon_0 + 1)^2 \qquad \text{Eq. (13.11)}$$

13.1.12 The Optimal Unit Contribution Margin

The optimal price change results in a new unit contribution margin:

$$[CM] = \frac{[P] - VC_0}{[P]} \qquad \text{Eq. (13.12)}$$

where [P] is the optimal price given by Equation (13.6).

13.2 The Normalized Formulas

Equations (13.6), (13.9), and (13.11) may be "normalized" meaning they can be expressed so that they are independent of the original conditions:

$$\frac{[P]}{P_0} = \frac{\mathcal{E}_0 + 1}{2\,\mathcal{E}_0} \qquad (13.6A)$$

$$\frac{[Q]}{Q_0} = \frac{\mathcal{E}_0 + 1}{2} \qquad (13.9A)$$

$$\frac{[R]}{R_0} = \frac{(\mathcal{E}_0 + 1)^2}{4\,\mathcal{E}_0} \qquad (13.11A)$$

The first and third of these expressions are very useful because they allow one to compute and tabulate the normalized optimal price and sales revenue, respectively, for any product or service on the market.

13.3 Reference Tables

Using diverse formulas to obtain the desired information can seem like a tedious chore and marketers and pricers would obviously prefer another means. One way would be to use the formulas to electronically compute and store the relevant data. This is the recommended method for active pricers with multiple products to keep track of. For the occasional user, charts and reference tables are a useful alternative.

Figure 13.1 is a graphical representation of Equation (13.3) for the optimal percentage price change for sales revenue maximization as a function of the price elasticity of demand. It shows, as one would expect, that the curve crosses the horizontal (P.E.D) axis at 1.0 (unitary elasticity), i.e., at the optimal price elasticity [ϵ]. At this P.E.D. no price change is required, i.e., it is the point of maximum achievable sales revenue. As the graph clearly shows, price elasticities below this point ($\epsilon_0 < 1.0$) require a price increase, while P.E.D.s in the elastic range ($\epsilon_0 > 1.0$) call for a price reduction.

Figure 13-1
Optimal Percentage Price Changes for Revenue Maximization

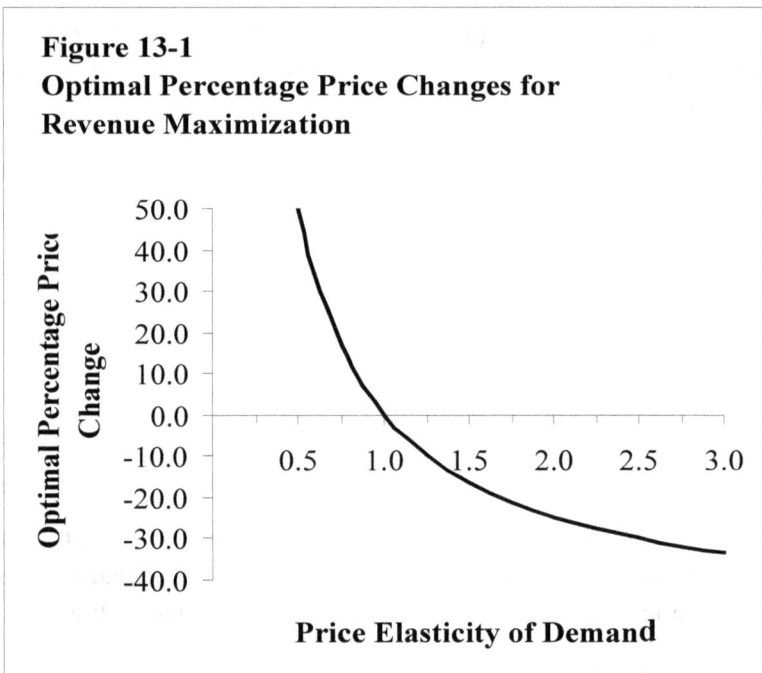

Table 13-1 (at the end of this chapter) entitled "Price Optimization for Maximum Revenue" is a listing of the two most important parameters, namely, the optimal percentage price changes and maximum percentage sales revenue changes for P.E.D.s from 0.25 to 3.00. These computations are based on Equations (13.3) and (13.10), respectively. The table allows a fast and easy means of solving common pricing problems associated with revenue maximization. Most of the other parameter values for which the formulas were given above, such as optimum price, optimum quantity, and maximum sales revenue, are derived from these two tabulations without much further effort.

Figure 13-2 is a graphical representation of Equations (13.6A) and (13.11A). The two graphs show that as the optimal prices decrease with increasing P.E.D. levels, revenues decrease until the P.E.D. is 1.0 after which they rise again.

Figure 13-2
Optimal Price & Maximum Revenue
(Normalized)

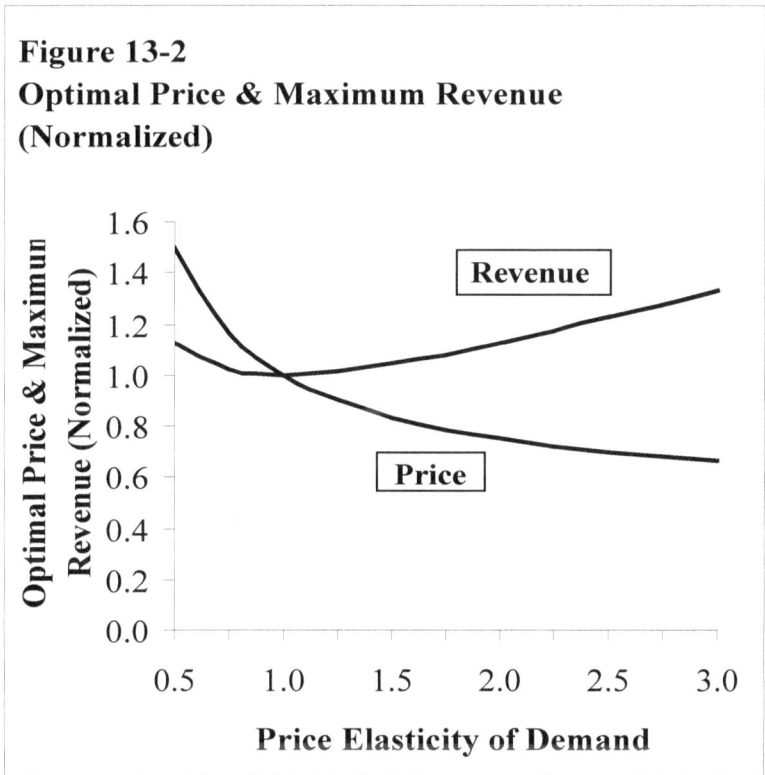

Table 13-2 entitled "Optimal Price & Maximum Revenue (Normalized)" is another tool for easily obtaining answers to revenue maximization problems. This table too is based on Equations (13.6A) and (13.11A) and allows the pricer to determine the optimal price and maximum revenue for any product or service provided a good estimate of the P.E.D. prior to the price adjustment is available.

A precautionary note regarding use of Tables 13-1 and 13-2 is in order. When Equations (13.6), (13.10), and (13.11) were developed in Section 13.1 above, the optimal percentage price change [▲P] given by Equation (13.3) was incorporated in these expressions. This means that the pricer must ensure that the price change required by Equation (13.3) is implemented prior to use of these table. If this is not done, the values listed will not yield valid results.

13.4 Application

The following illustrative example will show how the above formulas may be used to analyze and solve a revenue pricing problem either mathematically, by use of the tables, or graphically.

Illustrative Example: Humperdinck's Party Supplies

Humperdinck's is a distributor of supplies commonly used by business firms, churches, clubs, and other organizations for their occasional parties, picnics, and other festivities. The company is owned and operated by Engelbert Humperdinck who decided to start his own business after an unprofitable venture writing children's operas back in the Old Country. Engelbert buys his supplies such as paper plates, towels, utensils, napkins, and decorative items in bulk and repackages these to fill individual orders.

One of the most popular of Humperdinck's packages, called PartyTime-3, sells for $25 and costs Engelbert $10. Sales average about 200 per month. He wants to grow his business and is willing to cut his price by as much as 20% which he estimates will raise demand by about a third (35%). Unfortunately, he has no clue as to how a 10% or 20% price reduction would affect his sales revenue. Would dollar sales increase or decrease and by how much?

13.4.1 Formula Solution

Using the twelve formulas in the sequence presented above, one obtains these results.

i) Suppose, the PartyTime-3 price was reduced by 10%, what would be the impact on sales revenue? Since the P.E.D. is estimated to be 1.75 (35% / 20%), one has from Equation (13.1):

$$\blacktriangle R = -1.75\,(-0.10)^2 + (1 - 1.75)(-0.10) = 0.0575$$

Thus, a 10% price reduction would increase monthly revenue by about 6%.

ii) The monthly revenue after the 10% price reduction would be:

$$R_1 = R_0\,(1 + \blacktriangle R) = \$5.000\,(1 + 0.0575) = \$5{,}287.50$$

The same result is obtained more directly from Equation (13.2):

$$R_1 = \$5{,}000\,\{1 - 1.75\,(-0.10)^2 + (1 - 1.75)(-0.10)\} = \$5{,}287.50$$

iii) The optimal percentage price change is found from Equation (13.3):

$$[\blacktriangle P] = (1 - 1.75) / (2)(1.75) = -0.2143$$

Thus, the optimal price change is a price reduction of 21.4%. This is very close to the price adjustment Engelbert had originally planned.

iv) Since the P.E.D. is 1.75 and therefore more than 1.0, by our General Pricing Rule of Thumb (1), a price reduction is called for. This was shown above to amount to 21.4%.

v) The range of percentage price changes that will add to revenue extends from 0 to 2 × (– 0.2143) or from 0 to a price reduction of 42.9%. This means that the favorable price range extends from the present $25 down to $14.30 ($25 × 0.571).

vi) The optimal price for the PartyTime-3 package is:

$$[P] = P_0\,(1 + [\blacktriangle P] = \$25\,(1 - 0.2143) = \$19.64$$

The same result may be obtained more directly from Equation (13.6):

$$[P] = \$25\,(1.75 + 1) / (2)(1.75) = \$19.64$$

vii) Under the given conditions, revenue will be generated only in the price range given by Equation (13.7):

$$0 < P_1 < \$25 \; (1.75 + 1) / 1.75$$
$$0 < P_1 < \$39.3$$

viii) From Equation (13.8), the optimal percentage quantity change is:

$$[\blacktriangle Q] = (1.75 - 1) / 2 = 0.375$$

Thus the 21.4% price reduction will cause a volume increase of 37.5%.

ix) The optimal quantity is therefore:

$$[Q] = Q_0 \; (1 + \blacktriangle Q) = 200 \; (1 + 0.375) = 275$$

The same result may be obtained more directly from Equation (13.9):

$$[Q] = 200 \; (1.75 + 1) / 2 = 275$$

x) The optimal revenue change is by Equation (13.10):

$$[\blacktriangle R] = (1.75) \; (- 0.2143)^2 = 0.0804$$

Thus, the optimal sales revenue increase is about 8%.

xi) The maximum sales revenue after the optimal price change will be:

$$[R] = R_0 \; (1 + [\blacktriangle R]) = \$5{,}000 \; (1 + 0.0804) = \$5{,}402$$

The same result is also obtained from Equation (13.11):

$$[R] = \$5{,}000 \; (1 + 1.75)^2 / (4)(1.75) = \$5{,}402$$

xii) The unit contribution margin after the optimal price change is found from Equation (13.12):

$$[CM] = (\$19.64 - \$10.00) / \$19.64 = 0.491$$

Hence, the price reduction would reduce the unit contribution margin from the present 60% to about 49%.

13.4.2 Reference Table Solution

Engelbert could also use Tables 13-1 and 13-2 at the end of the chapter to quickly give him some answers.

i) Table 13-1

For a P.E.D. of 1.75, $[\blacktriangle P] = (21.4\%)$ according to the table. This price reduction will give Engelbert an optimal price of $[P] = \$25 \times (1-0.214) = \$19.65$. Similarly, the table shows $[\blacktriangle R] = 8.0\%$ giving him a maximum revenue after the price change of $[R] = \$5,000 \times (1 + 0.080) = \$5,400$. These results closely agree with the formula solutions.

ii) Table 13-2

For a P.E.D. of 1.75, the table gives Engelbert $[P] / P_0 = 0.786$ and therefore $[P] = \$25 \times 0.786 = \$19.65$ for the optimal price. Similarly, the table lists $[R] / R_0 = 1.080$ so that the maximum revenue at that price is $[R] = \$5,000 \times 1.080 = \$5,400$. These results too agree with the ones above. As previously noted, Engelbert would have had to reduce the PartyTime-3 net price to $19.65 before using the listed values in the two tables.

13.4.3 Graphical Solution

One may also arrive at these results using a graphical approach. Thus, if one inserts the PartyTime-3 parameter values in Equation (13.2) for revenue after a price change one obtains:

$$R_1 = \$5,000 \ \{1 - 1.75 \ (\blacktriangle P)^2 - 0.75 \ \blacktriangle P)\}$$

where, $\qquad \blacktriangle P = (P_1 - P_0) / P_0 = (P_1 - \$25) / \$25$

Thus if $P_1 = \$5$, for example, one has $\blacktriangle P = (\$5 - \$25) / \$25 = -0.80$ resulting in a revenue of $R_1 = \$2,400$.

Figure 13-3 shows the completed graph of revenue versus price. It may be noted that the curve peaks at a price of about $20, the optimal price $[P]$, and a monthly revenue of $5,400. These values match the prior results obtained by formula.

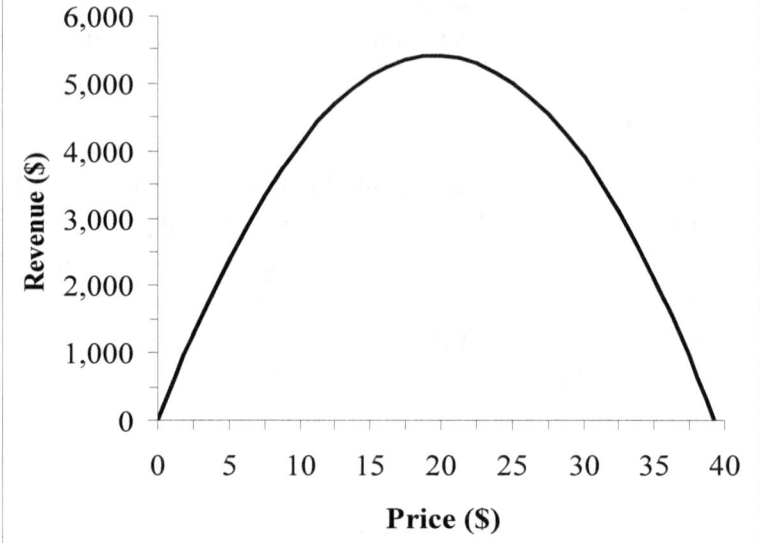

Figure 13-3
Revenue for PartyTime-3 (A)

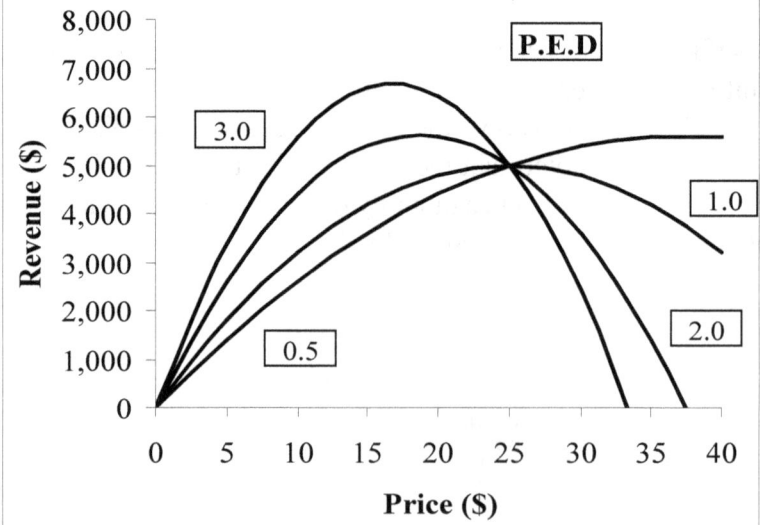

Figure 13-4
Revenue for PartyTime-3 (B)

Sometimes it's advantageous to plot the same graph for different P.E.D.s for comparison purposes especially since the exact P.E.D. levels are difficult to ascertain. Figure 13-4 shows the PartyTime-3 sales revenue as a function of price for price elasticities of demand of 0.5, 1.0, 2.0 and 3.0. All four curves intersect at a price of $25 and monthly sales revenue of $5,000 because these were the initial conditions before any price changes. Clearly evident from these curves is that the larger the P.E.D., the higher is the maximum achievable sales revenue and the smaller the optimal price.

13.4.4 Conclusion

Engelbert was correct in assuming that his PartyTime-3 package was overpriced since his goal was to maximize sales revenue. A price reduction from $25 to about $20 would give him a nearly 40% increase in sales volume but only a modest 8% increase in sales revenue from $5,000 to $5,400 per month. This is the best he can hope to do given the present conditions of price, incremental cost, and price elasticity of demand. PartyTime-3 suffers from the fact that it is a largely undifferentiated commodity-type product with only its name giving it some uniqueness. Engelbert will now have to use his entrepreneurial talents and marketing skills to come up with something else.

13.5 Pricing Guidelines (VII)

The above formulas and Figures 13-1 through 13-4 lead to five additional pricing propositions.

Pricing Proposition 11

For any product or service there exists one and only one optimal sell price for revenue maximization and all price points below or above this optimal price will result in less than maximum sales revenue for that product or service.

Pricing Proposition 12

Price adjustments for sales revenue maximization:

a. The optimal price change for sales revenue maximization depends on only one parameter, namely, the product's price elasticity of demand.

b. Where the pricing objective is to maximize sales revenue for a given product or service and its price elasticity of demand ϵ_0 does not equal 1.0 (unitary elasticity) an incremental price adjustment in the amount of

$$[\blacktriangle P] = \frac{1 - \epsilon_0}{2\,\epsilon_0} \times 100\%$$

is required.

Pricing Proposition 13

The larger the deviation from the optimal price for sales revenue maximization, the greater will be the rate of sales revenue decline so that if the sell price is below the optimal level and is further reduced or is above the optimal level and is further increased, the adverse effects on sales revenue will be magnified.

Pricing Proposition 14

For sales revenue maximization,

a) the required optimal price change is positive below unitary price elasticity of demand ($\epsilon_0 = 0$) and negative thereafter and,

b) optimal price reductions lead to reductions in maximum sales revenue until unitary price elasticity of demand is reached when further optimal price reductions result in increasing maximum sales revenue.

Pricing Proposition 15

In all practical cases, the unit contribution margin after an optimal price change for revenue maximization will always be less than before the price change.

In the next chapter we turn to the somewhat more complex topic of total contribution and profit maximization.

Notes

1. André Gabor, *Pricing*, 30-31.

2. J. P. Gould and C. E. Ferguson, *Microeconomic Theory*, 111.

Table 13-1
Price Optimization for Maximum Revenue

P.E.D. (ϵ_0)	Optimal Price Change [▲P] %	Maximum Revenue Change [▲R] %	P.E.D. (ϵ_0)	Optimal Price Change [▲P] %	Maximum Revenue Change [▲R] %
0.25	150.0	67.5	1.65	(19.7)	6.4
0.30	116.7	40.8	1.70	(20.6)	7.2
0.35	92.9	30.2	1.75	(21.4)	8.0
0.40	75.0	22.5	1.80	(22.2)	8.9
0.45	61.1	16.8	1.85	(23.0)	9.8
0.50	50.1	12.5	1.90	(23.7)	10.7
0.55	40.9	9.2	1.95	(24.4)	11.6
0.60	33.3	6.7	2.00	(25.0)	12.5
0.65	26.9	4.7	2.05	(25.6)	13.4
0.70	21.4	3.2	2.10	(26.2)	14.4
0.75	16.7	2.1	2.15	(26.7)	15.4
0.80	12.5	1.3	2.20	(27.3)	16.4
0.85	8.8	0.7	2.25	(27.8)	17.4
0/90	5.6	0.3	2.30	(28.3)	18.4
0.95	2.6	0.1	2.35	(28.7)	19.4
1.00	0.0	0.0	2.40	(29.2)	20.4
1.05	(2.4)	0.1	2.45	(29.6)	21.5
1.10	(4.5)	0.2	2.50	(30.0)	22.5
1.15	(6.5)	0.5	2.55	(30.4)	23.6
1.20	(8.3)	0.8	2.60	(30.8)	24.6
1.25	(10.0)	1.3	2.65	(31.1)	25.7
1.30	(11.5)	1.7	2.70	(31.5)	26.8
1.35	(13.0)	2.3	2.75	(31.8)	27.8
1.40	(14.3)	2.9	2.80	(32.1)	28.9
1.45	(15.5)	3.5	2.85	(32.5)	30.0
1.50	(16.7)	4.2	2.90	(32.8)	31.1
1.55	(17.7)	4.9	2.95	(33.1)	32.2
1.60	(18.8)	5.6	3.00	(33.3)	33.3

Table 13-2
Optimal Price & Maximum Revenue (Normalized)

P.E.D. (ϵ_0)	Optimal Price [P] / P_0	Maximum Revenue [R] / R_0	P.E.D. (ϵ_0)	Optimal Price [P] / P_0	Maximum Revenue [R] / R_0
0.25	2.500	1.563	**1.65**	0.803	1.064
0.30	2.167	1.408	**1.70**	0.794	1.072
0.35	1.929	1.302	**1.75**	0.786	1.080
0.40	1.750	1.225	**1.80**	0.778	1.089
0.45	1.611	1.168	**1.85**	0.770	1.098
0.50	1.500	1.125	**1.90**	0.763	1.107
0.55	1.409	1.092	**1.95**	0.756	1.116
0.60	1.333	1.067	**2.00**	0.750	1.125
0.65	1.269	1.047	**2.05**	0.744	1.134
0.70	1.214	1.032	**2.10**	0.738	1.144
0.75	1.167	1.021	**2.15**	0.733	1.154
0.80	1.125	1.013	**2.20**	0.727	1.164
0.85	1.088	1.007	**2.25**	0.722	1.174
0.90	1.056	1.003	**2.30**	0.717	1.184
0.95	1.026	1.001	**2.35**	0.713	1.194
1.00	1.000	1.000	**2.40**	0.708	1.204
1.05	0.976	1.001	**2.45**	0.704	1.215
1.10	0.955	1.002	**2.50**	0.700	1.225
1.15	0.935	1.005	**2.55**	0.696	1.236
1.20	0.917	1.008	**2.60**	0.692	1.246
1.25	0.900	1.013	**2.65**	0.689	1.257
1.30	0.885	1.017	**2.70**	0.685	1.268
1.35	0.870	1.023	**2.75**	0.682	1.278
1.40	0.857	1.029	**2.80**	0.679	1.289
1.45	0.845	1.035	**2.85**	0.675	1.300
1.50	0.833	1.042	**2.90**	0.672	1.311
1.55	0.823	1.049	**2.95**	0.669	1.322
1.60	0.813	1.056	**3.00**	0.667	1.333

CHAPTER

14

Pricing for Maximum Profit

*There is always a price that maximizes profit. A price
which is too high is as bad as a price which is too low.[1]*

Profit maximization is the ultimate goal of most firms for
diverse reasons even though they may focus more on sales revenue,
market share, or some other marketing or financial objective in the
short term. Managers are consequently vitally interested in selling
their products and services at the most profitable prices. This chapter
provides the market-based formulas and pricing guidelines by which
a marketer can ensure that the total contribution generated by each
of the firm's products and services is maximized.

In this chapter's presentation of the formulas, graphs, and
tables we shall follow the same sequence as that used in the previous
chapter on revenue maximization. An illustrative example is worked
out to show how a price optimization problem for maximizing total
contribution can be solved both mathematically and graphically.
Next important relationship, namely, that between price, sales
volume, and profitability is examined. The chapter concludes with
some final pricing propositions and observations. In the Appendix,
the interested reader will find a hypothetical case study from the fast
foods business further illustrating use of this optimization technique.

The formulas ideally lend themselves to electronic computations and storage of pertinent data so that the active price setter with a multitude of products and price adjustment requirements can solve profit maximization problems speedily and with a minimum of effort. The reference tables shown are meant for pricers with more limited price optimization requirements.

14.1 The Profit Maximizer Formulas

The sixteen formulas appearing below start with the basic profit equations, namely, Equations (3.1) and (3.5) of Chapter 3 whereby profit is the difference between revenue and total cost:

$$I = R - C$$

$$I = (P - VC) Q - F$$

where,

$I = $ Profit (\$)
$R = $ Revenue (\$)
$C = $ Total cost (\$)
$P = $ Price (\$)
$VC = $ Unit variable cost (\$)
$Q = $ Quantity (units)
$F = $ Total indirect fixed cost (\$)

If one can assume that the price change is incrementally small so that VC and F do not change with the price change and if one lets the subscripts 0 and 1 designate the parameters before and after such a price change, respectively, and lets Δ designate the dollar change resulting from this incremental price change, one obtains for this special case with $VC_1 = VC_0$ and $F_1 = F_0$:

$$\Delta I = \Delta K = (P_1 - VC_0) Q_1 - (P_0 - VC_0) Q_0$$

where ΔK is the change in total contribution.

14.1.1 The Contribution (Profit) Impact Formula (PIF)

Of considerable interest to a marketer is the impact of an incremental percentage price change for a product or service on its total contribution and profit. Using the above expression for ΔK, some basic algebraic manipulations lead to a formula that allows a pricer to compute the percentage total contribution (profit) change as a result of an incremental percentage price change:

$$\blacktriangle K = \frac{1}{CM_0} \{-\mathcal{E}_0 (\blacktriangle P)^2 + (1-\mathcal{E}_0\, CM_0)\, \blacktriangle P\} \qquad \text{Eq. (14.1)}$$

where, $\qquad \blacktriangle P = (P_1 - P_0)\,/\,P_0$

As usual, the symbol $\blacktriangle$ stands for a percentage change expressed as a decimal. As may be seen, this computation makes use of two familiar quantities, namely, the percentage unit contribution margin CM_0 and the price elasticity of demand $\mathcal{E}_0$ at the present price-volume operating point (P_0, Q_0). Equation (14.1) may properly be called the *profit impact formula* or PIF and will be so referred to in this book.

14.1.2 The Contribution after a Percentage Price Change

$$\text{Since } K_1 = K_0\,(1 + \blacktriangle K),$$

Equation (14.1) may be extended to allow computation of the new total contribution after the incremental price change:

$$K_1 = R_0 \{-\mathcal{E}_0 (\blacktriangle P)^2 + \qquad\qquad \text{Eq. (14.2)}$$
$$(1 - \mathcal{E}_0\, CM_0)\, \blacktriangle P + CM_0\}$$

Both Equations (14.1) and (14.2) are parabolas that rise to a peak and return to zero.

14.1.3 The Optimal Percentage Price Change

By differentiating the formula for $\blacktriangle K$ given in Equation (14.1) and setting the result equal to 0, it can be shown that the optimal percentage price change to achieve maximum contribution and profit is given by the expression:

$$\blacktriangle P^* = \frac{1 - \mathcal{E}_0\, CM_0}{2\, \mathcal{E}_0} \qquad \text{Eq. (14.3)}$$

Hence, the optimal incremental price change for profit maximization is a function of both the price elasticity of demand and the unit contribution margin prior to the price change but nothing else.

14.1.4 The Optimal Condition

Conditions are optimal when no price change is required to achieve maximum contribution and profit. If one sets Eq. (14.3) equal to zero ($\blacktriangle P^* = 0$), this occurs when the P.E.D. equals the reciprocal of the unit contribution margin:

$$\epsilon^* = \frac{1}{CM_0\,(\%)} \qquad \text{Eq. (14.4)}$$

where ϵ^* is the optimal P.E.D. for profit maximization. This important relationship is well-known to economists.[2] In this book, it also appears as Equation (7.12) of Chapter 7 (Isoprofit Analysis) and Table 8-1 of Chapter 8 (General Pricing Rule of Thumb 1). It tells the pricer in which direction prices must be adjusted if this condition is not met. Here we go a significant step further and in Equation (14.3) give the pricer a formula by which the exact amount of the necessary incremental price change may be computed.

14.1.5 The Price Range for Positive Contribution Changes

Almost as important as the optimal price for maximum total contribution is knowing the range of prices that will add to total contribution. This information may be obtained by setting the PIF of Equation (14.1) equal to zero to find its roots, i.e., the two points at which the percentage total contribution change $\blacktriangle K$ equals zero. This occurs when:

$$\blacktriangle P = 0; \quad \frac{1 - \epsilon_0\, CM_0}{\epsilon_0} \qquad \text{Eq. (14.5)}$$

Comparing the second root of Equation (14.5) with Equation (14.3), it is seen to be twice the optimal percentage price change for contribution maximization. Hence the price range for positive contribution changes extends from $\blacktriangle P = 0$ to $\blacktriangle P = 2 \times \blacktriangle P^*$.

14.1.6 The Optimal Price

The optimal price is the original price P_0 plus the optimal incremental price change as given by Equation (14.3):

$$P^* = \frac{P_0}{2\,\epsilon_0}\,\{1 + \epsilon_0\,(2 - CM_0)\} \qquad \text{Eq. (14.6)}$$

The optimal price is seen to depend on three parameters only, namely, the original sell price and the P.E.D. and unit contribution margin at that price.[3]

14.1.7 The Total Contribution Price Range

Sales revenue can generate total contribution only within a limited price range under the given conditions. This range is:

$$VC_0 < P_1 < \frac{P_0\,(\epsilon_0 + 1)}{\epsilon_0} \qquad \text{Eq. (14.7)}$$

The lower price limit is the unit variable cost VC_0 since no contribution is generated below this price point while the upper limit is identical to the sales revenue price range of Equation (13.7) of Chapter 13 because there can be no contribution without sales.

14.1.8 The Optimal Percentage Quantity Change

From the defining relationship between the P.E.D., price, and quantity one obtains from Equation (14.3):

$$\blacktriangle Q^* = \frac{\epsilon_0\,CM_0 - 1}{2} \qquad \text{Eq. (14.8)}$$

14.1.9 The Optimal Quantity

The optimal quantity is the original quantity Q_0 plus the optimal incremental quantity change as given by Equation (14.8):

$$Q^* = \frac{Q_0}{2}\,(\epsilon_0\,CM_0 + 1) \qquad \text{Eq. (14.9)}$$

14.1.10 The Maximum Total Contribution Change

The change in total contribution as a result of an optimal price change is found by inserting the optimal price change $\blacktriangle P^*$ of Equation (14.3) into Equation (14.1):

$$\blacktriangle K^* = \frac{\epsilon_0}{CM_0} (\blacktriangle P^*)^2 \qquad \text{Eq. (14.10)}$$

This formula relates, in compact form, the maximum total contribution change, the initial unit price elasticity of demand and contribution margin, and the optimal percentage price change.

14.1.11 The Maximum Total Contribution

The maximum total contribution is the original contribution K_0 plus the maximum contribution change of Equation (14.10):

$$K^* = \frac{R_0}{4\,\epsilon_0} (\epsilon_0\, CM_0 + 1)^2 \qquad \text{Eq. (14.11)}$$

The maximum total constitution that can be generated after an optimal price change, as given by Equation (14.3), is therefore a function only of the original sales revenue, price elasticity of demand, and unit contribution margin.

14.1.12 The Optimal Unit Contribution Margin

After the optimal price change, the unit contribution margin is given by:

$$CM^* = \frac{P^* - CV_0}{P^*} \qquad \text{Eq. (14.12)}$$

where the optimal price P^* is found from Equation (14.6).

14.1.13 The Optimal Sales Revenue

The marketer will also want to know the sales revenue after an optimal price change for profit maximization. This information may be obtained by inserting the optimal price change ▲P* given above into Equation (13.2) of Chapter 13 (Pricing for Maximum Revenue):

$$R^* = \frac{R_0}{4 \, \varepsilon_0} \{1 + \varepsilon_0{}^2 \, CM_0 \, (2 - CM_0) + 2 \, \varepsilon_0\} \qquad \text{Eq. (14.13)}$$

14.1.14 The Optimal Price Elasticity of Demand

The optimal P.E.D. is from Equation (14.4):

$$\varepsilon^* = \frac{1}{CM^*}$$

$$\varepsilon^* = \frac{P^*}{P^* - VC_0} \qquad \text{Eq.(14.14)}$$

Inserting Equation (14.6) into Equation (14.14) results in this expression for the optimal P.E.D. for contribution maximization:

$$\varepsilon^* = \frac{P_0 + \varepsilon_0 \, (P_0 + VC_0)}{P_0 + \varepsilon_0 \, (P_0 - VC_0)} \qquad \text{Eq. (14.15)}$$

According to this formula, the optimal price elasticity of demand for profit maximization is either 1.0 or larger than 1.0 and can never be less than 1.0 ($\varepsilon^* \geq 1.0$). In other words, the optimal price for profit maximization must always lie on the elastic portion of the product's demand curve.

14.1.15 A Comparison of Optimal Prices

In a practical case where the unit variable cost is not zero, the marketer will want to know how far apart the optimal prices for total contribution P* and sales revenue maximization [P] are. If one takes the difference between these two optimal prices as given by Equation (14.6) above and Equation (13.6) of Chapter 13 one obtains:

$$\Delta P = P^* - [P]$$

$$\Delta P = \frac{P_0}{2}(1 - CM_0) \qquad \text{Eq. (14.16)}$$

Clearly, as the percentage unit contribution margin CM_0 increases, the price difference between the two optimal prices gets smaller so that when $CM_0 = 1.0$ (100%) and $VC_0 = 0$, the price difference is zero.

14.2 The Normalized Formulas

Three of the formulas in our collection may be "normalized" to make them independent of the original conditions. These are Equation (14.6) for computing the optimal price P* for total contribution (profit) maximization, Equation (14.9) for the optimal quantity Q*, and Equation (14.11) for the maximum total contribution K*. Rewritten and normalized these become:

$$\frac{P^*}{P_0} = \frac{\{1 + \epsilon_0 (2 - CM_0)\}}{2 \epsilon_0} \qquad \text{Eq. (14.6A)}$$

$$\frac{Q^*}{Q_0} = \frac{(\epsilon_0 CM_0 + 1)}{2} \qquad \text{Eq. (14.9A)}$$

$$\frac{K^*}{R_0} = \frac{(\epsilon_0 CM_0 + 1)^2}{4 \epsilon_0} \qquad \text{Eq. (14.11A)}$$

14.3 Reference Tables

A very useful pricing tool is Table 14-1 entitled "Optimal Percentage Price Changes for Total Contribution (Profit) Maximization" at the end of this chapter which is based on Equation (14.3) above. It allows the pricer to quickly find the price change required to maximize total contribution and profit knowing the price elasticity of demand and percentage unit contribution margin of the product or service at the present price-volume operating point.

A graphical representation of Equation (14.3) is shown in

Figure 14-1 for unit contribution margins of 20%, 50%, and 80%. As one might expect, the curves for 80% and 50% cross the horizontal x-axis where the optimal price change is zero. This occurs at price elasticities of demand of 1.25 and 2.0, respectively, which are the optimal P.E.D.s ($\mathcal{E}^*$) for these two percentage contribution margins. The curve for a 20% contribution margin never crosses the horizontal axis because the optimal P.E.D. for this contribution margin is 5.0 and off the chart.

Figure 14-1 tells us that for profit maximization, i) the lower the unit contribution margin, the larger is the required price change (in absolute terms) at all P.E.D. levels, and ii) the required price changes decrease with increasing price elasticities of demand for all unit contribution margins.

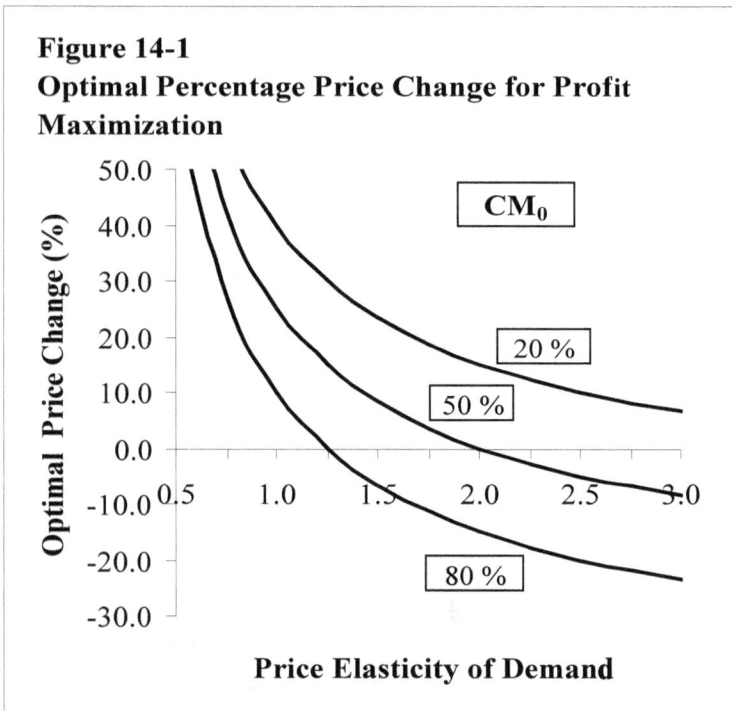

Figure 14-1
Optimal Percentage Price Change for Profit Maximization

Another useful pricing tool is the set of Tables 14-2 (1) and 14-2 (2) entitled "Optimal Price & Maximum Contribution (Normalized)" which are based on the normalized Equations (14-6A) and (14-11A) above. These allow the marketer to quickly determine the optimal prices and maximum total contribution (profit) for any product on the market.

This set of tables is meant as a sample only. For practical reasons, it covers only a limited range of price elasticities of demand, from 0.25 to 3.00 in steps of 0.25, and unit contribution margins of 20%, 30%, 50%, 70%, and 80%. Other listings with smaller P.E.D. and CM_0 increments may, of course, be easily developed and made available as an app.

The precautionary note mentioned in Section 13.3 of Chapter 13 (Pricing for Maximum Revenue) about the use of Tables 13-1 and 13-2 applies here as well. Because Table 14-2 (2) is based on formulas in which the optimal percentage price changes given by Equation (14.3) have been fully integrated, the values listed in this table are valid only after the optimal percentage price changes called for in Equation (14.3) have been implemented.

14.4 Application

The following illustrative example will show how the above formulas may be used to analyze and solve a profit pricing problem either mathematically, by use of the tables, or graphically.

Illustrative Example: Droneco Ltd. (II)

For this example, we return to Droneco which was introduced in Chapter 9 (Value Pricing) as a manufacturer of small surveillance drones for governmental and private use. One of the company's most popular models is the Firebird-7 which is being successfully used on the West Coast for spotting and monitoring wildfires. Once the drone has spotted such a fire, it hovers over it and sends back photographic images as well as real-time data including the fire's exact position, its intensity, the area covered, its speed and direction, and endangered structures in the fire's path.

The average net price of the Firebird-7 is $12,000 while the unit variable cost is $8,400 giving it a unit contribution margin of

$3,600 (30.0%). Monthly sales are 10 vehicles for a sales revenue of $120,000 and total contribution of $36,000. The marketing manager has estimated that a 10% price increase will reduce sales volume by only 15% (P.E.D. of 1.5). Management would like to make an incremental price change for this model to maximize profit.

In solving this pricing problem, we shall first follow the sequence of formulas given above and then use the shortcut provided by Tables 14-1 and 14-2 to get some quick answers. The analysis ends with the familiar graphical technique using just Equations (13.2) and (14.2) for sales revenue and total contribution, respectively, to plot the two functions.

14.4.1 Formula Solution

The above sixteen formulas will be applied in the exact sequence given.

i) Suppose, the Firebird-7 price was increased by 10%, what would be the impact on total contribution? By the PIF of Equation (14.1) one obtains:

$$\blacktriangle K = 1 / 0.30 \{- 1.5 (0.10)^2 + (1 - 1.5 \times 0.30) (0.10)\} = 0.133$$

Thus, a 10% price increase would raise monthly total contribution by 13.3%.

ii) The monthly total contribution after the price change would simply be the contribution prior to the price change plus the added contribution from the price change:

$$K_1 = K_0 (1 + \blacktriangle K) = \$36,000 (1 + 0.1333) = \$40,800$$

The same result is obtained directly from Equation (14.2):

$$K_1 = \$120,000 \{- 1.5 (0.10)^2 + (1 - 1.5 \times 0.30) 0.10 + 0.30\}$$
$$K_1 = \$40,800$$

iii) The optimal percentage price change is found from Equation (14.3):

$$\blacktriangle P^* = (1 - 1.5 \times 0.30) / (2 \times 1.5) = 0.1833$$

The optimal incremental price adjustment for profit maximization is therefore a price increase of 18.3%

iv) By Equation (14.4) the optimal P.E.D. requiring no price change is $\epsilon^* = 1 / CM_0 = 1 / 0.30 = 3.33$. Since the estimated P.E.D. in the present case is $\epsilon_0 = 1.50$ so that $\epsilon_0 < \epsilon^*$, by the General Pricing Rule of Thumb (1) given in Table 8-1 of Chapter 8, the price should be raised. This was indeed found to be the case above.

v) From Equation (14.5), the end points for positive contribution changes are:

$$\blacktriangle P = 0 \text{ and } \blacktriangle P = (1 - 1.5 \times 0.30) / 1.5 = 0.367$$

Hence, the price range for positive total contribution changes extends from $12,000 to $16,400 ($12,000 × 1.367).

vi) The optimal price is the original price plus the incremental price increase for profit maximization:

$$P^* = \$12,000 \ (1 + 0.1833) = \$14,200$$

The same result may also be obtained directly from Equation (14.6):

$$P^* = \$12,000 \ \{1 + 1.5 \ (2 - 0.30)\} / \ (2 \times 1.5) = \$14,200$$

vii) The range of prices for which the sales revenue generates total contribution is given by Equation (14.7):

$$\$8,400 < P_1 < \$12,000 \ (1.5 + 1) / 1.5$$
$$\$8,400 < P_1 < \$20,000$$

viii) The optimal percentage quantity change is obtained from Equation (14.8):

$$\blacktriangle Q^* = (1.5 \times 0.30 - 1) / 2 = -0.275$$

Thus, the 18.3% price increase comes at the expense of a 27.5% drop in sales volume.

ix) The optimal quantity sold is the original quantity plus the incremental quantity change due to the price change:

$$Q^* = 10 \ (1 - 0.275) = 7.25$$

One can obtain the same result by use of Equation (14.9):

$$Q^* = (10 / 2) \ (1.5 \times 0.30 + 1) = 7.25$$

x) The maximum total contribution change may be computed from Equation (14.10):

$$\blacktriangle K^* = 1.5 \ (0.1833)^2 / 0.30 = 0.168$$

Thus, the 18.3% price increase results in a 16.8% profit increase.

xi) The maximum total contribution is the original total contribution plus the added total contribution from the price increase:

$$K^* = \$36,000 \ (1 + 0.168) = \$42,050$$

Using Equation (14.11) the same result is obtained directly:

$$K^* = \$120,000 / 6.0 \ \{(1.5 \times 0.30 + 1)^2\} = \$42,050$$

xii) Equation (14.12) gives the optimal unit contribution margin:

$$CM^* = (\$14,200 - \$8,400) / \$14,200 = 0.408$$

Hence, the price increase resulted in a substantial contribution margin increase from 30.0% to 40.8%.

xiii) The optimal sales revenue is by Equation (14.13):

$$R^* = \$120,000 / 6.0 \ \{1 + (1.5)^2 \ (0.30) \ (2 - 0.30) + 3.0\} = \$103,000$$

This represents a sales revenue reduction of about 14%.

xiv) The optimal P.E.D. after the optimal price change is found by Equation (14.14):

$$\epsilon^* = \$14,200 / (\$14,200 - \$8,400) = 2.45$$

This result may be verified using Equation (14.15):

$$\epsilon^* = \{\$12,000 + 1.5 \ (\$12,000 + \$8,400)\} / \{\$12,000 + 1.5$$
$$(\$12,000 - \$8,400)\} = 2.45$$

This represents a P.E.D. increase of over 63% pushing the new price-volume operating point further into the elastic region.

xv) The price difference between the optimal prices for total contribution maximization P* and sales revenue maximization [P] is given by Equation (14.16):

$$\Delta P = \$12,000 \, (1 - 0.30) / 2 = \$4,200$$

This is as expected because by Equation (13.6) of Chapter 13, the optimal price for sales revenue maximization is:

$$[P] = \$12,000 \, (1.5 + 1) / (2 \times 1.5) = \$10,000$$

This is $4,200 less than the optimal price for total contribution computed in item vi) above.

14.4.2 Reference Table Solution

For some quick answers, management could also check out the two tables shown at the end of this chapter, namely, Table 14-1 (Optimal Price Change for Total Contribution Maximization) and Table 14-2 (Optimal Price and Maximum Total Contribution - Normalized).

i) Table 14-1

The initial values for Firebird-7 were given as $P_0 = \$12,000$, $\varepsilon_0 = 1.5$, $CM_0 = 30\%$, and $R_0 = \$120,000$. From Table 14-1, the optimal price change $\blacktriangle P*$ for profit maximization is seen to be 18.3% giving an optimal price of

$$P* = P_0 \, (1 + \blacktriangle P* \,) = \$12,000 \, (1 + 0.183) = \$14,196$$

which is close to the formula result of $14,200.

ii) Table 14-2

From Tables 14-2 (1) and 14-2 (2) one obtains, respectively, $P* / P_0 = 1.183$ and $K* / R_0 = 0.350$ which gives us an optimal price and maximum total contribution, respectively, of

$$P* = \$12,000 \times 1.183 = \$14.196, \text{ and}$$
$$K* = \$120,000 \times 0.350 = \$42,000$$

which both again closely match the formula results. As mentioned before, the values listed in Table 14-2 (2) presuppose that the price change called for by Eq (14.3), here an 18.3% price increase, has been implemented.

14.4.3 Graphical Solution

To plot the graph for total contribution, we apply Equation (14.2) using the initial operating point values, namely, $R_0 = \$120,000$, $\varepsilon_0 = 1.5$, and $CM_0 = 30\%$ to obtain:

Figure 14-2
Revenue & Toatal Contribution for Firebird -7
Original Parameter Estimates

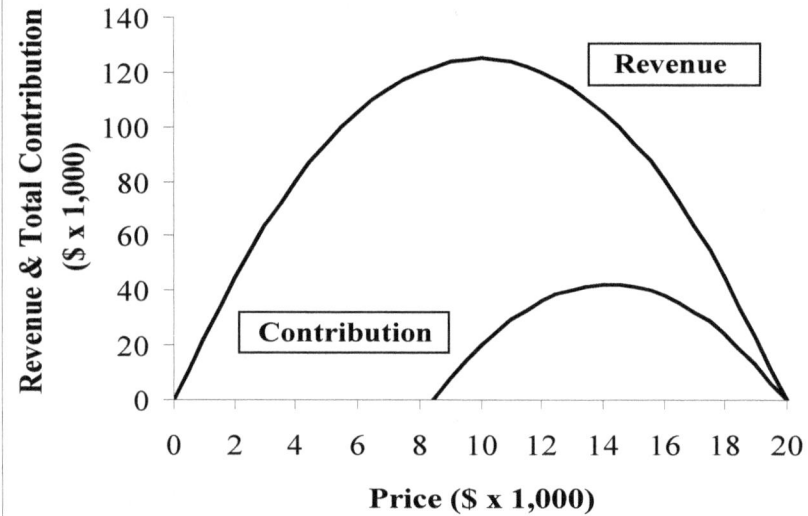

$K_1 = \$120,000 \{-1.5 \,(\blacktriangle P)^2 + 0.55 \,\blacktriangle P + 0.30\}$

where $\blacktriangle P = (P_1 - P_0) / P_0 = (P_1 - 12,000) / 12,000$.

The curve, given in Figure 14-2 and labeled "Contribution," shows total contribution to peak at around \$40,000 at a price of about \$15,000 which is consistent with previous results.

The sales revenue after an incremental price change $\blacktriangle P$ is found by use of Equation (13.2) in Chapter 13:

$$R_1 = R_0 \{1 - \varepsilon_0 \,(\blacktriangle P)^2 + (1 - \varepsilon_0) \,\blacktriangle P\} \qquad \text{Eq. (13.2)}$$

Inserting the initial values, one obtains:

$$: \quad R_1 = \$120{,}000 \ \{1 - 1.5\,(\blacktriangle P)^2 - 0.5\ \blacktriangle P\}$$

This curve in Figure 14-2 and labeled "Revenue" shows the optimal price and maximum sales revenue at the peak of the total contribution curve to be about $15,000 and $100,000, respectively. This confirms the earlier formula results, which gave us the more precise values of P* = $14,200 and R* = $103,000, respectively.

Total contribution is seen to be positive within the price range of $8,400 to $20,000 the lower limit being the unit variable cost VC_0 below which no contribution is generated. The optimal price for profit maximization is found exactly at the midpoint of this price range. These results agree with those obtained by formula.

Viewing the two curves of Figure 14-2 together, a significant point is that total contribution towards overhead and profit is earned at a narrow price range only which here extends from $8,400 to $20,000. Any lower prices can result in very large sales but these will not be profitable. These lower prices are obviously very favorable to the buyer but not to the seller although they are not entirely without benefit to the firm as they may, for instance, help keep unit variable costs down. The range of prices for which optimal price changes lead to positive total contribution changes is even more confined and here from $12,000 to $16,400.

Because it's difficult to obtain accurate estimates of the major pricing parameters, the price elasticity of demand and the unit contribution margin, the obvious solution is to plot curves for a number of these parameters to evaluate their impact on the favorable price ranges and total contributions.

Figure 14-3, which is also based on Equation (14.2) above, shows the Firebird-7 total contributions for price elasticities of demand of 1.0 and 2.0 and unit contribution margins of 30% and 70%, respectively, at various prices from 0 to $24,000. Interesting is the difference in the spread of favorable prices and the size of the maximum achievable total contributions with changes in these two parameters. The profitable price ranges are clearly a function of the price elasticity of demand while the size of total contribution depends mostly on the unit contribution margin. Larger unit margins result in higher profits as one would expect.

14.4.4 Conclusion

Our analysis has shown that the Firebird-7 surveillance drone is under-priced in view of the goal of maximum total contribution and profit. The price requires an upward adjustment of about 18% to $14,200 which will result in a total contribution and profit increase of about 17% to $42,050. With the adjusted price, the monthly sales volume will decline from 10 to 7 units and the sales revenue from $120,000 to $103,000. This all presupposes, of course, that management's two parameter estimates were correct. Since this is not assured, other parameters need to be evaluated as previously indicated.

Figure 14-3
Total Contribution for Firebird-7: Diverse Parameter Estimates

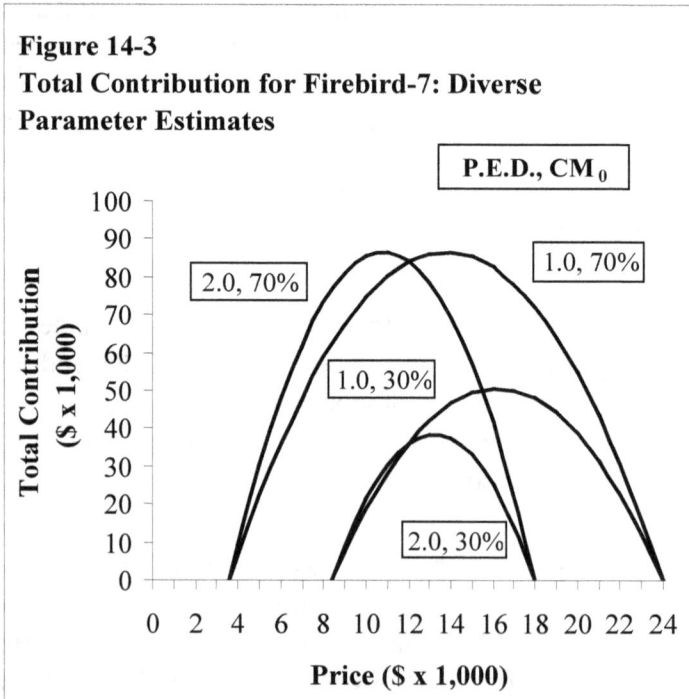

P.E.D., CM_0

2.0, 70%   1.0, 70%   1.0, 30%   2.0, 30%

Total Contribution ($ x 1,000)

Price ($ x 1,000)

Considering the new and higher Firebird-7 prices the question arises whether the other Droneco models now require repricing in order to keep a logical sequence in price and value as has been proposed. (See the Weber-Fechner Law discussed in Section 9.4 of Chapter 9). Not necessarily. To the extent that other models are designed for and marketed to product-market segments other than wildfire surveillance, they will face completely different demand curves and price elasticities of demand and should therefore be priced accordingly. Only models serving the same product-market segment need to be priced so as to reflect value differences.

14.5 Sales Volume vs. Total Contribution

The business sections of major dailies and other media often report on the quarterly financial results of major companies. Sales revenue and earnings changes are obviously of much interest especially to investors in these firms. Sometimes the news is good with hefty increases in both revenue and earnings. Most often it is less favorable with either sales revenue or earnings increasing while the other is declining.

The question often asked is whether these movements in sales and earnings can serve as a clue about the firms' price levels and, more specifically, whether this information is sufficient to tell management whether or not its prices need adjustment and, if so, in which direction. The answer is affirmative but only if one considers the relationship between sales volume (quantity sold) and total contribution or profit.

Figure 14-4 shows two typical total contribution curves labeled K which are seen to closely resemble the ones shown in Figure 12-2 of Chapter 12 and Figures 14-2 and 14-3 of the present chapter. Also shown and labeled Q are the linear price response curves showing the number of units sold at each price level during a given time period. In the left-hand graph, the movement of K is in the clockwise direction, as indicated by the two arrows, and the right-hand graph by movement in the counterclockwise direction also shown by two arrows. One can identity four pricing situations:

Figure 14-4
Total Contribution & Sales Volume Changes vs. Price

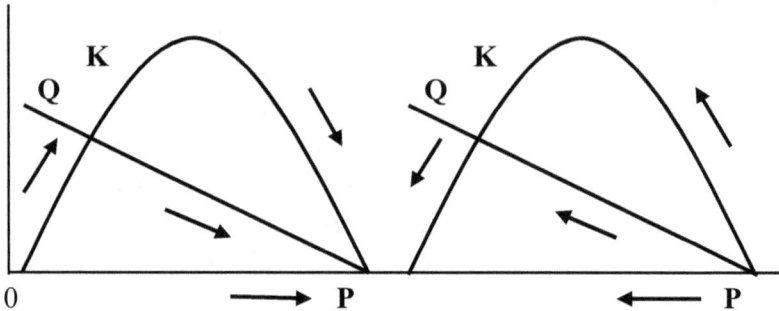

i) In the left-hand graph, as contribution K increases toward the maximum value (reached when the price P is at P*), sales volume Q is seen to decrease. By the law of demand, a quantity reduction is accompanied by a price increase. Since the movement to a higher value of K is favorable, the direction of the price change is also favorable, i.e., a further price increase is called for.

ii) In the left-hand graph, after contribution K has peaked at K* and is declining, sales volume Q continues to drop while the price P is increasing. Since the reduction in K is unfavorable, its decline must be reversed by decreasing the price P and increasing quantity Q.

iii) In the right-hand graph, as contribution K is rising so is sales volume Q. An increasing sales volume means a reduction in price P. Since an increasing K is favorable, the price movement is favorable also and the price should continue to be reduced.

iv) In the right-hand graph, after contribution has peaked, sales volume Q continues to increase while the price drops. Since the reduction in K is unfavorable, the situation must be reversed and the price increased with a consequent reduction in sales volume Q.

14.6 Pricing Guidelines (VIII)

The above observations lead to the last five pricing propositions and a second general pricing rule of thumb.

Pricing Proposition 16

For any product or service there exists one and only one optimal sell price for total contribution and profit maximization and all price points below or above this optimal price will result in less than maximum total contribution and profit for that product or service.

Pricing Proposition 17

a. The optimal price change for total contribution and profit maximization depends on only two parameters, namely, the product's unit contribution margin and its price elasticity of demand at the price-volume operating point (P_0, Q_0) prior to the price change.

b. Where the pricing objective is to maximize total contribution and profit for a given product or service and its price elasticity of demand ϵ_0 does not equal $1 / CM_0$, an incremental price adjustment in the amount of

$$\blacktriangle P^* = \frac{1 - \epsilon_0 \, CM_0}{2 \, \epsilon_0} \times 100\%$$

is required.

Pricing Proposition 18

The larger the deviation from the optimal price for total contribution and profit maximization, the greater will be the rate of decline in total contribution and profit so that if the sell price is below the optimal level and is further reduced or is above the optimal level and is further increased, the negative effects will be multiplied.

Pricing Proposition 19

For total contribution and profit maximization,

a) the lower the unit contribution margin, the larger is the required price change (in absolute terms) at all P.E.D. levels, and

b) the required price changes decrease with increasing price elasticities of demand for all unit contribution margins.

Pricing Proposition 20

In all practical cases, the unit contribution margin after an optimal price change for total contribution and profit maximization will always be higher than before the change.

General Pricing Rule of Thumb (2)

To increase contribution and profit for a given product, service or line of products or services, lower or raise prices depending on whether sales volumes and total contributions (profits) are changing in the same or opposite directions—

i) lower prices if the changes are in the same direction, and
ii) raise prices if the changes are in opposite directions.

The company's accounting department should be able to furnish the data on the number of units sold and the total contribution dollars generated by these sales over some interval of time so that appropriate price adjustments can be made where necessary.

Illustrative Example: West Valley Auto Sales

West Valley Auto Sales markets the automobiles of one of the top three American makes and has been very profitable over the years. The firm tracks monthly volume sales by brand name and model type along with the total contribution dollars earned. General manager Kate Windsor has recently noticed a disturbing trend over the past three months for one of their most popular models.

While the number of cars sold has been on the rise each month, the profitability of these sales has been significantly declining. She is at a loss to explain the situation because there have not been any formal price changes or special promotions for that brand nor was anything else undertaken that could have caused the trend.

Analyzing the problem, Kate realized that it could have resulted from any number of factors but that the pricing option was most likely the key especially since her sales force has considerable discretion in setting individual prices. The West Valley scenario fits situation iv) described above of increasing quantity sales Q and declining total contribution K, i.e., the optimum price level for contribution maximization has been passed and prices are declining when they should be rising.

In line with the above General Pricing Rule of Thumb (2), Kate has now decided to enlist her salespeople in a concerted effort to halt the suspected price erosion and stabilize prices by issuing new guidelines on available price discretion. In addition, she is considering an upward price adjustment as well after she has completed her analysis to include obtaining some good estimates of the price elasticities of demand for the various makes and models in the company's inventory.

14.7 Concluding Comments

Price optimization offers the marketer an alternative to isoprofit analysis (see Chapter 7) for analyzing price changes with the goal of improving contribution and profits. There are differences and similarities between the two techniques and the price-setter may come to prefer one over the other or use the two in combination. With isoprofit (also equal-profit or break-even sales) analysis, the marketer asks, "Will a price change of x percent be profitable?" With price optimization the question is, "What price must we charge to maximize profit and what will be that profit?"

Both techniques depend on knowing two quantities, namely, the price elasticity of demand and the unit contribution margin. In price optimization use of the P.E.D. is explicit because it enters directly into the formulas. In isoprofit analysis the requirement to know the P.E.D. is implicit because the marketer must estimate by what percentage sales volume will change as a result of the contemplated percentage price change. Knowing this ratio is, of course, equivalent to knowing the price elasticity of demand.

Clearly then, having good and valid estimates of these two parameters, namely, the P.E.D. and the unit contribution margin is crucially important in evaluating price change options for any product or service and by any method the marketer may choose. It will be incumbent on the firm's cost accounting department to arrive at accurate values for the average unit variable cost VC_0, the average net sell price P_0, and the average unit contribution margin CM_0 for the specific target market in which the product or service is being offered. As previously noted, the marketer must become very knowledgeable about the price sensitivity of his or her products and services, i.e., how incremental price changes will affect the quantities sold in the specific market segment, the target market, in which the product or service is being offered.

Whether the pricing goal is maximum sales revenue or total contribution and profit, the analyses in this and the previous chapter point out one inescapable fact. Because each product or service has a unique optimal price at any given time and place and it is usually not feasible to determine and implement optimal prices for very large assortments of products and services, most products and services offered by firms are likely to be either under- or overpriced resulting in less than achievable sales revenues or profits.

Notes

1. Robert Dolan and Hermann Simon, *Power Pricing*, 28.

2. The British economist A. P. Learner graphically demonstrated that at the point of maximum profit "The elasticity of demand is equal to the price divided by the difference between price and marginal cost—it is the inverse of our formula for the measurement of the degree of monopoly power," 169-170. See A. P. Learner, "The Concept of Monopoly and the Measurement of Monopoly Power," *The Review of Economic Studies*, Volume 1, Issue 3, June 1934, 157-175.

It is easy to show that the optimal condition for profit maximization as given by Equation (14.4) above is the equivalent of the formula

$$MR = P - \frac{P}{\epsilon}$$

found in many economic texts. See, for example, J. P. Gould and C. E. Ferguson, *Microeconomic Theory*, 112, and Ross Eckert and Richard Leftwich, *The Price System and Resource Allocation*, 356. Since economic theory holds that at the optimal price for profit maximization, marginal revenue equals marginal cost ($MR = MC$) and since marginal cost can be approximated by the unit variable cost ($MC = VC$), replacing MR with VC in the above equation and transposing terms one obtains:

$$\mathsf{E} = \cfrac{P}{P-VC} = \cfrac{1}{CM\,(\%)} \quad \text{QED}$$

3. The so-called Amoroso-Robinson relation, named after the two economists who introduced it, describes the relationship between marginal revenue, optimal price, and P.E.D. for a specific product x:

$$\frac{\partial R}{\partial x} = P\left(1 + \frac{1}{\mathsf{E}}\right)$$

where R = revenue, P = optimal price, and E = price elasticity ($\mathsf{E} < 0$).

Price consultants and authors Simon and Fassnacht have reformulated the Amoroso-Robinson relation giving this expression:

$$P^* = \frac{\mathsf{E}}{1 + \mathsf{E}}\,C'$$

where P* = product's optimal price in each market segment, E = segment-specific price elasticity of demand, and C' = segment-specific marginal cost. (The authors do not follow the usual practice of including a minus sign in their definition of price elasticity of demand).

Regarding the usefulness of the Amoroso-Robinson relation, Simon and Fassnacht noted: "The optimal price is thus an elasticity-based markup on marginal costs. What is shown [in their equation above], however, does not solve for the optimal price P*; rather it is simply a reformulation for the necessary condition 'marginal revenue = marginal cost.'" Nevertheless, the authors found that the Amoroso-Robinson relation provides a strong theoretical basis for the pricing rules of thumb employed by managers in diverse industries where cost-plus pricing is the norm. See Hermann Simon and Martin Fassnacht, *Price Management*, 187, 216, 492.

Table 14-1
Optimal Percentage Price Changes for Total Contribution (Profit) Maximization

CM₀ (%)	Price Elasticity of Demand (E_0)												
	0.5	0.6	0.7	0.8	0.9	1.0	1.1	1.2	1.3	1.4	1.5	1.6	1.7
5	97.5	80.8	68.9	60.0	53.1	47.5	43.0	39.2	36.0	33.2	30.8	28.8	26.9
10	95.0	78.3	66.4	57.5	50.6	45.0	40.5	36.7	33.5	30.7	28.3	26.3	24.4
15	92.5	75.8	63.9	55.0	48.1	42.5	38.0	34.2	31.0	28.2	25.8	23.8	21.9
20	90.0	73.3	61.4	52.5	45.6	40.0	35.5	31.7	28.5	25.7	23.3	21.3	19.4
25	87.5	70.8	58.9	50.0	43.1	37.5	33.0	29.2	26.0	23.2	20.8	18.8	16.9
30	85.0	68.3	56.4	47.5	40.6	35.0	30.5	26.7	23.5	20.7	18.3	16.3	14.4
35	82.5	65.8	53.9	45.0	38.1	32.5	28.0	24.2	21.0	18.2	15.8	13.8	11.9
40	80.0	63.3	51.4	42.5	35.6	30.0	25.5	21.7	18.5	15.7	13.3	11.3	9.4
45	77.5	60.8	48.9	40.0	33.1	27.5	23.0	19.2	16.0	13.2	10.8	8.8	6.9
50	75.0	58.3	46.4	37.5	30.6	25.0	20.5	16.7	13.5	10.7	8.3	6.3	4.4
55	72.5	55.8	43.9	35.0	28.1	22.5	18.0	14.2	11.0	8.2	5.8	3.8	1.9
60	70.0	53.3	41.4	32.5	25.6	20.0	15.5	11.7	8.5	5.7	3.3	0.0	(0.6)
65	67.5	50.8	38.9	30.0	23.1	17.5	13.0	9.2	6.0	3.2	0.8	(1.3)	(3.1)
70	65.0	48.3	36.4	27.5	20.6	15.0	10.5	6.7	3.5	0.7	(1.7)	(3.8)	(5.6)
75	62.5	45.8	33.9	25.0	18.1	12.5	8.0	4.2	1.0	(1.8)	(4.2)	(6.3)	(8.1)
80	60.0	43.3	31.4	22.5	15.6	10.0	5.5	1.7	(1.5)	(4.3)	(6.7)	(8.8)	(10.6)
85	57.5	40.8	28.9	20.0	13.1	7.5	3.0	(0.8)	(4.0)	(6.8)	(9.2)	(11.3)	(13.1)
90	55.0	38.3	26.4	17.5	10.6	5.0	0.5	(3.3)	(6.5)	(9.3)	(11.7)	(13.8)	(15.6)
95	52.5	35.8	23.9	15.0	8.1	2.5	(2.0)	(5.8)	(9.0)	(11.8)	(14.2)	(16.3)	(18.1)
100	50.0	33.3	21.4	12.5	5.6	0.0	(4.6)	(8.3)	(11.5)	(14.3)	(16.7)	(18.8)	(20.6)

Table 14-1
Optimal Percentage Price Changes for Total Contribution (Profit) Maximization

CM₀ (%)	Price Elasticity of Demand ε_0												
	1.8	1.9	2.0	2.1	2.2	2.3	2.4	2.5	2.6	2.7	2.8	2.9	3.0
5	25.3	23.8	22.5	21.3	20.2	19.2	18.3	17.5	16.7	16.0	15.4	14.7	14.2
10	22.8	21.3	20.0	18.8	17.7	16.7	15.8	15.0	14.2	13.5	12.9	12.2	11.7
15	20.3	18.8	17.5	16.3	15.2	14.2	13.3	12.5	11.7	11.0	10.4	9.7	9.2
20	17.8	16.3	15.0	13.8	12.7	11.7	10.8	10.0	9.2	8.5	7.9	7.2	6.7
25	15.3	13.8	12.5	11.3	10.2	9.2	8.3	7.5	6.7	6.0	5.4	4.7	4.2
30	12.8	11.3	10.0	8.8	7.7	6.7	5.8	5.0	4.2	3.5	2.9	2.2	1.7
35	10.3	8.8	7.5	6.3	5.2	4.2	3.3	2.5	1.7	1.0	0.4	(0.3)	(0.8)
40	7.8	6.3	5.0	3.8	2.7	1.7	0.8	0.0	(0.8)	(1.5)	(2.1)	(2.8)	(3.3)
45	5.3	3.8	2.5	1.3	0.2	(0.8)	(1.7)	(2.5)	(3.3)	(4.0)	(4.6)	(5.3)	(5.8)
50	2.8	1.3	0.0	(1.2)	(2.3)	(3.3)	(4.2)	(5.0)	(5.8)	(6.5)	(7.1)	(7.8)	(8.3)
55	0.3	(1.2)	(2.5)	(3.7)	(4.8)	(5.8)	(6.7)	(7.5)	(8.3)	(9.0)	(9.6)	(10.3)	(10.8)
60	(2.2)	(3.7)	(5.0)	(6.2)	(7.3)	(8.3)	(9.2)	(10.0)	(10.8)	(11.5)	(12.1)	(12.8)	(13.3)
65	(4.7)	(6.2)	(7.5)	(8.7)	(9.8)	(10.8)	(11.7)	(12.5)	(13.3)	(14.0)	(14.6)	(15.3)	(15.8)
70	(7.2)	(8.7)	(10.0)	(11.2)	(12.3)	(13.3)	(14.2)	(15.0)	(15.8)	(16.5)	(17.1)	(17.8)	(18.3)
75	(9.7)	(11.2)	(12.5)	(13.7)	(14.8)	(15.8)	(16.7)	(17.5)	(18.3)	(19.0)	(19.6)	(20.3)	(20.8)
80	(12.2)	(13.7)	(15.0)	(16.2)	(17.3)	(18.3)	(19.2)	(20.0)	(20.8)	(21.5)	(22.1)	(22.8)	(23.3)
85	(14.7)	(16.2)	(17.5)	(18.7)	(19.8)	(20.8)	(21.7)	(22.5)	(23.3)	(24.0)	(24.6)	(25.3)	(25.8)
90	(17.2)	(18.7)	(20.0)	(21.2)	(22.3)	(23.3)	(24.2)	(25.0)	(25.8)	(26.5)	(27.1)	(27.8)	(28.3)
95	(19.7)	(21.2)	(22.5)	(23.7)	(24.8)	(25.8)	(26.7)	(27.5)	(28.3)	(29.0)	(29.6)	(30.3)	(30.8)
100	(22.2)	(23.7)	(25.0)	(26.2)	(27.3)	(28.3)	(29.2)	(30.0)	(30.8)	(31.5)	(32.1)	(32.8)	(33.3)

Table 14-2 (1)
Optimal Price & Maximum Contribution (Normalized)

P.E.D. (ϵ_0)	CM_0 (%)	Optimal Price ($P*/P_0$)	P.E.D. (ϵ_0)	CM_0 (%)	Optimal Price ($P*/P_0$)
0.25	20	2.600	1.75	50	1.036
0.50	20	1.900	2.00	50	1.000
0.75	20	1.567	2.25	50	0.972
1.00	20	1.400	2.50	50	0.950
1.25	20	1.300	2.75	50	0.932
1.50	20	1.233	3.00	50	0.917
1.75	20	1.186	0.25	70	2.650
2.00	20	1.150	0.50	70	1.650
2.25	20	1.122	0.75	70	1.317
2.50	20	1.100	1.00	70	1.150
2.75	20	1.082	1.25	70	1.050
3.00	20	1.067	1.50	70	0.983
0.25	30	2.850	1.75	70	0.936
0.50	30	1.850	2.00	70	0.900
0.75	30	1.517	2.25	70	0.872
1.00	30	1.350	2.50	70	0.850
1.25	30	1.250	2.75	70	0.832
1.50	30	1.183	3.00	70	0.817
1.75	30	1.136	0.25	80	2.600
2.00	30	1.100	0.50	80	1.600
2.25	30	1.072	0.75	80	1.267
2.50	30	1.050	1.00	80	1.100
2.75	30	1.032	1.25	80	1.000
3.00	30	1.017	1.50	80	0.933
0.25	50	2.750	1.75	80	0.886
0.50	50	1.750	2.00	80	0.850
0.75	50	1.417	2.25	80	0.822
1.00	50	1.250	2.50	80	0.800
1.25	50	1.150	2.75	80	0.782
1.50	50	1.083	3.00	80	0.767

Table 14-2 (2)
Optimal Price & Maximum Contribution (Normalized)

P.E.D. (ϵ_0)	CM_0 (%)	Maximum Contribution K^*/R_0	P.E.D. (ϵ_0)	CM_0 (%)	Maximum Contribution K^*/R_0
0.25	20	1.103	1.75	50	0.502
0.50	20	0.605	2.00	50	0.500
0.75	20	0.441	2.25	50	0.502
1.00	20	0.360	2.50	50	0.506
1.25	20	0.313	2.75	50	0.513
1.50	20	0.282	3.00	50	0.521
1.75	20	0.260	0.25	70	1.381
2.00	20	0.245	0.50	70	0.911
2.25	20	0.234	0.75	70	0.775
2.50	20	0.225	1.00	70	0.723
2.75	20	0.218	1.25	70	0.703
3.00	20	0.213	1.50	70	0.700
0.25	30	1.156	1.75	70	0.707
0.50	30	0.661	2.00	70	0.720
0.75	30	0.500	2.25	70	0.737
1.00	30	0.423	2.50	70	0.756
1.25	30	0.378	2.75	70	0.778
1.50	30	0.350	3.00	70	0.801
1.75	30	0.332	0.25	80	1.440
2.00	30	0.320	0.50	80	0.980
2.25	30	0.312	0.75	80	0.853
2.50	30	0.306	1.00	80	0.810
2.75	30	0.303	1.25	80	0.800
3.00	30	0.301	1.50	80	0.807
0.25	50	1.266	1.75	80	0.823
0.50	50	0.781	2.00	80	0.845
0.75	50	0.630	2.25	80	0.871
1.00	50	0.563	2.50	80	0.900
1.25	50	0.528	2.75	80	0.931
1.50	50	0.510	3.00	80	0.963

CHAPTER

15

Pricing and the Law

Antitrust laws in general, and the Sherman Act in particular, are the Magna Carta of free enterprise. They are as important to the preservation of economic freedom and our free enterprise system as the Bill of Rights is to the protection of our fundamental personal freedoms.[1]

Laws and regulations, both federal and state, have a major impact on business conduct especially in the domain of pricing. The reason is obvious. Anticompetitive pricing practices can do substantial harm to a free enterprise system which presupposes prices set by market forces and not by monopolies and cartels or agreements among rival firms to reduce or eliminate competition.

15.1 An Overview

It is important for the marketer to know what the boundaries of legal conduct are since ignorance of the law can lead to losses on two fronts. On one hand, managers may become too conservative and risk-averse in their pricing practices and find in "cost-plus" or a similar suboptimal pricing scheme a safe haven. They thereby forego the significant sales and profit opportunities that can result from market oriented pricing. On the other hand, managers may engage in conduct which is proscribed and suffer the often costly consequences. Some of these are chronicled in Section 15.2 below.

The law is complex and ever changing in response to new legislation and especially court decisions as judges continue to apply existing law to new cases and sometimes reinterpret the law resulting in legal precedents. Even though this author holds a law degree with a concentration in antitrust law and is therefore qualified to write on the subject, formal legal advice is beyond the scope of *Pricing the Profitable Sale*. This chapter cannot and is not intended to serve as a substitute for sound, up-to-date legal counsel provided by an in-house legal department or outside attorneys with antitrust experience. Rather, this brief survey is meant merely to set forth and discuss the major legal issues facing the typical manager with pricing responsibilities.

This chapter begins with some prominent antitrust cases reported in the media in the past. Excerpts from the major statutes such as the Sherman and Clayton acts are presented next followed by how these impact various business practices including price fixing, predatory pricing, resale price maintenance, conscious parallelism, and price signaling. To afford the reader a better understanding of the court opinions and the underlying issues, some of the actual court cases out of which these arose are briefly discussed. The important topic of price discrimination and the Robinson-Patman Act are discussed next. Since antitrust laws are not unique to the United States, there follows a brief overview of applicable European Union laws. The chapter ends with some thoughts on pricing and ethics.

15.2 A Sampling of Antitrust Cases in the Media

When firms and their managements run afoul of the law the penalties incurred can be severe including large fines and even imprisonment for guilty executives and managers. Most cases are settled without a formal trial as a result of plea bargaining while still others are dropped for lack of sufficient evidence. A small sampling of antitrust cases reported in the print media in recent years follows.

* Vitamin price fixing draws record $755 million in fines

Chicago Tribune, May 21, 1999, 3.

Synopsis: Two companies, Hoffman-LaRoche of Switzerland and BASF of Germany entered a plea deal with the Justice department agreeing to pay $750 million in fines. The firms were accused of price-fixing and bid-rigging in the vitamin industry which caused American consumers to pay inflated prices.

* Prison for ADM execs

Chicago Tribune, July 10, 1999, 1.

Synopsis: Two senior executives from Archer Daniels Midland Co. were convicted on charges of conspiring with Japanese and Korean firms to fix the world-wide price of the livestock feed additive lysine. Each received a two year prison sentence and was fined $350,000.

* U.S. Will Not Pursue Price-Fixing Case Against Mercedes-Benz Dealers

The New York Times, December 25, 2003, B1.

Synopsis: The Department of Justice had charged Mercedes-Benz dealers from New York, New Jersey, and Connecticut of having fixed prices at secret dealer meetings. The case was initiated by a disgruntled Mercedes dealer who was dropped after unauthorized discounting. The Justice Department decided not to prosecute.

* 4 Agree to Jail Sentences in Chip Price-Fixing Case

The New York Times, December 3, 2004, B3.

Synopsis: Four marketing and sales executives from Infineon Technologies (three German and one American) entered a plea deal with the Justice Department. They had been accused of conspiring with competitors to fix prices in computer memories.

* Visa and MasterCard Settle Lawsuit but Merchants Aren't Celebrating

The New York Times, August 9, 2012, B6.

Synopsis: In a civil suit brought by 7 million retail merchants Visa and MasterCard agreed to a $7.3 billion settlement. The two credit card companies were accused of colluding, separately, with banks to eliminate competition and increase their transactions fees.

* U.S. Now Paints Apple as 'Ringmaster' in Its Lawsuit on E-Book Price-Fixing

The New York Times, May 15, 2013, B1.

Synopsis: The Justice Department charged Apple and five publishers (Hachette, HarperCollins, Macmillan, Penguin, and Simon & Schuster) with conspiring to fix e-book prices at a level above the standard $9.99 charged by Amazon. The publishers agreed to settle the charges leaving Apple the only defendant.

* Companies Admit They Fixed Prices of Car Parts

The New York Times, September 27, 2013, B1.

Synopsis: Nine Japanese automotive suppliers including Hitachi Automotive and Mitsubishi Electric agreed to plead guilty to criminal conspiracy charges and pay more than $740 million in fines. Over 25 million cars sold in the U.S. were affected by the illegal conduct.

As may be noted, all the above news items involved price-fixing charges but not all antitrust cases are, of course, of that nature. Price fixing typically results in the biggest penalties and such cases are therefore the most newsworthy. More recently, the pricing power and monopolistic practices by the world's biggest and most profitable firms are increasingly being challenged by the antitrust authorities in both the United States and the European Union.

15.3 U.S. Antitrust Enforcement

The antitrust laws of the United States are enforced by the Antitrust Division of the Department of Justice (DOJ) and the Federal Trade Commission (FTC). The Justice Department has authority over the Sherman Act, the primary federal law to combat antitrust violations, and is empowered to bring both civil and criminal actions while the FTC is confined to civil actions only. Both the DOJ and the FTC have jurisdiction over the Robinson-Patman Act which deals with price discrimination. The antitrust laws also allow private civil actions by any person who is injured in his or her business or property. Relief can take the form of an injunction forbidding the unlawful conduct or damages equal to three times the economic damage actually incurred (known as "treble damages)." Over 80% of DOJ and FTC antitrust cases are never tried but settled by so-called consent decrees in which the defendant agrees to curtail or modify its conduct.

15.4 Monopolies and Monopolizing

The Sherman Act represents a turning point in buyer protection. It can be said that it changed the legal principle of seller - buyer relations from *caveat emptor* or "buyer beware" to *caveat venditor* or "seller beware." The Act dates to 1890 and was the country's first federal antitrust statute. It was enacted to ensure competition in the marketplace and to prevent the establishment of monopolies and cartels with power to restrict output, increase prices, and earn monopoly profits at the expense of consumers. The Sherman Act was meant to codify the English common law precedents in the area of restraints of trade. The authors of the statute realized that its open-ended provisions could not stand on their own and encouraged the courts to examine the question of illegal versus legal conduct on a case-by-case basis. Indeed, the case literature of Supreme Court and Court of Appeals decisions is quite voluminous.

15.4.1 The Sherman Act

Excerpts from Sections 1, 2 and 3 of the Sherman Act, the three most important ones, are reproduced below.

Section 1. Every contract, combination in the form of trust or otherwise, or conspiracy, in restraint of trade or commerce among the several States, or with foreign nations, is declared to be illegal. Every person who shall make any contract or engage in any combination or conspiracy hereby declared to be illegal shall be deemed guilty of a felony, and, on conviction thereof, shall be punished by fine not exceeding $10,000,000 if a corporation, or, if any other person, $350,000, or by imprisonment not exceeding three years, or by both said punishments, in the discretion of the court. [15 U.S.C. § 1]

Section 2. Every person who shall monopolize, or attempt to monopolize, or combine or conspire with any other person or persons, to monopolize any part of the trade or commerce among the several States, or with foreign nations, shall be deemed guilty of a felony, and, on conviction thereof, shall be punished by fine not exceeding $10,000,000 if a corporation, or, if any other person, $350,000, or by imprisonment not exceeding three years, or by both said punishments, in the discretion of the court. [15 U.S.C. § 2].

Section 3. Every contract, combination in form of trust or otherwise, or conspiracy in restraint of trade or commerce in any Territory of the United States…is herby declared illegal. Every person who shall make any such contract or engage in such combination or conspiracy shall be deemed guilty of a felony, and, upon conviction thereof, shall be punished by fine not exceeding one million dollars if a corporation, or, if any other person, one hundred thousand dollars, or by imprisonment not exceeding three years, or by both punishments, in the discretion of the Court. [15 U.S. Code § 3].

Note: Section 7 of the Act holds that wherever "person" or "persons" is used in the Act it is to include corporations and associations.

15.4.2 The Clayton Act

A second important statute which requires attention by managers engaged in pricing is the Clayton Act of 1914 which was enacted to prevent anticompetitive practices in their incipiency. The pertinent provisions of the Act are given below.

Section 2: This section has been replaced by the Robinson-Patman Act.

Section 3. It shall be unlawful for any person engaged in commerce, in the course of such commerce, to lease or make a sale or contract for sale of goods, wares, merchandise, machinery, supplies, or other commodities, whether patented or unpatented, for use, consumption, or resale within the United States or any Territory thereof…or fix a price charged therefore, or discount from, or rebate upon, such price, on condition, agreement, or understanding that the lessee or purchaser thereof shall not use or deal in the goods, wares, merchandise, machinery, supplies, or other commodities of a competitor or competitors of the lessor or seller, where the effect of such lease, sale, or contract for sale of such condition, agreement, or understanding may be to substantially lessen competition or tend to create a monopoly in any line of commerce. [15 U.S. Code § 14].

Section 4 (a). Except as provided in subsection (b), any person who shall be injured in his business or property by reason of anything forbidden in the antitrust laws may sue therefore in any district court of the United States in the district the defendant resides or is found or has an agent, without respect to the amount in controversy, and shall recover threefold the damages by him sustained and the cost of suit, including reasonable attorney's fees.
[15 U.S. Code § 15].

15.4.3 The Stare Decisis Doctrine

Stare decisis is an important component of the Anglo-American common law. It means "to stand on decided cases" and requires judges to follow precedent. Cases decided by the Supreme Court become the law of the land and all lower courts are bound by its rulings. Most cases do not reach the Supreme Court. Some cases tried in a federal District Court are appealed to the federal Circuit Court for the circuit with jurisdiction in that area of the country. The decisions of the circuit courts are published and then becomes part of the case law for that jurisdiction. Even the Supreme Court decides cases on the basis of stare decisis but has the option of overturning previous rulings when new reasonings have undermined their doctrinal underpinnings.

15.4.4 Antitrust Injury and Standing

Not explicitly in the statute and judicially created is the requirement of *antitrust injury* which means that the plaintiff must plead and prove to have suffered injury as a direct result of the unlawful conduct of the defendant. In the *Brunswick Corp.* case Brunswick Corporation, a large operator of bowling centers across the United States, was sued because it had acquired and operated over two hundred defaulting bowling centers during a seven-year period. The suit alleged that under the antitrust laws these acquisitions were illegal because they might substantially lessen competition or tend to create a monopoly. The Court rejected that claim stating that the antitrust laws were enacted for the *protection of competition, not competitors.*[2]

According to the *Brunswick Doctrine*, in a private damage action for treble damages, *Plaintiffs must prove antitrust injury, which is to say injury of the type the antitrust laws were intended to prevent and that flow from that which makes defendants' acts unlawful. The injury should reflect the anticompetitive effect either of the violation or of the anticompetitive acts made possible by the violation.* Antitrust injury is also closely related to the judicial concept of *standing*, i.e., whether a plaintiff can sue claiming antitrust violation in a federal court. Generally, without antitrust injury a plaintiff will have no standing.

15.4.5 Judicial Antitrust Standards

The courts have set two standards in evaluating anticompetitive conduct. Some conduct such as price fixing by competitors is *per se* (in itself) illegal while other conduct falls under the *rule of reason* standard. Where an activity has been found to be blatantly anticompetitive it is considered per se illegal and courts are not required to make further inquiries whether the activity is reasonable or not. Under the rule of reason standard, on the other hand, the trial court makes more factual inquiries to determine whether the challenged conduct is unreasonably anticompetitive and thereby illegal. Regarding the usage trend of the two standards, antitrust authors Sullivan and Harrison have observed that "the per se rule of illegality is applied less and less frequently."[3]

15.4.6 Monopolizing and Market Power

Section 2 of the Sherman Act makes monopolizing or attempting to monopolize any portion of the trade among the States a felony. This has led courts to look into the concept of market power. What is market power? In *DuPont*, the Justice Department brought a civil action against Du Pont alleging monopolization of the market for cellophane.[4] At one time the company was producing about 75% of U.S. cellophane making a considerable profit on the product. The District Court found, and the Supreme Court affirmed, that there were substitute wrapping products on the market for consumers to choose from and therefore no antitrust violation. The Supreme Court defined monopoly power thus: *A party has monopoly power if it has, over any part of the trade or commerce among the several States, a power of controlling prices or unreasonably restricting competition.... Monopoly power is the power to control prices or exclude competition.*

Courts have used a quantitative measure known as the *Lerner Index* (named for economist Abba Lerner) to assess market power:

$$L = (P - C) / P \qquad \text{Eq. (15.1)}$$

where L is the Lerner Index, P is the firm's profit maximizing price and C the marginal cost at the profit maximizing output."[5] The larger the Lerner Index, the greater is the firm's market power. Because the data required to calculate the Lerner Index are often not available, courts have used *market share* as a proxy. However, computing market share, the ratio of the firm's sales and total industry sales, is just as problematic.

The reader will recall from Equation (14.14) of Chapter 14 that a product's optimal price P*, optimal price elasticity of demand ε* at that price, and the unit variable cost VC_0 are related by:

$$\varepsilon^* = P^* / (P^* - VC_0) \qquad \text{Eq. (15.2)}$$

If we invert both sides of Equation (15.2), we obtain:

$$L = 1 / \varepsilon^* = (P^* - VC_0) / P^*$$

$$L = CM^* \qquad \text{Eq. (15.3)}$$

This means that the Lerner Index is directly proportional to the optimal contribution margin CM* and inversely proportional to the optimal price elasticity of demand. Thus, the higher the CM* and the smaller the optimal P.E.D., the greater will be the market power of that product in the given market. Products with inelastic demand ($\varepsilon < 1.0$) and high unit profit margins are, of course, characteristic of a monopoly.

But the Lerner Index appears basically flawed because a firm can have a large contribution margin and still have no market power because of inadequate sales. Hence, Firm A with a market share of just 25% can have considerably more market power than Firm B with a 75% market share if its total contribution dollars are substantially higher than those of its competitor. In this writer's opinion, a more realistic Market Power Index (MPI) would be:

$$MPI = K^* / R^* \qquad \text{Eq. (15.4)}$$

where K* is the maximum total contribution as given by Eq. (14.11) of Chapter 14 and R* the maximum sales revenue at K* as given by Eq. (14.13). The larger this ratio, the larger would be the firm's market power of its product or products in the given market. Besides being a better indicator of market power than the Lerner Index, the MPI would be easier to compute because all the data would be readily available from company records.

15.5 Restraints of Trade

The courts distinguish between *horizontal* and *vertical* restraints of trade. Horizontal restraints generally involve collusion among unrelated entities such as between companies competing in the same product-market. Vertical restraints exist if the illegal activity is among related entities at different organizational levels such as between a manufacturer and its dealers. Agreements among competitors to fix prices, divide territories and markets, or restrict output are examples of horizontal restraints. As previously noted, horizontal restraints of trade are the most egregious of antitrust offenses and the most severely punished. As a general rule, courts have been more tolerant in cases of vertical restraints and generally apply the rule of reason.[6]

It should come as no surprise that express, signed agreements between competitors are rarely found but that is not much of a shield for wrongdoers. From early on the courts have held that an express agreement is not necessary to establish a Section 1 violation and the existence of such an agreement could be inferred from conduct and circumstantial evidence.

15.5.1 Horizontal Restraints of Trade

The two most prevalent violations of the antitrust laws are price fixing among competitors and territory allocations.

Price Fixing

The temptation by executives and managers of competing firms to conspire to fix prices is large. Jeffrey Sonnenfeld and Paul Lawrence, both associated with the Harvard Business School, have identified several industry and company characteristics that are conducive to price-fixing schemes.[7] For the industry, these include i) overcapacity, ii) undifferentiated products, iii) contact with competitors, and iv) large, price-sensitive customers. Company characteristics include i) a collusion culture, ii) high rewards for profits, iii) decentralized pricing decisions, iv) widespread trade association participation, v) reactive rather than proactive legal staff, and vi) loose ethics rules. It goes without saying that where these conditions exist special company efforts are required to move from the "danger zone" to the "safety zone."

Among the many antitrust cases involving price fixing we shall look at just one in which the Court clearly articulated the per se rule making horizontal price fixing illegal. In *Trenton Potteries*, twenty individuals and twenty-three corporations were convicted of conspiring to fix prices in the manufacture and sale of vitreous bathroom fixtures.[8] The group were members of a trade organization, the Sanitary Potters' Association, which controlled the manufacture and distribution of 82% of such fixtures produced in the United States. An issue was whether the prices charged were reasonable. In applying the per se rule, the Court stated: *The power to fix prices, whether reasonably exercised or not, involves power to control the market and to fix arbitrary and unreasonable prices... uniform price fixing by those controlling in any substantial manner a trade or business in interstate commerce is prohibited by the Sherman law, despite the reasonableness of the prices agreed on.*

Market and Customer Allocation

Rather than fixing prices for products and services, firms have at times engaged in *market allocation* schemes whereby each competitor is granted a given percentage of the total market, or each is given a certain territory in which the others will not compete, or else customers are divided up among the competitors. These are horizontal restraints of trade and, not surprisingly, the courts have made these per se illegal. In the *Topco* case (see Note 1) the Supreme Court rejected the District Court's rule of reason analysis stating: *This Court has reiterated time and time again that horizontal territorial limitations...are naked restraints of trade with no purpose except stifling of competition.* On remand, the trial court, over the government's objection, permitted Topco to designate areas of "primary responsibility" for each member and for reasonable compensation where one member sold in another's primary area.

15.5.2 Vertical Restraints of Trade

As previously noted, courts have typically been more charitable in dealing with conspiracies to fix prices among producers and members of their distribution chains. Unlike in horizontal restraints, here the rule of reason prevails as judges try to determine if the defendants' conduct has led to the type of damages the antitrust laws were meant to prevent.

An interesting case involved both vertical and horizontal price-fixing. Sullivan and Harrison classified it as a vertical price-fixing case and therefore entitled to rule of reason treatment.[9] The defendant was Apple, the world's leading maker of smartphones. In *U.S. v. Apple Inc.*, the government alleged that Apple had conspired with the five largest publishing companies in the country (Hachette Book Group, HarperCollins Publishers, Macmillan Publishers, Penguin Group, and Simon & Schuster) to raise the price of e-books in violation of the Sherman Act.[10] The conspiracy, initiated by an Apple executive, arose because Amazon charged only $9.99 for its e-books which made it difficult for the publishers to compete with their more profitable printed versions.

The court ruled that the conduct was so egregious to be a per se offense. There was overwhelming evidence of a conspiracy that included executives of the publishers regularly meeting in private dining rooms in New York restaurants to work out a scheme by which the publishers would raise the price of e-books and Apple receive a 30% commission on e-books sold in its iBookstore. The publishers pleaded guilty and settled with the government but Apple decided to fight the case claiming that it never intended to raise prices, that there was no evidence that e-book prices rose, and that the publishers' price setting was a case of parallel decision-making.

In its decision the circuit court found that *Apple had orchestrated a conspiracy among the Publisher Defendants to raise the price of e-books* and that the conspiracy was blatant enough to *constitute a per se violation of the Sherman Act and, in the alternative, unreasonably restrained trade under the rule of reason.* The Supreme Court declined to hear Apple's appeal. The lower court fined Apple $450 million.

Resale Price Maintenance (RPM)

Companies are much interested in the prices their products are sold for at the wholesale and retail levels. For image reasons, luxury goods firms may wish to establish minimum prices at which their products may be purchased or they may want to do business with certain select retailers only. Other firms prefer to set maximum resale prices in order to ensure adequate sales and to prevent price gouging by channel members. These are vertical restraints of trade and may involve vertical price-fixing schemes. The terminology in general use for these practices is resale price maintenance (RPM). The question has been, In light of the antitrust laws, is retail price maintenance legal? The courts have distinguished between maximum resale price maintenance and minimum resale price maintenance and treated them differently because of their different antitrust implications.

Resale price maintenance had traditionally been illegal under the English common law. Once a trader had acquired the goods from the seller, she could dispose of them any way she pleased, i.e., give them away or resell them at any price she chose without further interference from the seller. This rule of law became part of American antitrust law and its interpretation by the courts has until recent times held that retail price maintenance, both minimum and maximum, by sellers was anticompetitive and on its face per se illegal.

The Case Law

The per se rule against resale price maintenance was established in 1911 in the Supreme Court's ruling in *Dr. Miles* in which a manufacturer of proprietary medicines, wanting to maintain minimum retail prices, had signed agreements with certain wholesalers, jobbers and retailers to adhere to its resale prices.[11] The company was sued by a wholesaler who desired to purchase these medicines but refused to sign a contract. The defendant's argument was that under the common law it had the right to determine to whom it would sell and therefore also the terms of sale.

The Court disagreed and affirmed the decision of the circuit court that the agreements were invalid under the common law and in violation of the antitrust laws. Specifically, the Court held that *where commodities have passed into the channels of trade and are owned by dealers, the validity of agreements to prevent competition and to maintain prices is not to be determined by the circumstances...the complainant having sold its product at prices satisfactory to itself, the public is entitled to whatever advantage may be derived from competition in the subsequent traffic.*

Albrecht v. The Herald, decided in 1968, was a case in maximum retail price maintenance. In that case Albrecht, a newspaper distributor with an assigned territory, refused to abide by the maximum subscriber price imposed by the paper whereupon its management hired an agent to contact Albrecht's subscribers to switch to a new distributor the paper had hired.[12] The jury found for the defendant holding that *The Herald's* conduct was entirely unilateral and lawful. The circuit court affirmed but, citing an earlier case, the Supreme Court reversed ruling that agreements to fix maximum prices, *no less than those to fix minimum prices, cripple the freedom of traders and thereby restrain their ability to sell in accordance with their own judgment.*

In 1997, the Court overturned the *Albrecht rule* and in *State Oil Co. v. Khan* held that maximum price-fixing schemes should be analyzed by the rule of reason rather than by the stricter per se rule.[13] In that case, a gasoline wholesaler, State Oil Co., attempted to force a gasoline station owner, Barkat Khan, to sell its products at certain maximum prices. Khan resisted and sued alleging the practice was unlawful under the antitrust laws. He won his case in the circuit court but the Supreme Court overturned its previous rulings holding that maximum price-fixing could be pro-competitive.

The final end to the per se rule for vertical price fixing came in a 2007 decision when the Court ruled in *Leegin* that minimum price fixing cases too were entitled to a rule of reason analysis.[14] Leegin produced leather apparel and to protect the quality image of its offerings required its dealers not to sell below certain recommended prices. When it discovered one of its dealers to be offering 20% discounts, it refused to make further sales to it. The dealer's parent company, PSKS, sued alleging that Leegin had violated the antitrust laws when it entered into agreements with its dealers. After the district court ruled in favor of PSKS, Leegin appealed to the Supreme Court to overturn *Dr. Miles*. The Court did holding that manufacturer-imposed minimum resale prices were not per se illegal under the antitrust laws because the practice *can lead retailers to compete efficiently for customer sales in ways other than to cut retail prices.*

The Colgate Doctrine

Notwithstanding all the Court's decisions on the legality or illegality of vertical price restraints, the marketer can take heart in a doctrine first annunciated in 1919 in *United States v. Colgate*.[15] The government had alleged that the defended had sent letters and circulars to its distributors and retailers showing uniform prices to be charged, urging its dealers to adhere to these prices, and had terminated sales to dealers who did not adhere to the suggested prices. The indictment charged that the defendant's insistence for channel members to adhere to its published prices amounted to restrictive agreements between the manufacturer and its dealers in violation of the Sherman Act. The trial court ruled for the defendant stating that Colgate had no agreements with its dealers but acted entirely unilaterally. The Supreme Court affirmed.

According to the *Colgate Doctrine*, resale price maintenance is legal as long as there is no agreement between the manufacturer and the distributor, retailer or any other distribution channel member. The Sherman Act encompasses only contracts and agreements. As the Court in Colgate so eloquently stated: *In the absence of any purpose to create or maintain a monopoly, the Act does not restrict the long recognized right of trader or manufacturer engaged in an entirely private business, feely to exercise his own independent discretion as to parties with whom he will deal; and, of course, he may announce in advance the circumstances under which he will refuse to sell....* In other words, the seller may unilaterally declare the price his product is to be sold for and the terms of sale and refuse to make further sales to a dealer who does not adhere to his pricing policy and other terms of sale such as a suggested retail price [SRP] for his product or products.

15.5.3 Predatory Pricing

A firm is said to engage in *predatory pricing* if it prices a product or products below cost to drive competitors from the market so that it may afterwards charge higher prices and recoup its losses while earning monopoly profits. Such conduct appears to be anticompetitive and courts have agreed to hear complaints based on predatory pricing theories but only reluctantly because the antitrust laws are meant to guard the public from inflated prices due to collusion among competitors while predatory prices are the result of competitor rivalries that bring down prices which is in line with the intent of the antitrust laws.

Subsidizing Theory

One early legal theory advanced by plaintiffs was that their competitor was subsidizing below-cost prices in their market with profits from higher prices charged in another. That was the major argument made by *Zenith Radio* when it accused Japanese television manufacturer Matsushita Electric of conspiring with others to under-price their television sets in the U.S. while charging higher prices in Japan.[16] The Supreme Court affirmed a summary judgment against the plaintiff because its conspiracy theory did not seem plausible. The Court questioned the likelihood that a firm could recoup its losses during the period of predation after it had achieved monopoly power and noted that *predatory pricing schemes are rarely tried, and even more rarely successful.* And as Sullivan and Harrison noted: "Today, the notion that a predator uses one market to subsidize another has been abandoned."[17]

The Areeda-Turner Test

To assist the courts in assessing whether a price is to be considered predatory or not, Professors P. Areeda and D. Turner proposed a test which has since come to be known by their names. According to the *Areeda-Turner Test* prices below reasonable anticipated short-run marginal costs should be considered predatory. Because marginal cost is difficult to compute, this quantity has been replaced by average variable cost so that the revised test is: A price at or above anticipated average variable cost (AVC) should be presumed lawful while a price below this cost should conclusively be presumed unlawful.[18]

Based on previous material in *Pricing the Profitable Sale*, this test makes perfect sense. Thus, the quantity "average variable cost" in the Areeda-Turner Test is what we have herein called the "unit variable cost" (VC). We know that a price at or below this cost will generate zero or negative contribution dollars and we have consequently labeled it the *price floor*. Under ordinary circumstances, it would be foolish to sell below that price because each additional sale would lead to a unit contribution loss equal to the difference between the sell price and the unit variable cost ($P - VC$) and a total loss of $(P - VC) \times Q$ where Q is the quantity sold and $P < VC$.

A New Standard

The most important decision on this topic has come with *Brooke Group* in which the Supreme Court set the bar for a plaintiff to succeed so high that it is not likely to prevail in a predatory pricing case.[19] The cigarette industry, a highly concentrated oligopoly, is known for its occasional price wars and *Brooke Group* was an outgrowth of such a battle. In its lawsuit Liggett alleged that its rival Brown & Williamson Tobacco was granting its wholesalers volume discounts resulting in prices below cost intended to pressure Liggett to raise prices on its generic cigarettes which would help preserve Brown & William's super profits on its branded cigarettes.

In its analysis of the case, the Court combined provisions in the Section 2 of the Sherman Act and the Robinson-Patman Act (see Section 15.7 below) to announce a new standard. In the Court's opinion *Evidence of below cost pricing is not alone sufficient to permit an inference of probable recoupment and injury to competition. The plaintiff must demonstrate that there is a likelihood that the scheme alleged would cause a rise in prices above a competitive level sufficient to compensate for the amounts expended on the predation, including the time value of money.* Using this more restrictive standard, the Court held for the defendant.

15.6 Communications Among Competitors

In Sections 8.3 and 8.4 of Chapter 8 we discussed oligopolies and leadership pricing, respectively, and stated that oligopolies tend to be very *interdependent* and that engaging in *leadership pricing* is one way they attempt to prevent direct price competition and possible price wars. It was also pointed out that a prudent price leader gives the price followers advance public notice of its intention to make a major price change so that they will not be taken by surprise and react in a negative way.

In legal parlance acting in concert with other members of an oligopoly is known as *conscious parallelism* and announcing a price change as *price signaling*. Clearly, these activities could be termed tacit collusion and the question is whether they are legal under the antitrust laws. Generally speaking, the courts have treated oligopolistic conduct with kid gloves presuming it to be a natural component of doing business in a free market economy.

15.6.1 Conscious Parallelism

Conscious parallelism is legal with an important caveat. The verdict for the defendants in *Theatre Enterprises* states: *This Court has never held that proof of parallel business behavior conclusively establishes agreement or, phrased differently, that such behavior itself constitutes a Sherman Act offense. Circumstantial evidence of consciously parallel behavior may have made heavy inroads into the traditional judicial attitude toward conspiracy but "conscious parallelism" has not yet read conspiracy out of the Sherman Act entirely.*[20] This case was a treble damage civil action in which Theatre Enterprises sued Paramount alleging the defendant had violated the antitrust laws by conspiring to restrict "first run" pictures to downtown theaters and suburban theaters to subsequent runs. The jury held for the defendants and the circuit court affirmed. Since it was found that the conduct of the defendants stemmed from independent action rather an agreement, tacit or express, the Court affirmed judgment for the defendants.

15.6.2 Price Signaling

The practice of giving advance public notice of a price change, which may facilitate tacit price collusion among oligopolies, may be presumed legal based on a case brought by the FTC against DuPont and Ethyl, the country's two leading producers of lead antiknock gasoline additives. In the *DuPont* case, the two firms were petitioning the Second Circuit Court to vacate an FTC cease and desist order which had alleged "unfair methods of competition" and "unfair acts and practices" in violation of Section 5 of the FTC Act. and, specifically, that the defendants had, among several other non-collusive practices, i) used a 30-day price change advance notice clause in all contracts, and ii) given advance price change notices to the press thereby "substantially lessening competition by facilitating price parallelism at non-competitive levels higher than might have otherwise existed."[21]

The Second Circuit vacated the order and in a strongly worded opinion that was highly critical of the FTC and its rulings in general rejected the Commission's analysis and enunciated this rule of law: *Before business conduct in an oligopolistic industry may be labeled "unfair" within the meaning of § 5 a minimum standard demands that, absent a tacit agreement, at least some indicia of oppressiveness must exist such as (1) evidence of anticompetitive intent or purpose on the part of the producer charged, or (2) the absence of an independent legitimate business reason for its conduct.* Specifically, the court held that *The mere existence of an oligopolistic market structure in which a small group of manufacturers engage in consciously parallel pricing of an identical product does not violate the antitrust laws.*

15.7 Price Discrimination

As we saw in Section 10.3 (Chapter 10), one of the accepted marketing practices for maximizing sales revenue or profits for products and services is to customize prices to accommodate different customer groups with different value perceptions. In target segments with high price sensitivity, the marketer will typically charge less than in ones where demand is inelastic and customers are able and willing to pay more. Usually these products are very similar and can be produced and marketed with no or little cost differences. The question is, Is price discrimination, while profitable, also legal? Price discrimination is illegal only if certain stringent conditions exist and none of the available defenses are met.

Price discrimination in the marketplace is made unlawful by § 2(a)-(f) of the Robinson-Patman Act (the "Act") which amends § 2 of the Clayton Act. This Act has seen less enforcement activity at the federal level in recent years possibly because it seems to run counter to conventional antitrust legislation which seeks to protect the consumer. Robinson-Patman was enacted in 1936 to protect small independent retailers from encroachment by chain stores which were able to extract price concessions from producers as a result of their greater buying power.

Consequently the Act has been highly controversial. As Sullivan and Harrison have noted: "This Depression era Act was passed principally to protect competitors. Arguments based on economic theory suggest that it may actually cause prices to increase and output to decrease. Consequently, the Act is viewed by many as misguided in the context of modern antitrust theory."[22]

Due to the fact that price discrimination is impacted by not only the Robinson-Patman Act but also the Sherman and Clayton acts and that these were written with different antitrust goals in mind, the case law in this area of antitrust litigation is unusually complex and largely unsettled. In this book we shall cite just a few of the most important cases.

15.7.1 The Robinson-Patman Act

The two most important sections of the Robison-Patman Act Amendments to §2 of the Clayton Act are reproduced below:

Section 2(a) It shall be unlawful for any person engaged in commerce, in the course of such commerce, either directly or indirectly, to discriminate in price between different purchasers of commodities of like grade and quality, where either or any of the purchases involved in such discrimination are in commerce, where such commodities are sold for use, consumption, or resale within the United States or any Territory thereof or the District of Columbia or any insular possession or other place under the jurisdiction of the United States, and where the effect of such discrimination may be substantially to lessen competition or tend to create a monopoly in any line of commerce, or to injure, destroy, or prevent competition with any person who either grants or knowingly receives the benefit of such discrimination, or with customers of either of them: *Provided,* That nothing herein contained shall prevent differentials which make only due allowance for differences in the cost of manufacture, sale, or delivery resulting from the differing methods or quantities in which such commodities are to such purchasers sold or delivered: *Provided, however,* That the Federal Trade Commission may, after due investigation and hearing to all interested parties, fix and establish quantity limits, and revise the same as it finds necessary, as to particular commodities or classes of commodities, where it finds that available purchasers in greater quantities are so few as to render differentials on account thereof unjustly discriminatory or promotive of monopoly in any line of commerce; and the foregoing shall then not be construed to permit differentials based on differences in quantities greater than those so fixed and established: *And provided further,* That nothing herein contained shall prevent persons engaged in selling goods, wares, or merchandise in commerce from selecting their own customers in bona fide transactions and not in restraint of trade: *And provided* *further*, That nothing herein contained shall prevent price changes from time to time where in response to changing conditions affecting the market for or the marketability of the goods concerned, such as but not limited to actual or imminent deterioration of perishable goods, obsolescence of seasonal goods, distress sales under court process, or sales in good faith in discontinuance of business in the goods concerned.

Section 2(b) Upon proof being made, at any hearing on a complaint under this section, that there has been discrimination in price or services or facilities furnished, the burden of rebutting the prima facie case thus made by showing justification shall be upon the person charged with a violation of this section, and unless justification shall be affirmatively shown, the Commission is authorized to issue an order terminating the discrimination: *Provided, however*, That nothing herein contained shall prevent a seller rebutting the pima facie case thus made by showing that his lower price or the furnishing of services or facilities to any purchaser or purchasers was made in good faith to meet an equally low price of a competitor, or the services or facilities furnished by a competitor. [15 U.S.C. § 13].

15.7.2 Elements of a Prima Facie Case

For a *prima facie* case of illegal price discrimination under the Robinson-Patman Act five elements must be present and proved:

i) *Interstate Commerce*

Congress is authorized to regulate commerce among the States by Section 8 of Article I of the U. S. Constitution and therefore the antitrust laws, including the Robinson- Patman Act, require that the sales take place in interstate commerce. The courts have used the terms "stream of commerce" or "flow of commerce" in describing sales under these provisions.

ii) *Two Prices and Two Sales*

By a 1974 Supreme Court decision in *Gulf Oil*, there must have been at least two reasonably contemporaneous sales to different purchasers and at least one of these must have crossed state lines.[23] In this case Coop, a paving company, sued certain asphalt producers alleging they had committed several antitrust law violations and sought injunctive relief and treble damages. The Court found that the market for asphalt was exclusively and necessarily local and that Coop had failed to show that the alleged restraints would affect the interstate liquid asphalt market. The Court held that it lacked jurisdiction over intrastate claims of antitrust violations.

iii) Price Discrimination

In an important 1960 decision in *Anheuser-Busch*, the Supreme Court ruled that price discrimination means merely a price difference.[24] Without this ruling, price discrimination would be difficult to litigate since it would require weighing the economics in each case. While the term price discrimination is still used, the question prosecutors and courts ask is, Did the seller charge different buyers different prices for the same goods?

Because the Act contains no express reference to functional discounts this topic has been the subject of much litigation including the *Morton Salt* (1948), *Texaco* (1990), and *Smith Wholesale* (2007) cases.[25] A functional discount is a means by which a seller reimburses its distribution chain for services rendered (holding inventory, servicing retailers, advertising etc.) with the most "upstream" members of the chain (distributors, wholesalers) receiving the largest discounts.

In *Morton Salt*, the producers of table salt had offered substantial discounts to customers that bought salt in greater than carload lots. The FTC found Morton guilty of price discrimination. The Court of Appeals reversed and the Supreme Court reversed again. The company had argued that the discounts were available to all. The Supreme Court found that since only five companies qualified for the largest discount, functionally they were not. The ruling has been interpreted to mean that functional discounts are not illegal provided they are equally available to all buyers. The court explained that *in enacting the Robison-Patman Act Congress was especially concerned with protecting small businesses which were unable to buy in quantities, such as the merchants here who purchased in less-than-carload lots.*

In *Texaco*, Hasbrouck and a group of gasoline station owners who were Texaco customers sued after the company gave two distributors substantial discounts making it impossible for the retailers to compete with the distributors' own stations. The Court found that the services performed by the distributors were insubstantial and did not merit the large discounts. The plaintiffs were awarded treble damages for antitrust injuries. In the Court's opinion *A legitimate functional discount that constitutes a reasonable reimbursement for the purchaser's actual market functions does not violate the Act. However, the Act does not tolerate a functional discount that is completely untethered either to the supplier's savings or the wholesaler's costs.*

In *Smith Wholesale*, the plaintiffs, distributors of Phillip Morris cigarettes to retail outlets, alleged that the cigarette company's discount schedule, which was based on the percentage of their total cigarette sales that were of the defendant's brand, was discriminatory and unlawful under the Act. The Court of Appeals found no violation and affirmed the District Court's summary judgment for the defendant holding that *a discount equally and realistically available to all purchasers of a like commodity does not discriminate in price within the meaning of § 13(a).*

iv) Commodities of "Like Grade and Quality"

The leading case regarding this requirement is *Borden Co.* in which the FTC found Borden, a milk producer, to be in violation of the Act because it charged different prices for its branded and private label evaporated milk even though the two were chemically identical.[26] On appeal, the Circuit Court set aside the FTC ruling holding that the branded and private label milk were different products. The Supreme Court reversed holding that a public preference for a name brand for which it was willing to pay a higher price did not establish that the two products were different. The

Court suggested the lower court consider the cost justification and competitive injury provisions of the Act. On remand, the Circuit Court allowed Borden's price differential after finding that it caused no substantial competitive injury.

v) Injury to Competition

The Act requires a showing that the effect of such price discrimination *may be substantially to lessen competition*. In *primary-line* price discrimination the injury is to a competitor of the price discriminator (usually in the form of lost sales and profits) while in *secondary-line* injury the seller's disfavored customer may sue the price discriminating seller if it suffers injury competing with the favored customer. *Utah Pie* is the foremost primary-line discrimination case.[27] The petitioner, a local producer of frozen desert pies, alleged that certain large national competitors had entered the Utah market charging lower prices than they did in neighboring states resulting in a substantial loss in petitioner's market share. The jury sided with the petitioner, the Court of Appeals reversed, and the Supreme Court reversed again finding for the petitioner and awarding treble damages. The Court held that there was sufficient evidence by which the jury could find competitive injury. As to secondary-line price discrimination, the *Morton Salt* case cited above dealt with that situation.

15.7.3 Defenses

The Act makes three defenses available to rebut a prima facie case of price discrimination.

i) Cost Justification

A price discriminator may escape liability by showing, according to § 2(a) of the Act, that price differentials *make only due allowance for differences in the cost of manufacture, sale, or delivery*. The cost defense was unsuccessfully used in an earlier *Borden* case in which the government alleged the company had discriminated in milk prices to independent grocery stores and grocery store chains.[28] The grocery chains received a flat discount that was lower than the best volume discounts available to the independents. The trial court found for the defendants.

On direct appeal, the Supreme Court reversed holding that the *Robison-Patman Act contemplates both in express wording and legislative history, a showing of actual cost differences.* According to the opinion, Borden had used faulty methodology in arriving at its cost differentials that would make the price differentials legal. As Sullivan and Harrison have noted "The [cost] defense, for the most part, has not been of great value to defendants."[29]

ii) Meeting Competition

Section 2(b) of the Act allows rebuttal of the prima facie case by showing that the lower price *was made in good faith to meet an equally low price of a competitor.* The defense allows meeting but not beating a competitor's price. Unlike the cost justification defense, this defense is more effective and has been successfully raised by several defendants.

A major issue with the meeting competition defense has been whether an exchange of price information among competitors for purposes of taking advantage of this defense in the Robinson-Patman Act is lawful. In *U.S. Gypsum* the manufacturers of gypsum board routinely called competing producers to determine the prices currently being offered to specific customers.[30] The Government criminally indicted various companies and their officials of price-fixing in violation of the Sherman Act. The company and a number of executives and managers were convicted in the District Court after a jury trial. The Circuit Court reversed and the Supreme Court affirmed the ruling of the lower court.

The primary issue in this case was whether intent is one of the elements in a criminal charge under the Sherman Act. The Court ruled that *A defendant's state of mind or intent is an element of a criminal antitrust offence which must be established by evidences and inferences drawn therefrom....* It found no such intent here.

On the issue of interseller price information exchange the Court held that *A good faith belief, rather than an absolute certainty, that a price concession is being offered to meet an equally low price of a competitor suffices to invoke the § 2(b) defense; exchange of price information, even when putatively for the purpose of Robinson-Patman Act compliance must remain subject to close scrutiny under the Sherman Act.*

Furthermore the Court held that *The good faith standard remains the benchmark against which the seller's conduct is to be evaluated, and we agree with the Government and the FTC that this standard can be satisfied by efforts falling short of interseller verification in most circumstances....* The Court faulted the lower court for treating interseller price verification as an exception to liability under the Sherman Act. Despite the price information exchange, the Court ruled for the defendants.

iii) Changing Conditions

This defense *in response to changing conditions* allows the anticompetitive sale of goods that are perishable and about to spoil, or have become obsolete and been discontinued, or offered to clear out inventory because the seller is going out of business.

15.8 European Union Antitrust Law

Multinational companies must satisfy the legal requirement of more than one jurisdiction which, in the case of firms with operations in both the United States and the European Union (EU), means that they are subject to both American and European antitrust laws. In the EU, antitrust laws are enforced by the European Commission (EC) and, specifically, the Directorate General for Competition. The EC is the executive arm of the EU and is located in Brussels, Belgium. Its decisions can be appealed to the General Court and from there to the European Court of Justice (ECJ). The ECJ hears cases involving questions of law only. The EU antitrust law is contained in Articles 101 and 102 of the Treaty on the Functioning of the European Union.

Article 101: This article prohibits all agreements and concerted practices which may affect trade between member states and which have as their object or affect the prevention, restriction, or distortion of competition within the European Union including horizontal (price-fixing or market sharing) and vertical agreements. The EC can levy fines of up to 10% of a company's annual worldwide sales on conviction. It is also empowered to grant total immunity to a firm that is the first to submit actionable evidence of wrongful conduct. Private suits for damages based on EC antitrust violations can be brought in the courts of member countries.

Article 102: Article 102 prohibits firms from holding a dominant position in a market and abusing that position. In assessing dominance, the EC analyzes the relevant product-market and the firm's market share. The relevant product-market is made up of all products/services which customers consider to be substitutes in terms of their characteristics, prices, and intended use. Market share is considered a strong indicator in assessing dominance—the higher a company's market share and the longer the time it has been held, the more dominant it is. If market share lies below 40%, dominance is not considered likely.

European antitrust law has been strongly influenced by American law which has a longer history but there are major differences in the substantive law due to different socioeconomic objectives of the U.S. and EU antitrust laws. Furthermore, because of the different systems of law there are also procedural differences. The American system is based on the *common law* of England in which case law (sometimes called judge-made law) is a major component. European law, known as the *civil law* has its origin in the *Corpus Juris Civilis* of ancient Rome and adjudication is based on the codified law with less reliance on case law. It is therefore important for American businesses with European operations to seek legal counsel from attorneys knowledgeable in EU antitrust law and procedure and not to rely solely on advice obtained from domestic counsel.

15.9 Managers and the Law

In this brief presentation, we have dealt with only the most important areas of antitrust law that would be of interest to managers in their ongoing activities of pricing their companies' products. This being a pricing book, only issues and cases directly related to pricing have been covered. There is a whole body of antitrust law that pertains to non-price antitrust violations. Among the topics not covered herein are bundling of products and services, concerted refusals to deal, consignment sales, exclusive dealings, licensing agreements, mergers, promotional discrimination, and tying arrangements.

Because antitrust law is complex and business activity is equally so, uncertainty about the legality of various contemplated pricing initiatives by managers is inevitable. The courts are partly to blame because the annunciated opinions and rules of law are often vague and ambiguous leading to endless speculation by academics and practitioners alike as to their real meaning. In addition, each case coming before a court is unique in the facts and circumstance and the court's opinion is necessarily tailored to that specific case. This makes it difficult to know with certainty if the ruling in that case applies to a case in which the facts and circumstances are somewhat different.

Yet, as we have seen, there is certain conduct which the statutes and courts have held as being unlawful and especially egregious. First among these is conspiring with competitors to restrain trade in interstate commerce and especially to fix prices in violation of the Sherman Act. Business executives and managers with pricing responsibilities are cautioned to be ever vigilant. While most would never contemplate entering a price-fixing conspiracy with a competitor, they may still be in danger of inadvertently being drawn into one.

Special precaution is recommended in interactions with

competitors such as during trade shows or similar events. Discussions about pricing and prices of competing products should never be a topic and if it comes up, the prudent manager should excuse herself and leave. Similarly, phone conversations between competitors are subject to being monitored and recorded. Private suits especially should be cause for concern because of the provision of Section 4(a) of the Clayton Act which allows any person who has suffered injury to his business or property as a result of an antirust violation to recover treble damages plus the cost of suit.

15.10 Ethics in Pricing

A pricing practice may be profitable and it may be legal but that does not mean that it is also ethical. Ethics involves moral values and standards and on many issues people in business will disagree on what is acceptable and what is not. This section of *Pricing the Profitable Sale* is not intended to offer guidelines or judgments but merely to point out that ethics is part of pricing just as the law is part of it. Undoubtedly, there are people who would even consider perceived value pricing wrongful and unethical because, unlike cost-plus pricing, it seems to set no limit to profits and corporate greed. This author would strongly disagree with that notion.

As was pointed out in the Introduction already, there is nothing unethical in pricing ones goods and services to make a profit. That is the whole purpose of business in a free market economy. As we know a firm, in order to exist and survive, must be profitable or at least break even. Clearly then, if a firm's objective is to make a profit, it might as well seek to maximize it. That is why profits increase with rising prices until an optimum price point is reached and then decline again to zero. It is only logical for marketers to price at this optimal level dictated by market forces and customer demand if conditions permit them to do so.

While pricing for profit cannot be classified as unethical, there are occasions when the practice becomes patently or borderline so. Price gouging is such an area. Many states have no laws against this practice and while it may be legal it is arguable not very ethical if individuals and families suffer financial damage as a result. Price gouging usually arises with an unusual shortage of goods and services due to unforeseen circumstances such as has been the case with the present Covid-19 pandemic and the war in Ukraine. Natural disasters like hurricanes also encourage price gouging. Gasoline stations have been known to suddenly raise pump prices to exorbitant levels or change payment terms to cash only while grocery stores may substantially raise prices on basic food items in short supply.

Ethical issues are also common in industries in which prices are not free to move but are controlled by dominant and unregulated entities determined to extract monopoly profits from a captive customer base with few options. The healthcare and pharmaceutical industries are often cited as primary examples. Thus, hospitals have been found to charge uninsured patient exorbitant fees for even minor surgical procedures. Pharmaceutical companies have earned excessive profits on life-saving drugs even though their development was wholly or partially funded by Government. Some drug companies with expiring patents have been known to pay off generic producers to delay marketing a generic replacement drug so that they can continue earning outsized profits on their regular brands.

Fortunately, most unethical practices eventually become known and the media and social networks can be expected to spread the word. In the most egregious cases new regulations and laws are eventually enacted to protect the public. More often though, unethical pricing just earns the offending business very bad publicity creating sufficient ill will to impact the bottom line. It almost goes without saying but pricing that is both lawful and ethical will in the long run also be the most profitable.

Notes

1. *United States vs. Topco Associates, Inc.* [405 U.S. 596 (1972)]. In *Topco*, a number of small grocery chains had banded together to obtain quality merchandise under private labels in order to compete more effectively with the larger national and regional chains. The government charged that Topco had conspired with member firms for each firm to sell only Topco-controlled brands within the marketing territory allocated to it and refrain from selling Topco-controlled brands outside such territory. The Court held that dividing markets is a per se violation of Section § 1 of the Sherman Act because the scheme's purpose was to stifle competition.

2. *Brunswick Corp. v. Pueblo Bowl-O-Mat, Inc.* [429 U.S. 477 (1977)].

3. E. Thomas Sullivan and Jeffrey L Harrison, *Understanding Antitrust and Its Economic Implications*, 137.

4. *United States v. E I. Du Pont De Nemours & Co.* [131 U.S. 377 (1956)].

5. Sullivan and Harrison, supra at 25-26.

6. Sullivan and Harrison, supra at 205.

7. Jeffrey A. Sonnenfeld and Paul R. Lawrence, "Why Do Companies Succumb to Price Fixing?" *Harvard Business Review*,

July-August 1978, 9.

8. *United States v. Trenton Potteries Co.* [273 U.S. 392 (1927)].

9. Sullivan and Harrison, supra at 125.

10. *United States v. Apple Inc.* [791 F.3d 290, 296 (2d Cir. 2015)].

11. *Dr. Miles Medical Co. v. Park & Sons* [220 U.S. 373 (1911)].

12 *Albrecht v. The Herald Co.* [390 U.S. 145 (1968].

13. *State Oil Co. v. Khan* [552 U.S. 3 (1997)].

14. *Leegin Creative Leather Products, Inc. v. PSKS, Inc.* [551 U.S. 877 (2007)].

15. *United States v. Colgate & Company* [250 U.S. 300 (1919)].

16. *Matsushita Electric Industry Co. v. Zenith Radio* [475 U.S. 574 (1986)].

17. Sullivan and Harrison, supra at 305.

18. Sullivan and Harrison, supra at 309-310.

19. *Brooke Group Ltd. v. Brown & Williamson Tobacco* [509 U.S. 209 (1993)].

20. *Theatre Enterprises v. Paramount Film Distributing*

Corp. [346 U.S. 537 (1954)].

21. *E. I. Du Pont De Nemours & Co. v. Federal Trade Commission* [729 F.2d 128 (2d Cir. 1984)].

22. Sullivan and Harrison, supra at 385.

23. *Gulf Oil Corp. v. Copp Paving Co.* [419 U.S. 186 (1974)].

24. *FTC v. Anheuser-Busch, Inc.* [363 U.S. 536 (1960)].

25. *FTC v. Morton Salt Co.* [334 U.S. 37 (1948)]; *Texaco, Inc. v. Hasbrouck* [496 U.S. 543 (1990)]; and *Smith Wholesale Co. v. Phillip Morris USA, Inc.* [477 F.3d 854 (6th Cir. 2007)].

26. *FTC v. Borden Co.* [383 U.S. 637 (1966)].

27. *Utah Pie Co. v. Continental Baking Co.* [386 U.S. 685 (1967)].

28. *U.S. v. Borden Co.* [370 U.S. 460 (1962)].

29. Sullivan and Harrison, supra at 405.

30. *U.S. v. United States Gypsum Co.* [438 U.S. 422 (1978)]

APPENDIX

I. Formula Derivations

Optimal Prices on Linear Price Response Curve

A. Optimal Price for Sales Revenue Maximization

The linear price response curve of Figure 10-1 of Chapter 10 has the equation:

$$Q = Q_M - (Q_M / P_M) P$$

Sales revenue is therefore:

$$R = P \times Q$$

$$R = -\frac{Q_M}{P_M} P^2 + Q_M P$$

This expression for sales revenue R versus price P has the shape of a parabola whose maximum value is obtained by taking the first derivative of R with respect to P and setting the result equal to zero:

$$\frac{\partial R}{\partial P} = -\frac{2 Q_M}{P_M} P + Q_M = 0$$

$$[P] = \frac{P_M}{2} \qquad \text{QED} \qquad \text{Eq. (A.1)}$$

In words, the optimal price for sales revenue maximization is one-half of the maximum (reservation) price P_M. This means that [P] lies at the midpoint of the PRC where the price elasticity of demand is equal to one.

B. Optimal Price for Total Contribution (Profit) Maximization

Total contribution is the difference between sales revenue and total variable cost:

$$K = R - V = R - VC_0 Q$$

Since,

$$R = -\frac{Q_M}{P_M} P^2 + Q_M P$$

and

$$Q = Q_M - \frac{Q_M}{P_M} P$$

from Section A above, one obtains:

$$K = -\frac{Q_M}{P_M} P^2 + \frac{Q_M (P_M + VC_0)}{P_M} P - VC_0 Q_M$$

This equation for total contribution too has the shape of a parabola which can be differentiated with respect to P and the result set equal to zero to obtain the optimal price P* that will maximize total contribution:

$$\frac{\partial K}{\partial P} = -\frac{2 Q_M}{P_M} P + \frac{Q_M (P_M + VC_0)}{P_M} = 0$$

$$P^* = \frac{P_M + VC_0}{2} \qquad\qquad \text{QED} \qquad\qquad \text{Eq. (A.2)}$$

In words, the optimal price for total contribution (profit) maximization is one-half the sum of the maximum (reservation) price and the product's unit variable cost. Thus, P* is located at the midpoint of that section of the PRC between the unit variable cost VC_0 and the reservation price P_M.

Note

Can the sell prices for revenue maximization and contribution (profit) maximization ever be equal? To find out we set Equation (A.1) equal to Equation (A.2):

$$[P] = P^*$$

$$\frac{P_M}{2} = \frac{P_M + VC_0}{2}$$

The answer is "yes" but only if VC_0, the product's average unit variable cost, is zero. At all other times, the price that maximizes total contribution P* will always be higher than the price that maximizes sales revenue [P].

II. Hypothetical Case Studies

A. Revenue Maximization: The Metropolitan Transit Authority - Midwest (MTA)

The Metropolitan Transit Authority - Midwest (MTA) provides public transportation services for a major Midwestern city and surrounding suburbs offering about 1.8 million rides a day. The MTA has over 13,000 employees while its rolling stock includes 1,200 rapid transit cars and 2,200 buses. The authority has been plagued by severe financial, service, and organizational problems for several years. A succession of public transportation professionals has been unable to turn the company around. There have been four executive directors in three years with the last one, who came from another major city with impeccable transportation credentials, serving just a year and a half before resigning. The city's leading daily, the *Herald Tribune*, has characterized the MTA as being "in shambles through years of waste, mismanagement, political intrigue, and fiscal famine."

In order to stem the tide of red ink from the MTA, the city's popular but increasingly exasperated mayor, Richard J. Dooley, has recently decided to make a major management change. Rather than pick another transportation expert for the vacancy, Mr. Dooley reached out to the business community and hired a retired commercial real estate mogul named Robert Belforte to lead the MTA. The mayor believes that the only way the MTA can be made profitable is to have it run like a business and that a successful businessman like Mr. Belforte would be a logical choice.

Mr. Belforte assumed his new position in February of this year and in mid-July the *Herald Tribune* introduced him to the general public in their *Herald Tribune Magazine*, a supplement to their Sunday issue. In this lengthy article with the heading "Mr. Fixit. Robert Belforte is taking a hard-nosed business approach at the MTA, but he admits he may be in for the ride of his life," Mr. Belforte frankly admitted, with no apologies given, that "I have no qualifications for this job." He does have a strong belief, he told the interviewer, that the customer is numero uno and this must be reflected in the attitude of MTA employees who previously thought their jobs were mostly about driving trains and buses rather than serving the public.

Robert Belforte wasted no time in transforming this unwieldy bureaucracy into a modern business corporation. When he took over, the executive director had twenty-five individuals reporting to him including eight deputy executive directors with each deputy running his own fiefdom. Not surprisingly, there was little coordination of activities among them to ensure an effective and efficient operation. Bolstered by a recent report from a prestigious management consulting firm commissioned by the MTA board, Mr. Belforte cut the number of deputies to three whom he renamed vice presidents while he himself took the title of president. The new titles were meant to promote a business model within the organization. To reduce costs, he closed down a number of rapid transit stations that were rarely used but were also served by bus routes. To improve service, Mr. Belforte introduced printed time schedules for all rapid transit and bus routes and installed a system of controls to maintain departure and arrival times. Other cost reduction and service improvement ideas are in the planning stage.

The major problem at the MTA now as ever are insufficient funds for daily operations and capital improvements. This year's operating expenses are expected to come to $780 million. Just over half of expenses are typically covered by fares collected from passengers. A subsidy from the Regional Transportation Authority in the form of a percentage of sales taxes plus state matching funds and some federal funds pay for most of the remaining outlays. Typically there is still a shortfall which last year amounted to $51 million. Another one is expected for this year especially since the latest recession has reduced the amount of sales taxes being collected.

On January 1 of the year, and before Mr. Belforte came on board, the MTA raised fares across the board. Prior to this date, a rush hour fare cost $1.25 while the non-rush hour (off-peak) fare was $1.00. Before the fare changes went into effect, MTA officials had presented the MTA board with five fare proposals all of which provided for fare increases. The option favored by the board was the one with the highest fare increase (20%), the largest expected increase in fare revenue ($34.5 million), and the smallest anticipated decline in ridership (4.6%). After public hearings, the MTA board approved this option and the new fare structure was implemented. Rush-hour fares are now $1.50 while off-peak fares were raised to $1.15. The cost for transfers was raised from 25 cents to 30 cents.

A few months into the new fare structure, MTA officials became alarmed when they noticed that ridership had dropped by 10% which was over twice of the 4.6% they had anticipated. By April, Mr. Belforte had become convinced that the fare increase instituted by his predecessor had been a big mistake. He subsequently informed the MTA board of his opinion and proposed that an immediate fare cut of 50 cents to $1.00 be implemented. The new fare would apply to both rush-hour and off-peak hour traffic. He proposed to start with Sundays only and, if the experiment proved successful, extend it to the entire week.

Fare reduction enjoys broad popular support both not only with MTA's new management team but outside as well. Mr. Belforte favors a fare reduction because in his business experience price reductions have always led to increases in both demand and sales revenue. In the July *Herald Tribune* interview he is quoted as saying "We believe service reductions and fare increases are self-defeating in that they cut ridership and lower revenues." The *Herald Tribune* has voiced strong support. In an April editorial headed "MTA should try fare-cutting gamble," the paper had advised that "decreasing fares would have the long-term value of increasing ridership—the MTA's best hope for the future." The MTA board is known to have strong doubts about fare reductions as a means of generating additional sales revenue and has not yet acted on Mr. Belforte's proposal.

Analysis

The information available to us is insufficient to make a complete analysis of the problems faced by the MTA. Among missing statistics are the number of fare paying customers using the MTA trains and buses on a daily basis, the proportion of full to discounted fares (available to students and seniors), the proportion of daily rush hour to off-peak passengers, the number of weekly and monthly passes sold at a discount, and the sales revenues generated by each category. Yet despite this information shortfall we can, with the help of the formulas and a general pricing rules of thumb in *Pricing the Profitable Sale*, evaluate the pricing options available to MTA's management and board and develop some recommendations. The three main pricing options are i) keep the 20% fare increase implemented at the beginning of the year, ii) implement a fare structure using the optimal fare and maximum fare revenue change as computed by the pricing formulas, and iii) reduce fares to $1.00 across-the-board as proposed by the new MTA president and his team.

i) Keep present fare schedule: The finding that the fare increase led to a 10% reduction in ridership can be used to estimate the P.E.D.s for the rush hour and off-peak segments as follows.

Ridership Segment	Fare Before	After	Change Fare	Rides	Estim. P.E.D.
Rush hour	$1.25	$1.50	20.0%	(10.0%)	0.50
Off-peak	$1.00	$1.15	15.0%	(10.0%)	0.67

By Equation (13.1) of Chapter 13, the percentage sales revenue change as a percentage price change will be:

$$\blacktriangle R = - \epsilon_0 (\blacktriangle P)^2 + (1 - \epsilon_0) \blacktriangle P$$

For the rush hour segment:

$$\blacktriangle R = - (0.50)(0.20)^2 + (1 - 0.50)(0.20) = 0.080$$

For the off-peak segment:

$$\blacktriangle R = - (0.67)(0.15)^2 + (1 - 0.67)(0.15) = 0.035$$

Conclusion: The new fare structure will generate additional sales revenue of 8.0% and 3.5% for the rush hour and off-peak segments, respectively.

ii) *Implement optimal fare schedule*: The optimal fare, optimal ridership change, and maximum fare revenue change can be computed using Equations (13.3), (13.8), and (13.10) of Chapter 13 as follows:

For the rush hour segment:

$$[\blacktriangle P] = (1 - \epsilon_0) / 2 \epsilon_0 = (1 - 0.50) / (2)(0.50) = 0.50$$
$$[P] = P_0 (1 + \blacktriangle P) = (\$1.25)(1 + 0.50) = \$1.87$$
$$[\blacktriangle Q] = (\epsilon_0 - 1) / 2 = (0.50 - 1) / 2 = (0.25)$$
$$[\blacktriangle R] = \epsilon_0 [\blacktriangle P]^2 = (0.50)(0.50)^2 = 0.125$$

For the off-peak segment:

$$[\blacktriangle P] = (1 - 0.67) / (2)(0.67) = 0.25$$
$$[P] = \$1.00 (1 + 0.25) = \$1.25$$
$$[\blacktriangle Q] = (0.67 - 1) / 2 = (0.17)$$
$$[\blacktriangle R] = (0.67)(0.25)^2 = 0.042$$

Conclusion: For the rush hour segment, the optimal fare is $1.87 which would reduce ridership by 25% and add 12.5% to fare revenue. For the off-peak segment, the optimal fare is $1.25 resulting in a ridership drop of 17% and additional fare revenue of 4.2%.

iii) Reduce fares: For this option, the estimated P.E.D.s are:

Ridership Segment	Fare Before	Fare After	Change Fare	Change Rides	Estim. P.E.D.
Rush hour	$1.50	$1.00	(33.3%)	10.0%	0.30
Off-peak	$1.15	$1.00	(15.0%)	10.0%	0.67

For the rush hour segment:

$$\blacktriangle R = -(0.30)(-0.333)^2 + (1 - 0.30)(-0.333) = (0.266)$$

For the off-peak segment:

$$\blacktriangle R = -(0.67)(-0.150)^2 + (1 - 0.67)(-0.150) = (0.065)$$

Conclusion: A fare reduction to $1.00 for both rush hour and off-peak traffic would reduce fare revenue by 26.6% and 6.5% from present levels, respectively.

Recommendation

Remarkable about this case is the very low price elasticities of demand found for MTA's transportation services but these are likely to be typical of the public transportation sector. The reason is that individuals working in the city's offices and retail establishments have few alternatives other than drive their own vehicles to town. This is not a viable option for most because city parking tends to be both restricted and expensive. Economically speaking, public transportation companies, like the MTA, are operating government-sanctioned monopolies. Their demand curves are therefore inelastic and steep. This, in turn, has significant pricing implications. According to our first general pricing rule of thumb (see Table 8-1,

Chapter 8) whenever demand is inelastic, i.e. the P.E.D. is less than 1.0, a price increase is always called for if the pricing goal is to maximize revenue.

It appears, therefore, that the decision of the MTA board and previous administration to raise fares in January of this year was absolutely correct and the only viable option. The calculations above show that fare revenues for rush hour and off-peak hour traffic will add additional revenues of 8.0% and 3.5%, respectively. Clearly, these fares should be kept in place. Under no circumstances should the MTA board agree to a fare reduction as proposed by the new MTA management. Such an across-the-board reduction to $1.00 would not add to revenue but cut it substantially—by 27% and 7% for the rush hour and off-peak hour segments, respectively.

The optimum price adjustments necessary for maximum revenue improvements, namely 50% and 25% for the rush hour and of-peak hour segments, respectively, would not have been realistic as they would have caused a mass exodus from the system. As the computations above show, with fares at $1.90 and $1.25 for the two segments, the estimated ridership drops would have been 25% and 17%, respectively. Such a fare schedule would most likely have met with vociferous protests from riders who would have argued that the new fares were excessive and unfair and should be rescinded. These system users would have contended that as tax payers they were entitled to have their fares subsidized from public funds and not be made to carry the entire burden.

The MTA board must have wisely decided to raise fares by only a reasonable amount with the prospect of more and smaller increases in the future. That is why the board is not likely to follow the recommendations of the new administration and the editors of the *Herald Tribune* to cut fares. It simply would not make any sense.

If Mr. Belforte experienced an increase in sales revenue when cutting prices in his business career, it was because the commercial real estate market is very competitive and demand curves for properties tend to be more elastic. In such circumstances, i.e., where the P.E.D. is larger than 1.0, a lowering of prices does indeed lead to higher revenues. This is not the case in public transportation. Clearly, Mayor Dooley was unaware of the differences among businesses and may have picked the wrong businessman for the job at least as far as the fare issue was concerned. Mr. Belforte's other efforts improving the system were certainly praiseworthy.

B. Profit Maximization: Fritzel's Restaurant

Fritzel's is a West Coast fast foods restaurant that, unlike other establishments of its kind, caters mostly to older adults and seniors. Its varied menu includes such old favorites as hamburger, Italian beef, and Reuben sandwiches, Chicago style hot dogs, homemade potato and lentil soups, and potato pancakes along with an assortment of desserts and gourmet coffees. The restaurant's homey décor with wood-paneled walls and sturdy wood furnishings plus the soft background music of popular hit tunes from the 1950s and 1960s is intended to appeal to an older clientele. Fritzel's is the American Dream come true of Fritz Strudel who was known as Fritzel when he grew up in his native Austria. Before his present venture, Fritz was chef for a restaurant specializing in Austro-Hungarian cuisine including Hungarian goulash, Sauerbraten, Wienerschnitzel, Frikadellen (German-style hamburgers), Kohlrouladen (stuffed cabbage rolls), Semmelknödel (large bread dumplings), and Spätzle.

One of Fritzel's most popular menu items is a gourmet hamburger sandwich Fritz created especially for mature taste buds. Unlike the typical hamburger of the big chains, which Mr. Strudel has described as a "soggy mess," his is a firmer product with a patty made of select, low-fat ground beef, chopped onion, minced garlic, and paprika. In lieu of the standard hamburger bun the patty is served on a Brötchen, a classic German bread roll with a crisp crust and chewy interior, which Fritz prepares according to an original recipe. This hamburger had no special name until a customer once jokingly asked for a Fritzelburger. The name took hold and Fritz's gourmet hamburger is now known by that name.

A couple of days ago Fritz got into a conversation with one of his regulars named Wendy. After complementing him on the meal she had just enjoyed, Wendy casually asked Fritz how business was going. Fritz replied that despite booming sales and the ten to twelve hours he put in each day, he was having considerable difficulty making a profit. It seems that after paying for supplies, employee wages, rent, utilities, insurance, and repairs and maintenance there was little left at the end of the month. Wendy now identified herself as Wendy Wiener, a partner in the well-known pricing consultancy of Wiener & Wurst, and offered to help him make his business profitable. She suspected that his menu was not priced correctly and offered Fritz to do a sample study for his Fritzelburger at a small introductory fee. Fritz readily agreed and the two began their collaboration.

The first thing Wendy wanted to know was how Fritz came up with the price of $3.60 for his Fritzelburger. Fritz explained that he had checked on the price of a standard hamburger sandwich offered by Roland's, a national hamburger chain one of whose restaurants was located less than three blocks from Fritzel's. Their price was $3.30 and he had added 30 cents for the extra ingredients, he said. "That was not the wisest thing you could have done, Fritz" Wendy told him. Why, she wanted to know, was he charging just a little more than a Roland's hamburger? "You are not competing with them or their hamburgers," she told Fritz, "and it therefore makes little sense to take Roland's menu prices as a guide. The Fritzelburger is a unique product with no real competition while the eating experience Fritzel's provides too is different and unique," Wendy explained. "You are entitled to charge your customers the full value you are offering them and for which most, if not all, will undoubtedly be willing to pay." To Fritz that made sense and he nodded in agreement.

Analysis

Wendy, who had recently acquired an advance copy of *Pricing the Profitable Sale* and decided to use the price optimization methods discussed there, needed to know two essential parameters, namely, the average unit contribution margin for the Fritzelburger and its sensitivity to price changes at the present price level. Coming up with a number for the product's unit contribution margin, Wendy knew, would not be easy because that is not commonly used in the restaurant business. There another metric known as the *profit margin* is popular. It is defined as the percentage of gross sales after all operating expenses are deducted including meal ingredients, wages, rent, utilities, and depreciation. In other words, direct, incremental costs are not separated out from indirect fixed costs. In the restaurant business profit margins tend to be very slim—on the order of just 5% on average.

To get an estimate for the CM_0 Wendy needed to determine the product's unit variable cost VC_0, i.e., the incremental cost directly attributable to the Fritzelburger. The most important components of

VC$_0$ were the ingredients that went into the product and the wages of the part-time employees. Since this was to be a preliminary analysis, Wendy accepted the numbers Fritz was able to furnish without further research. Accordingly, the unit variable cost was found to be $2.70 including $1.60 for the burger ingredients and $1.10 for wages and other incremental expenses. The unit contribution margin was therefore:

$$CM_0(\$) = P_0 - VC_0 = \$3.60 - \$2.70 = \$0.90$$
$$CM_0(\%) = CM_0(\$) / P_0 = \$0.90 / \$3.60 = 25.0\%$$

For obtaining a rough estimate of the P.E.D., Wendy proposed that this being August they run an "October Special" for the Fritzelburger in which during that month they reduce the price of this product by about 10% from $3.60 to $3.25. The promotion would be advertised by large signs outside and inside Fritzel's and in some print media. Wendy would first make an accurate count of the number of Fritzelburgers sold during next month, September, and compare these to the number sold during the October promotion. Obviously, she would have to drop one day's sales for October to have the same number of days for each month. Dividing the percentage quantity change by the known percentage price change would give her an estimate of the Fritzelburger's P.E.D. at the present price-volume operating point (P_0, Q_0).

This having been done, Wendy found that, on average, daily October sales of the Fritzelburger were up from September sales by 18% from 200 to 236. This meant that the product's P.E.D. was 18% / 10% or 1.80. Clearly, while demand was elastic it was not overly so. The elasticity number seemed reasonable since it represented a balance between two opposing factors. The uniqueness of the product would cause demand to be less elastic but seniors on a limited budget would make it higher. The relatively low P.E.D. also told Wendy that the Fritzelburger was under-priced. According to Equation (14.4) of Chapter 14, at a unit contribution margin of 25% the optimal P.E.D. (ε*) is 4.0 but since here it was only 1.8 (ε_0), by the first general pricing rule of thumb (Table 8-1, Chapter 8), a price increase was called for.

Wendy then developed more detailed results. From Table 14-1 (Chapter 14), she found that with a CM_0 of 25% and a P.E.D. of 1.8, the optimal percentage price change $\blacktriangle P*$ is 15.3%. With this basic information, she was able to arrive at these numbers:

* Optimal price: $P* = P_0 (1 + \blacktriangle P*) = \$3.60 \times 1.153 = \$4.15$

* Optimal sales volume: $Q* = Q_0 (1 + \blacktriangle Q*) = Q_0 (1 - \epsilon_0 \blacktriangle P*)$
  $Q* = 200 (1 - 1.80 \times 0.153) = 145$

* Optimal sales revenue: $R* = P* \, Q* = \$4.15 \times 145 = \$602$

* Optimal contrib. margin: $CM*(\$) = (P* - VC_0) = \$4.15 - \$2.70 = \$1.45$

* Optimal total contribution: $K* = CM*(\$) \times Q* = \$1.45 \times 145 = \$210$

* Optimal P.E.D.: $\epsilon* = 1 / CM*(\%) = 1 / 0.35 = 2.9$

In summary, Wendy found these daily sales and total contribution results for before and after an optimal Fritzelburger price change:

	Before	After
Price (P)	$3.60	$4.15
Sales Volume (Q)	200	145
Sales Revenue (R)	$720	$602
Total Contribution (K)	$180	$210
Unit Contribution Margin ($)	$0.90	$1.45
Unit Contribution Margin (%)	25%	35%
Price Elasticity of Demand (ϵ)	1.8	2.9

To graphically show the Fritzelburger's daily sales revenue and total contribution in relation to its price, Wendy plotted the two metrics using an electronic spreadsheet with curve plotting capabilities (Microsoft's Excel). The formula for sales revenue after an incremental price change is from Equation (13.2) of Chapter 13:

$$R_1 = R_0 \{1 - \epsilon_0 (\blacktriangle P)^2 + (1 - \epsilon_0) \blacktriangle P\}$$

Inserting the relevant parameter values for *before* listed above, one obtains:

$$R_1 = 720 \{1 - 1.8 (\blacktriangle P)^2 - 0.8 \blacktriangle P\}$$

where, $\blacktriangle P = (P_1 - 3.60) / 3.60$.

The total contribution after an incremental price change is given by Equation (14.2) of Chapter 14:

$$K_1 = R_0 \{-\text{\textepsilon}_0 (\blacktriangle P)^2 + (1 - \text{\textepsilon}_0\, CM_0)\blacktriangle P + CM_0\}$$

which in the present case becomes:

$$K_1 = 720\{-1.8\,(\blacktriangle P)^2 + 0.55\ \blacktriangle P + 0.25\}$$

where, $\blacktriangle P = (P_1 - 3.60)/3.60$.

Figure B-1
Sales Revenue & Total Contribution for the Fritzelburger

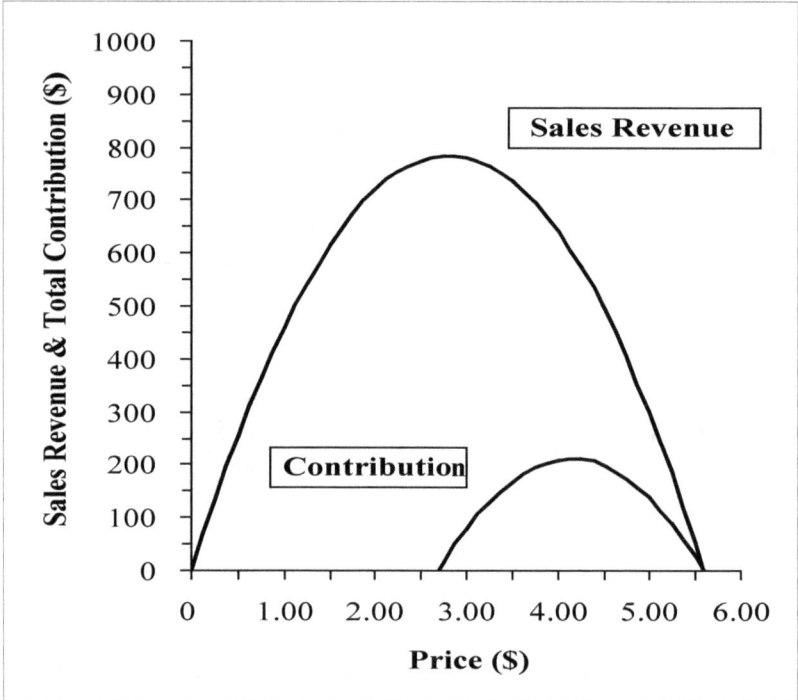

The resulting two curves for the Fritzelburger are shown in Figure B-1. Immediately apparent from this graph is the relatively small amount of daily total contribution dollars earned at all price levels in comparison to the substantial daily sales revenue for this product. The reason is, of course, the very low unit contribution margin. The highest daily total contribution achievable is seen to be about $210 at the optimal price P* of $4.15. Also observable is the fact that contribution does not begin to be generated until the Fritzelburger price is at least $2.70, i.e., the product's estimated unit variable cost (VC_0), while all sales below $2.70 are seen to produce losses. The sales revenue curve is seen to peak at about $800 reached at the optimal price for sales revenue maximization [P] of $2.80, a reduction of 22.2% from the present price of $3.60. At that price almost no contribution dollars would be generated as the contribution curve indicates.

Recommendations

All indications are, Wendy told Fritz, that he is selling his Fritzelburger significantly below its perceived value and is losing money on the product. She recommended a price increase to $3.99 in two incremental steps rather than one in order to make the increase more palatable for her customers. The first step should be from $3.60 to $3.79 and the second three months or so later to $3.99. People just hate price increases especially in frequently purchased items, she explained, and because the price of $3.60 has been out there for a couple of years, it has become firmly established in the minds of customers. A price beyond it will signal his customers that they are getting less value causing them to reconsider their available options including changing restaurants. She also advised Fritz that along with the increase in total contribution of about 16%, he could expect substantial drops in sales volume and revenue of about 28% and 16%, respectively.

Wendy talked to Fritz about the need to get a better estimate of his direct incremental (variable) cost for all his menu items. For the Fritzelburger his estimates were accepted without further research, she said, but if these were significantly off, it would change the recommended optimum price although she felt fairly confident that he was selling an underpriced product. If, after a more detailed cost analysis of his menu items, direct variable costs are found to be high in comparison to industry standards, Fritz must try to reduce them through more cost-effective purchase practices and other means since cost seemed to be his major problem, according to Wendy. He needed to bring these incremental costs down to improve his unit contribution margins.

Wendy suggested to Fritz that he begin implementing the recommended price change and, if he found the results to be positive, consider repricing his other popular menu items such as the Reuben sandwich and the sausage and potato pancake plate. She also let Fritz know that she would be happy to sign a retainer agreement with him on behalf of Wiener & Wurst that would offer continuing assistance for profit improvements to cover cost analyses and repricing of all or part of his menu items as well as recommendations on menu changes and other improvements.

Bibliography

Andersen, William R., and C. Paul Rogers III. *Antitrust Law: Policy and Practice*. New York: Matthew Bender, 1985.

Baker, Walter L., Michael V. Marn, and Craig C. Zawada. *The Price Advantage*. 2nd ed. Hoboken, NJ: John Wiley & Sons, 2010.

Dean, Joel. "Pricing Policies for New Products." *Harvard Business Review on Pricing*. Boston: Harvard Business School Publishing, 2008:101-131.

Dholakia, Utpal. *How to Price Effectively: A Guide for Managers and Entrepreneurs*. Book Design Templetes.com, 2017.

Dolan, Robert J., and Hermann Simon. *Power Pricing: How Managing Price Transforms the Bottom Line*. New York: The Free Press, 1996.

Eckert, Ross D., and Richard H. Leftwich. *The Price System and Resource Allocation*. 10th ed. Chicago: The Dryden Press, 1988.

Eiteman, Wilford J. *Price Determination in Oligopolistic and Monopolistic Situations*. (Michigan Business Reports No. 33). Ann Arbor: The University of Michigan, 1960.

Furtwengler, Dale: *Pricing For Profit: How To Command Higher Prices For Your Products and Services*. New York: AMACOM, 2010.

Gabor, André. *Pricing: Concepts and Methods for Effective Marketing*. 2nd ed. Hants, UK: Gower Publishing Company Ltd., 1988.

Gould, J. P., and C. E. Ferguson. *Microeconomic Theory*. 5th ed. Homewood, IL: Richard D. Irwin, Inc., 1980.

Kotler, Philip. *Marketing Management: Analysis, Planning, and Control*. 2nd ed. Englewood Cliffs, NJ: Prentice Hall, Inc., 1972.

Kotler, Philip and Kevin L. Keller. *Marketing Management*. 13th ed. Upper Saddle River, NJ: Pearson Education, Inc., 2009.

Levitt, Theodore. *The Marketing Mode: Pathways to Corporate Growth*. New York: McGraw-Hill Book Company, 1969.

Marn, Michael V., and Robert L. Rosiello. "Managing Price, Gaining Profit." *Harvard Business Review on Pricing*. Boston: Harvard Business School Publishing Corp., 2008: 45-73.

Mohammed, Rafi. *The 1% Windfall: How Successful Companies Use Price to Profit and Grow*. New York: HarperCollins Publishers, 2010.

Monroe, Kent B. *Pricing: Making Profitable Decisions*. 2nd ed. New York: McGraw-Hill, Inc., 1990.

Monroe, Kent B. *Pricing: Making Profitable Decisions*. 3rd ed. New York: McGraw-Hill Companies, 2003.

Morris, Michael H., and Gene Morris. *Market Oriented Pricing: Strategies for Management*. Lincolnwood, IL: NTC Business Books, 1992.

Nagle, Thomas T. and Georg Müller. *The Strategy and Tactics of Pricing: A Guide to Growing More Profitably*. 6th ed. New York: Routledge, 2018.

Oxenfeldt, Alfred R. *Pricing Strategies*. New York: AMACOM, 1975.

Phillips, Robert L. *Pricing and Revenue Optimization*. Stanford, CA: Stanford Business Books, 2005.

Rao, Akshay R., Mark E. Bergen, and Scott Davis. "How to Fight a Price War." *Harvard Business Review on Pricing*. Boston: Harvard Business School Publishing Corp., 2008: 75-100.

Risley, George. *Modern Industrial Marketing: A Decision-Making Approach*. New York: McGraw-Hill Book Company, 1972.

Simon, Hermann, Frank F. Bilstein, and Frank Luby. *Manage For Profit Not For Market Share: A Guide To Greater Profits In Highly Contested Markets*. Boston: Harvard Business Review Press, 2006.

Simon, Hermann and Martin Fassnacht. *Price Management: Strategy, Analysis, Decision, Implementation*. Cham, Switzerland: Springer Nature Switzerland AG, 2019.

Stiving, Mark. *Impact Pricing: Your Blueprint for Driving Profits*. Madison, WI: Entrepreneur Press, 2011.

Sullivan, E. Thomas, and Jeffrey L. Harrison. *Understanding Antitrust and Its Economic Implications*. 7th ed. Durham: Carolina Academic Press, 2019.

Tucker, Spencer A. *Pricing for Higher Profit: Criteria, Methods, Applications*. New York: McGraw-Hill Book Co., 1966.

Zell, Hans Peter. *Pricing For Profit: The Manager's Guide to Market Oriented Pricing*. Bloomington, IN: Xlibris, 2014.

Subject Index